MW00333772

# FROM NEWGATE TO DANNEMORA

*The Rise of the Penitentiary in New York, 1796–1848*

## About Fall Creek Books

Fall Creek Books is an imprint of Cornell University Press dedicated to making available again classic books that document the history, culture, natural history, and folkways of New York State. Presented in new paperback editions that faithfully reproduce the contents of the original editions, Fall Creek Books titles will appeal to all readers interested in New York and the state's rich past.

Thomas Eddy, 1758–1827, New York's first significant prison reformer. From an engraving in Samuel L. Knapp, *The Life of Thomas Eddy* (New York, 1834). Reprinted by courtesy of the New-York Historical Society.

# FROM NEWGATE TO DANNEMORA

*The Rise of the Penitentiary
in New York, 1796–1848*

By W. DAVID LEWIS

CORNELL UNIVERSITY PRESS
*Ithaca, New York*

Copyright © 1965 by Cornell University

All rights reserved

CORNELL UNIVERSITY PRESS

*First published 1965*

First printing, Cornell Paperbacks, 2009

Library of Congress Catalog Card Number: 64-8260

To Carolyn and the Children

# Preface

ONE of the advantages of a federal system of government, as James Bryce once noted, is the way it enables experiments of potentially wide significance to be made on a limited scale. If a study of the American past reveals many cases in which the states have used their power in an effort to uphold a faulty status quo, it also demonstrates that they have sometimes accepted their responsibilities in a creative manner, producing noteworthy chapters in the history of public welfare and serving, to use the words of Arthur M. Schlesinger, as "laboratories of social innovation." [1] Both aspects of state behavior—the negative and the positive—have been exemplified in the important areas of law enforcement and correction. Students of penology and government alike have lamented the existence of disparate and conflicting statutes and legal procedures, the occasional lack of effective cooperation between officials representing different jurisdictions, and the persistence of archaic penal methods in some parts of the country. On the other side of the picture, however, are examples of pioneering ventures at the state level that have been of great importance in the perennial fight against crime.

In this study I have traced the development of correctional policies in a key state during a critical era in the history of American reform movements. Starting with the adoption of its first modern penal code in 1796, New York for a time followed the lead

[1] Arthur M. Schlesinger, *The American as Reformer* (Cambridge, Mass., 1950), pp. 22, 26.

vii

of Pennsylvania in the treatment of offenders, but during the 1820's it became a significant innovating force in its own right by devising the Auburn system of penitentiary discipline, widely acclaimed and copied throughout the United States and abroad. The various features of this system reflected to a considerable degree the needs, fears, and attitudes prevailing in New York at the time of its adoption; as conditions changed in later years a number of modifications were made, thus providing an interesting record of interaction between a given mode of institutional operation and the environment in which it was developed. By the late 1840's, however, the impulse for prison reform had waned, and methods that were increasingly outmoded continued to be imposed upon most adult convicts for the rest of the nineteenth century despite periodic advances in the treatment of special groups of felons such as first offenders and the criminally insane. A distinct phase of correctional change had thus come to an end more than a decade before the Civil War.

With but few exceptions, professional historians have not been notably active in studying the evolution of law enforcement and correction in America.[2] This is unfortunate, because the way in which a community treats those who deviate from its standards of acceptable behavior often reveals much about its values and preoccupations. There is a need to interpret public responses to crime during various periods of our history in the light of broader trends that were concurrently evident in other fields of human activity.[3] In this book I have tried particularly to place the formative years of the Auburn system in a meaningful social context, because the relative harshness which characterized penal affairs at this time—

[2] This is particularly true in the period of almost thirty years since the appearance of Blake McKelvey's pioneering work, *American Prisons: A Study in American Social History Prior to 1915* (Chicago, 1936). A noteworthy exception, however, is Jack K. Williams, *Vogues in Villainy: Crime and Retribution in Ante-bellum South Carolina* (Columbia, S.C., 1959).

[3] For a valuable work on the development of public attitudes regarding certain types of crime and deviance, see David Brion Davis, *Homicide in American Fiction, 1798–1860: A Study in Social Values* (Ithaca, N.Y., 1957).

contrasting in many ways with the distinctly milder outlook prevailing both in the post-Revolutionary era and again briefly in the 1840's—seemed especially to require explanation. In seeking to account for this comparative stringency, I have emphasized the ways in which conservative reform impulses, prevailing public anxieties, and desires to produce conformity and social control helped to create an atmosphere within which a dominantly repressive penal philosophy could take root and flourish.

In the preparation of this study I have not proceeded from the assumption that my findings would be specifically applicable to questions involving the management of penitentiaries today; and I will be satisfied if they merely help add perspective to matters that are, or should be, of great public concern. I do believe that the history of prison reform in the period before the Civil War is relevant in a broad sense to the penal problems of the present time. Whatever our reactions may be to the methods of those who devised the Auburn system or the rival plan of complete solitary confinement adopted in Pennsylvania, we should remember that these men were trying to deal in a courageous and direct manner with difficulties arising from the very nature of a penitentiary. They knew from experience that separating offenders from the body of law-abiding citizens and throwing them together in an artificially created society composed almost entirely of felons could easily result not in rehabilitation but in even deeper degradation, besides giving rise to formidable administrative problems. The answers that they arrived at may not appeal to us, but the fundamental realities with which they tried to cope still obtain.

The completion of this book would not have been possible without the aid and encouragement of many persons. It is a pleasure to acknowledge their help while assuming full responsibility for any shortcomings that may remain. My father, Gordon C. Lewis, has worked for many years in the fields of law enforcement and correction, and many of his interests have become mine also. I would like to thank my brother-in-law and former teacher, Professor Ira V. Brown of the Pennsylvania State University, for first pointing out to me that the rise of the Auburn system deserved more study than had previously been given to it. I am under great obligation to Professor David Brion Davis of Cornell University, who was most generous with helpful criticism and advice during the preparation of this work. Among others who deserve thanks in this regard are Carroll C. Arnold of the Pennsylvania State University, Walter LaFeber of Cornell University, and Norman B. Wilkinson of the Eleutherian Mills–Hagley Foundation.

The staffs of various libraries and historical agencies were most cooperative during the course of my research, including those connected with the Cornell University Library, the Library of Congress, the New-York Historical Society, the New York State Library, the New York State Historical Association, the Morris Library of the University of Delaware, and the Eleutherian Mills Historical Library. I also appreciate the kindness of Warden Robert E. Murphy, whose staff provided me with a tour of Auburn prison and allowed me to inspect two buildings that remained from the ante-bellum period. The Social Science Research Center of Cornell University at one point aided my investigations with a travel grant, for which I would like to express my gratitude. I am also indebted to the editors of *New York History* and the *New-York Historical Society Quarterly* for publishing a pair of articles based substantially upon two chapters of the doctoral dissertation from which this book has developed.

Finally, my deepest thanks go to my wife, Carolyn, whose encouragement, editorial sense, and typing ability were frequently called upon and never found wanting.

W. DAVID LEWIS

*Eleutherian Mills–Hagley Foundation*
*Wilmington, Delaware*
*June, 1964*

# Contents

# Illustrations

# FROM NEWGATE TO DANNEMORA

*The Rise of the Penitentiary in New York, 1796–1848*

# Chapter I

# The Heritage

THE United States played a pioneering role in the development of modern correctional methods. From the early years of national independence to the coming of the Civil War, the achievements of American penal reformers won international respect and admiration. Distinguished foreign visitors, Alexis de Tocqueville among them, toured the prisons of the New World and wrote valuable treatises on the techniques they observed. Sightseeing Europeans traveling about the new nation seldom failed to include in their itineraries such institutions as the Eastern State Penitentiary at Philadelphia, the New York state prisons at Auburn and Sing Sing, or the Connecticut penitentiary at Wethersfield. American reformers quarreled heatedly about the relative merits of various penal methods, growing especially warm in their praise or denunciation of the rival Auburn and Pennsylvania systems of discipline. "Both have found such earnest, I may say passionate assailants and defenders," remarked a European onlooker, "that we are reminded of various theological controversies, and cannot but wish that their zeal was tempered with greater moderation." [1]

No American state was more deeply involved in penal pioneering during this period than New York, which revamped its old methods of punishment in 1796. Led by a Quaker merchant named

[1] Frederick von Raumer, *America and the American People,* trans. William W. Turner (New York, 1846), p. 233.

1

Thomas Eddy, reformers secured the passage of a law abolishing the death penalty for all but three crimes and prescribing lengthy prison sentences for most major offenses.[2] This action launched New York upon a course of penitentiary management which in time made it the avowed rival of the state from which it had all but copied its first modern penal code.

Of the various influences that induced New York to adopt new modes of punishment in 1796, the most immediate came from the neighboring state of Pennsylvania, where interest in prison reform was deeply rooted. The first assembly of Penn's colony, held at Chester in 1682, had enacted a system of laws punishing most crimes with hard labor in a "house of correction," and retaining the death penalty only for first-degree murder. This code represented a great departure from normal European methods of punishment, and has been regarded by modern scholars as a milestone in the history of penology, but it did not remain on the books very long. In an attempt to gain British sanction for the validity of court trials in which Quaker jurors were affirmed but not sworn, Pennsylvania legislators adopted many features of the harsh English code in 1718. Nevertheless, a precedent for mild penal methods had been set, and renewed efforts for reform awaited only the coming of independence.[3]

Following the removal of British restraints, Pennsylvania soon became a leader in adopting new methods of dealing with criminals. A brief experiment with forced labor "publicly and disgracefully imposed" was inaugurated in 1786, but humanitarians contended that such treatment merely destroyed the felon's sense of shame, and authorities turned to protracted confinement as a preferable policy. The legislature passed a series of laws prohibit-

[2] *Laws of the State of New York Passed at the Sessions of the Legislature Held in the Years 1789, 1790, 1791, 1792, 1793, 1794, 1795, and 1796 Inclusive* (Albany, 1887), III, 669–676.

[3] Harry Elmer Barnes, *The Evolution of Penology in Pennsylvania* (Indianapolis, 1927), pp. 31–55; Herbert W. K. Fitzroy, "The Punishment of Crime in Provincial Pennsylvania," *Pennsylvania Magazine of History and Biography*, LX (July, 1936), 242–269.

ing liquor in jails, establishing separation of the sexes among inmates, appointing official prison inspectors, separating debtors from felons, restricting indiscriminate visiting of jails, and providing solitary confinement for the most hardened offenders. Capital punishment was again reserved for first-degree murder. The Walnut Street Jail, a Philadelphia institution upon which construction had been started before the Revolution, now began receiving felons from all parts of the state.[4]

Applauding these developments, and applying most of the pressure which brought them about, was a group of citizens who in 1787 founded "The Philadelphia Society for Alleviating the Miseries of Public Prisons," which has been called "the first of the great modern prison reform societies."[5] Strong support for new methods came from members of the Society of Friends, reflecting the Quaker belief that any man—even a criminal—possessed a share of the divine "inner light" which could be reached and nurtured through proper treatment. The reform movement, however, was broadly based, enlisting the efforts of such men as Episcopal Bishop William White and the prominent physician Benjamin Rush. Inspiration also came from abroad through the writings of the great English prison reformer John Howard and the achievements of Sir Thomas Beevor, who had established a model jail at Wymondham, Norfolk.[6]

Influential citizens in New York observed the correctional reforms in Pennsylvania with interest. Especially conversant with the new measures was Thomas Eddy, who had been reared in Philadelphia and knew various humanitarians there. As a Tory in the

[4] Job R. Tyson, *Essay on the Penal Law of Pennsylvania* (Philadelphia, 1827), pp. 15–18, 49–54; Negley K. Teeters, *The Cradle of the Penitentiary: The Walnut Street Jail at Philadelphia, 1773–1835* (n.p., 1955), pp. 29–31.

[5] Barnes, *Evolution of Penology in Pennsylvania*, p. 81. For a detailed history of this society see Negley K. Teeters, *They Were in Prison* (Philadelphia, 1937), *passim*.

[6] Orlando F. Lewis, *The Development of American Prisons and Prison Customs, 1776–1845* (n.p., 1922), pp. 33–35; Teeters, *The Cradle of the Penitentiary*, pp. 31–32.

Revolution, Eddy had experienced a brief taste of wretched jail conditions. As a merchant, he had reason to desire a penal code in New York which would protect property more effectively than the ill-assorted and unevenly executed sanguinary punishments that prevailed there. As a Quaker, he believed that many criminals could be reformed if subjected to firm but humane treatment.[7]

Eddy, who eventually came to be known as the "John Howard of America," had few talents as a speaker and was not a profound thinker. Instead, he was a "quiet crusader" who knew how to interest the right people in his ideas and had marked abilities as a lobbyist.[8] In the course of exploring western New York for possible canal routes and sitting in on treaty negotiations with the Indians, he became well acquainted with General Philip Schuyler, father-in-law of Alexander Hamilton and a political star of the first magnitude in the Empire State. Keenly aware of the prestige which the General's name would bring to the cause of prison reform in New York, and of the power which Schuyler wielded as a state senator, Eddy persuaded his friend to visit Philadelphia with him in the winter of 1796 and inspect the Walnut Street Jail. Schuyler was impressed with the institution, and helped Eddy draft a bill for the establishment of a penitentiary system in New York after the two men returned home. In a strategic move, they arranged to have Ambrose Spencer, a powerful political leader, introduce the measure in the legislature, and Schuyler spoke strongly in its support. Eddy played his part during the debates by having copies of the Pennsylvania penal code distributed freely among the lawmakers and by being present as a lobbyist. When the act was passed on March 26, 1796, he was placed on a four-man committee

[7] For an extended account of Eddy's career, still valuable because of the original documents it contains, see Samuel L. Knapp, *The Life of Thomas Eddy* (New York, 1834), *passim*.

[8] Arthur A. Ekirch, "Thomas Eddy: His Ideas and Interests" (unpublished M.A. thesis, Columbia University, 1938), pp. 7, 37. A condensation of this thesis appears as "Thomas Eddy and the Beginnings of Prison Reform in New York," *Proceedings of the New York State Historical Association*, LXI (1943), 376–391.

empowered to build a state prison, and that body in turn gave him primary authority to supervise this task. Thereupon he "engaged the architect and the workmen, and went on in his own way with the whole concern." [9]

Guided by the experience of Pennsylvania and activated by the efforts of Thomas Eddy, New York had thus embarked upon an important social and institutional experiment. To understand the nature of this experiment, however, and to appreciate some of the problems that were encountered in carrying it out, it is necessary to look beyond the immediate circumstances from which the act of 1796 resulted. Like his humanitarian counterparts in Philadelphia, Eddy was a member of a trans-Atlantic community of the benevolently inclined. Throughout his career he carried on an extensive correspondence with European reformers who shared his interests. His theories on the treatment of criminals owed much to the writings of such men as Howard, Montesquieu, and Beccaria. [10] The penitentiary which he built in New York showed considerable European influence, even to the point of being named "Newgate" after the famous English institution. The development of prison reform in the Empire State must therefore be examined in light of the Old World's long experience in dealing with the problem of crime.

The roots of criminal justice are probably embedded in an age

[9] Knapp, *Life of Thomas Eddy*, pp. 56–57, and [Thomas Eddy], *An Account of the State Prison or Penitentiary House, in the City of New-York* (New York, 1801), pp. 12–13. Ironically, Edward Livingston, at this time a citizen of New York and later the most world-renowned American penal theorist, had little or nothing to do with the adoption of his native state's first modern prison legislation. A member of the federal Congress, he had been chairman of a committee on criminal and penal laws in 1794. He and his family, however, were political foes of the New York Federalists, under whose auspices the law of 1796 was passed. See William B. Hatcher, *Edward Livingston: Jeffersonian Republican and Jacksonian Democrat* (University, La., 1940), pp. 1–34 *passim*, and Charles H. Hunt, *Life of Edward Livingston* (New York, 1864), p. 83.

[10] Knapp, *Life of Thomas Eddy, passim*; [Eddy], *Account of the State Prison*, p. 6. On the significance of the trans-Atlantic connection in reform, see especially Michael Kraus, "Eighteenth Century Humanitarianism: Collaboration Between Europe and America," *Pennsylvania Magazine of History and Biography*, LX (July, 1936), 270–286.

when vengeance served as the primary motive for punishment. Retribution was initially meted out to the felon by his victims or their blood relatives, but in time societies selected officials to deal with offenders in the name of the group. The primordial thirst for revenge never completely disappeared, but it was eventually supplemented by religious or ethical considerations. The acts of a criminal, it was reasoned, angered not only his fellows but also the deities whom they worshiped. Unless culprits were apprehended and punished, the wrath of the gods might jeopardize the safety of the entire community. Some groups gradually came to believe in a supernatural moral order which was violated whenever a crime occurred, and to feel that the sense of disequilibrium resulting from such a violation could be removed only through the expiatory suffering of the guilty. Thus the concept of crime was blended with that of sin.[11]

Such ideas are potent. They existed in ante-bellum America, influencing prison reformers who took it for granted that the felon offended both man and God, and that the church as a guardian of moral order and social stability had an important part to play in the treatment of lawbreakers. By this time, however, other concepts had also assumed great significance. According to the theory of deterrence, inflicting pain on an offender was justifiable because it discouraged others from following his example. The idea of reformation, on the other hand, led many to believe that the treatment of a criminal, whether painful or otherwise, should make him a better person.[12] These two philosophies, not really antithetical but nevertheless difficult to reconcile in practice, were

[11] This discussion is based upon material scattered throughout a number of works on penology and criminology. See especially John L. Gillin, *Criminology and Penology* (rev. ed.; New York, 1935), pp. 195–206; Hans von Hentig, *Punishment: Its Origin, Purpose and Psychology* (London, 1937), *passim;* Bronislaw Malinowski, *Crime and Custom in Savage Society* (New York, 1932), p. 99; and Ray M. McConnell, *Criminal Responsibility and Social Constraint* (New York, 1912), p. 6. For the views of a scholar who minimizes the importance of vengeance in the origins of punishment, see Edwin H. Sutherland, *Principles of Criminology* (Chicago, 1934), pp. 299–302.

[12] These theories are discussed at length in McConnell, *Criminal Responsibility and Social Constraint,* pp. 60–112.

part of America's intellectual inheritance from the Old World.

The penal methods that prevailed throughout most of human history impress the modern reader as very severe and, in some cases, utterly cruel. Protracted institutional treatment was beyond the means of any but the most advanced societies, even had the desire to use it for curative ends been present. Such inflictions as whipping, maiming, and killing were attractive to law-enforcement officials not only because they could easily be witnessed by spectators and thus have some deterrent effect, but also because they were speedy and cheap. Occasionally it was profitable to confine felons and force them to row galleys, build public works, or to perform various other useful tasks. In other cases, as in ancient Greece, incarceration became a common alternative punishment for offenders who could not—or would not—pay fines.[13] By and large, however, the prison as a place of punishment or corrective treatment is a modern innovation. Until the eighteenth century it was usually only a place of temporary detention for untried suspects, political enemies of the state, holders of heterodox religious views, and insolvent debtors.[14]

One important organization, however, did manage to gain considerable experience over the centuries in providing institutional treatment for convicted offenders. During the Middle Ages the Roman Catholic Church gained special criminal jurisdiction, within certain limitations, over clergymen and members of religious orders. Excessively severe punishments could, and sometimes did, occur under the use of this authority; but the fact that most offenders preferred to be tried by ecclesiastical courts rather than by civil ones indicates that the penalties inflicted by the former were usually more lenient than those meted out by the latter. Because of this relative clemency, the privilege of "benefit of clergy" became more and more widely sought, and was gradually extended not only to a variety of minor church functionaries

[13] Irving Barkan, "Imprisonment as a Penalty in Ancient Athens," *Classical Philology*, XXXI (October, 1936), 338–341. On the gradual occurrence of the same phenomenon in England, see William Blackstone, *Commentaries on the Laws of England* (Oxford, 1765–1769), IV, 130–158, 209–245.

[14] Harry Elmer Barnes, *The Repression of Crime* (New York, 1926), p. 84.

but also to anybody who could read certain passages of Scripture.[15] Offenders tried by clerical courts could be sent on long pilgrimages or required to make protracted fasts. However, they might also be remanded to ecclesiastical prisons, where the punishment they experienced was justified as curative, being designed to bring about repentance and amendment of life. "The correctional system is Christian, it is Catholic, it is no new system," declared an Italian writer in the nineteenth century. "It had its birth in the monasteries, and a Pope gave it its baptismal name when it came into the world." [16]

Whatever the merits of this claim, the Church of Rome cannot easily be disregarded in discussing the rise of the modern penitentiary. Monastic institutions were designed in part for those who wished to spend lives of expiation and atonement, and the discipline practiced in them had much in common with the regimes imposed upon convicts by later European and American prison reformers. Subsistence upon coarse food or shortened rations; the wearing of distinctive, and in certain cases humiliating, garb; abstinence from sexual and other excitements; the contemplation of past transgressions, accompanied by resolutions to make future amendment; the use of a cellular form of living accommodation; and the encouragement or absolute requirement of silence —all these were features of monastic life which may conceivably have influenced the thinking of those who built and administered prisons in the late eighteenth and early nineteenth centuries. Interestingly, writers on penal reform in ante-bellum America occasionally noted the pertinence of early monastic precedents to their arguments.[17]

[15] See especially George Ives, *A History of Penal Methods* (London, 1914), pp. 29–54. On the use of "benefit of clergy" at a later time in England under the Anglican Church, see Arthur L. Cross, "The English Criminal Law and Benefit of Clergy during the Eighteenth and Early Nineteenth Centuries," *American Historical Review*, XXII (April, 1917), 544–565.

[16] Quoted in Harry Elmer Barnes and Negley K. Teeters, *New Horizons in Criminology* (1st ed.; New York, 1943), p. 502.

[17] See especially the anonymous article "Seclusion," *Pennsylvania Journal of Prison Discipline and Philanthropy*, IV (January, 1849), 4–8.

In ecclesiastical prisons, various types of discipline prevailed. Some inmates confined in these institutions were allowed much freedom in going about the grounds, but others were put in cells on restricted rations or thrown into dungeons and manacled with irons. Flogging, later to become a frequent and controversial practice at many nineteenth-century American penitentiaries, was used in a number of monasteries as well as in church prisons. A punishment particularly dreaded was absolute solitary confinement alleviated only by the infrequent visits of monks or other clerical officials, a type of treatment similar to that which was later to be imposed upon convicts under the Pennsylvania system.[18] Catholic establishments for juvenile delinquents were also significant in foreshadowing subsequent correctional developments. The famous Hospice of St. Michael in Rome influenced such reformers as John Howard, and some writers have attempted to trace a line of descent connecting this institution, the Maison de Force at Ghent, and the New York state prison at Auburn. Scholars have also found interesting anticipations of modern penological theories in the ideas of such Catholic thinkers as St. Thomas Aquinas, Dom Jean Mabillon, Fra Filippo Franci, and Pope Clement XI.[19]

From the sixteenth century onward, ecclesiastical leaders were not alone in considering what penal techniques might replace the expeditious but brutal methods that had prevailed for centuries. Because of a scarcity of laborers in certain areas, as in Germany after the wholesale carnage of the Thirty Years' War, it made more sense to conserve human resources than to waste them through frequent executions and maimings.[20] Some mercantilists who wanted to use judicial power as "a mechanism for providing

---

[18] Ives, *History of Penal Methods*, pp. 40–43.

[19] See especially three articles by Thorsten Sellin: "Filippo Franci—A Precursor of Modern Penology," *Journal of the American Institute of Criminal Law and Criminology*, XVIII (May, 1926), 104–112; "Dom Jean Mabillon—A Prison Reformer of the Seventeenth Century," *ibid.*, XVIII (February, 1927), 581–602; and "The House of Correction for Boys in the Hospice of St. Michael in Rome," *ibid.*, XX (February, 1930), 533–553.

[20] Georg Rusche and Otto Kirchheimer, *Punishment and Social Structure* (New York, 1939), pp. 8–52 *passim*.

society with labour and revenue under particularly advantageous conditions" were especially interested in punishments that would not kill or incapacitate. As Sir William Petty asked in 1662, "Why should not insolvent Thieves be rather punished with slavery than death?" [21] French "Repopulationists" later advocated penal reforms because of similar convictions, and the mercantilist minister Colbert encouraged a systematic policy of consigning offenders to the galleys. Magistrates, he believed, were wasting vital manpower through an overuse of capital punishment.[22]

Galley servitude, which was probably worse than death for many criminals who suffered it, was only one alternative to which various leaders resorted in the search for more intelligent penal policies. A development of particular significance was the evolution of the workhouse, an institution originally designed for the poor which became in time a type of correctional facility in which beggars, paupers, vagabonds, petty offenders, and even a number of actual felons labored at assigned tasks under close supervision. The Calvinist emphasis upon work as both a duty and a morally beneficial activity provided an additional stimulus for the widespread adoption of the workhouse idea. Dreading the strict regimes prevailing in such establishments, it was reasoned, potential inmates might make special efforts to lead law-abiding and self-supporting lives in order to avoid being placed in them; others who persisted in sloth, idleness, or delinquency might reform after a period of confinement. For both practical and theoretical reasons, therefore, workhouses spread rapidly after the mid-sixteenth century, when England began using the London Bridewell as a place of detention for paupers. They were especially popular in Germany and the Low Countries.[23]

[21] Quoted in Eli F. Heckscher, *Mercantilism,* trans. Mendel Shapiro (London, 1934), II, 297.

[22] Joseph J. Spengler, *French Predecessors of Malthus* (Durham, N.C., 1942), pp. 77, 94; Paul W. Bamford, "The Procurement of Oarsmen for French Galleys, 1660–1748," *American Historical Review,* LXV (October, 1959), 37.

[23] See especially Rusche and Kirchheimer, *Punishment and Social Structure,* pp. 41–52.

"With the creation and multiplication of workhouses," one writer has stated, "the foundation of the modern prison system was firmly laid." [24] In view of later industrial developments in American prisons, it is particularly interesting to note that many workhouses quickly came to be managed for profit. In some cases entire institutions were contracted out to private citizens who ran them as business ventures; in others, governmental bodies themselves undertook entrepreneurial functions. Various privileges were given to these combined penal and manufacturing enterprises; in Amsterdam, for example, a monopoly of the rasping of brazilwood for use in the dyeing industry was granted to a local house of correction. Like the prison workshops later to be established in such states as New York, the industrial departments of European workhouses speedily aroused the anger of free craftsmen, who tried to secure legal action against what they regarded as unfair competition.[25] It is also noteworthy that the famous Maison de Force, founded at Ghent in 1772 as a place of correction for offenders, mendicants, vagrants, and the like, was an outgrowth of the workhouse idea. Under the reign of Maria Theresa it had a regime of solitary confinement at night and congregate labor by day which was similar to the system later imposed upon convicts at Auburn prison.[26]

Early prison reformers in America, including those in New York, were familiar with the workhouse idea and aware of the types of discipline practiced at various European institutions. It is likely that knowledge of these establishments was carried to New

[24] Frederick H. Wines, *Punishment and Reformation: A Study of the Penitentiary System* (new ed.; New York, 1919), p. 118.

[25] Rusche and Kirchheimer, *Punishment and Social Structure*, pp. 43–44, 48–51; Thorsten Sellin, *Pioneering in Penology: The Amsterdam Houses of Correction in the Sixteenth and Seventeenth Centuries* (Philadelphia, 1944), p. 54.

[26] See particularly Charles Lucas, *Du Système Pénitentiaire en Europe et aux États-Unis* (Paris, 1828–1830), II, 243–262. I have not been able to determine conclusively that those who developed the Auburn system were influenced by the example of the Maison de Force. However, they could easily have found information about it in the works of John Howard.

Amsterdam by the first Dutch settlers, some of whom came on their way to embarkation through regions where workhouses were common.[27] Even though England did not utilize such institutions for the treatment of criminals to the extent that this was done on the Continent, the British did develop county houses of correction modeled upon the London Bridewell. Penal discipline was authorized by law in these establishments as early as 1609, and some knowledge of the techniques used in them must inevitably have crossed the Atlantic.[28] By 1735, New York City had a workhouse where disobedient slaves and servants were sent for punishment, various types of vagrants and runaways were forced to labor, and paupers were given alms in addition to employment in spinning or farming.[29] Later in the century John Howard supplied detailed information on European workhouses to American readers in his writings on prison reform.[30]

The workhouse gave responsible officials in both the Old World and the New a type of institution which, if efficiently managed, could eliminate financial objections to the protracted confinement of offenders. Equally important, it offered a type of penal treatment which would not grate upon the humanitarian sensibilities of citizens who throughout the eighteenth century found old methods of punishment increasingly bizarre and distasteful. If the foundation of the modern prison system had been laid, however, the penitentiary itself did not appear until the period of the American Revolution. In Europe, many felons—especially non-clergyable ones—continued to suffer brutal and time-honored inflictions. Offenders in eighteenth-century France, for example, could be burned at the stake, immersed in boiling liquids, drawn

[27] Sellin, *Pioneering in Penology*, p. 108.

[28] Sidney and Beatrice Webb, *English Prisons under Local Government* (New York, 1922), pp. 12–17.

[29] George W. Edwards, *New York as an Eighteenth Century Municipality, 1731–1766* (New York, 1917), pp. 98–99.

[30] John Howard, *The State of the Prisons in England and Wales . . . and an Account of Some Foreign Prisons* (Warrington, England, 1777), *passim*, especially pp. 119–133.

and quartered, broken on the wheel, mangled, mutilated, branded, flogged, or placed in the pillory.[31] The Swedish law code of 1734—actually a reform document—prescribed death for sixty-eight offenses.[32] In England there was a great extension of laws authorizing sanguinary punishments; of more than two hundred crimes which were capital in 1800, about two-thirds had become so within the previous hundred years. Executions were occasions of public diversion, with morbid mobs struggling for the best vantage points from which to witness the fate of the condemned and even paying large sums of money for what amounted to "box seats."[33] The entertainment value of spectacular punishments and the persistence of the idea that terror was necessary for the deterrence of crime contributed to the slowness with which modern methods were adopted, as did the existence of special provisions for large numbers of clergyable and other types of offenders. In England many criminals were deported to the American colonies because of such legal loopholes, particularly after 1717.[34]

Punishments in America were not usually as brutal or as frequently inflicted as those which prevailed in many areas of Europe, but were nevertheless copied from Old World practices. In colonial New York, for example, the jail was chiefly a place for debtors or for those awaiting trial. For over a century after the founding of New Amsterdam there was not even a separate prison building on Manhattan Island. If jail sentences were imposed, they usually supplemented other punishments or lasted but a short time. Under the code of laws introduced after the conquest of the colony by the

[31] Shelby T. McCloy, *The Humanitarian Movement in Eighteenth-Century France* (Lexington, Ky., 1957), pp. 173–175.

[32] Carl Ludwig von Bar *et al.*, *A History of Continental Criminal Law*, trans. Thomas S. Bell *et al.* (Boston, 1916), p. 296.

[33] C. Grant Robertson, *England under the Hanoverians* (London, 1911), p. 484; Leon Radzinowicz, *A History of English Criminal Law and Its Administration from 1750: The Movement for Reform, 1750–1833* (New York, 1948), pp. 175–178.

[34] Cross, "English Criminal Law and Benefit of Clergy," *passim;* Marcus W. Jernegan, *Laboring and Dependent Classes in Colonial America, 1607–1783* (reprinted ed.; New York, 1960), pp. 48–49.

Duke of York, eleven offenses were made capital, a number which had increased to sixteen by the late eighteenth century. Public whipping, pillorying, banishment, branding, stocking, and carting (tying a culprit to the tail of a wagon and dragging him ignominiously through the streets) were among the punishments imposed by the magistrates. Flogging was frequently employed, with judges sentencing offenders to as few as five or as many as one hundred and fifty lashes for a variety of crimes. One painful device, copied from military use, was a wooden horse with a sharp back upon which prisoners sat with weights and chains hung about their feet. After the British took over the colony this punishment was sometimes aggravated by placing steed and rider in a cart and jogging them up and down the streets, a method called "the horse of Mary Price" in honor of its first victim.[35]

The severity of penal justice in colonial New York, however, can easily be exaggerated. As in other American colonies, there was a chronic shortage of labor which made the wisdom of frequent executions or disabling penalties somewhat dubious. Fines were frequently used, especially in New York City, where the proceeds were split among informers, sheriffs, and the municipality. Juries hesitated to subject culprits to punishments, such as carting and pillorying, which rendered those who suffered them legally "infamous" and consequently unable to hold public office, bring actions at law, be witnesses in court proceedings, or hold property. Unlike the citizens of some other colonies, New Yorkers were comparatively tolerant of moral offenses, and accordingly less severe in punishing those guilty of them. Statistics on the incidence of capital inflictions, moreover, are distorted by the atypically large number of cases which occurred in such times of public hysteria as accompanied the attempted slave insurrection of 1741–1742.

[35] Barnes, *The Repression of Crime*, pp. 87–88; Elizabeth D. Lewis, "Old Prisons and Punishments," in *Historic New York: Being the Second Series of the Half Moon Papers*, ed. Maud W. Goodwin *et al.* (New York, 1899), pp. 83–94; Julius Goebel, Jr., and T. Raymond Naughton, *Law Enforcement in Colonial New York: A Study in Criminal Procedure* (New York, 1944), pp. 514–516, 709.

Criminal justice in early New York was no trifling matter, but it should not be portrayed in excessively dark hues.[36]

The tendency to be somewhat lenient in enforcing penal laws which were severe on paper was evident not only in America but also in Europe. Despite a growing list of capital statutes in England, for example, the number of criminals who were actually executed declined throughout the eighteenth century. This was not only because of the alternative of deportation but also because humanitarian juries often refused to convict offenders for minor delinquencies punishable by death. In addition, a proliferation of conflicting and imprecise laws enabled many criminals to take advantage of loopholes, particularly if they were able to retain clever lawyers.[37]

This state of affairs had disturbing implications. When citizens preferred in many cases to let palpably guilty men go free rather than to exact inhumane penalties, and when ill-drafted or inconsistent statutes were readily evaded and circumvented by the unscrupulous, would-be offenders were encouraged to believe that they could break the law with impunity. This not only nullified the deterrent aim of punishment but also made it difficult for victims of crime to gain restitution and impaired the security of property. On the other hand, if juries were to forget about humanitarian scruples and begin to implement increasingly harsh penal codes in an unflinching way, they would run the risk of further brutalizing the public and wasting more human resources. Even milder physical punishments which did not kill offenders but merely disfigured or humiliated them might, in the words of one

[36] Goebel and Naughton, *Law Enforcement in Colonial New York*, pp. 702–709, 718–719; T. Raymond Naughton, "Criminal Law in Colonial New York," *Proceedings of the New York State Historical Association*, XXXI (1933), p. 238; Arthur E. Peterson, *New York as an Eighteenth Century Municipality Prior to 1731* (New York, 1917), pp. 194–195.

[37] Radzinowicz, *English Criminal Law*, p. 151; Cross, "English Criminal Law and Benefit of Clergy," *passim;* G. M. Trevelyan, *English Social History: A Survey of Six Centuries* (London, 1942), p. 348; Coleman Phillipson, *Three Criminal Law Reformers: Beccaria, Bentham, Romilly* (London, 1923), pp. 164 ff.

reformer, cause such people to "lose all sense of shame out of sheer habituation to disgrace," and to remain criminals all their lives.[38] Dilemmas like these became of increasing concern to thoughtful eighteenth-century humanitarians, causing them to look for ways in which to modify existing criminal laws and penal practices.

Broadly speaking, such reformers can be divided into two main groups. One of these, representing the outlook of the Enlightenment, wanted above all else to make criminal law rational, to strip it of metaphysical concepts and purge it of superstition. The second group, inspired to a large degree by religious convictions, saw the offender as a child of God who should be treated with compassion and love. Both points of view were influenced by the growth of toleration and humanitarianism in the eighteenth century, but they formed a somewhat unstable combination. Prison reformers with pronounced religious ideas, John Howard among them, were apt to be hostile toward such rationalists as Voltaire. Christians who held that man sinned out of free moral choice and was accountable to God for his misdoings had reason to disapprove when French *philosophes* questioned the existence of free will.[39] On the other hand, such rationalists as Jeremy Bentham were critical of those whose sentiments and emotions governed their outlook on penal affairs.[40] Thus the eighteenth century handed down a mixed legacy to future generations of prison reformers.

Rationalists were appalled by the wanton and capricious cruelty, the reverence for outworn tradition, and the outright stupidity which typified the penal methods of their day. Above all else, they wanted a criminal code that would be predictable in its operations. Beginning with Montesquieu, they demanded punishments proportioned to the relative seriousness of offenses. They held that

[38] Phillipson, *Three Criminal Law Reformers*, pp. 61, 170–171, 291–294; William Eden (Lord Auckland), *Principles of Penal Law* (2nd ed.; London, 1771), pp. 13, 59, 62; Jonas Hanway, *Distributive Justice and Mercy* (London, 1781), pp. 11–14.

[39] See Derek L. Howard, *John Howard: Prison Reformer* (London, 1958), p. 34; Phillipson, *Three Criminal Law Reformers*, pp. 48–49.

[40] Élie Halévy, *The Growth of Philosophic Radicalism*, trans. Mary Morris (London, 1928), p. 69.

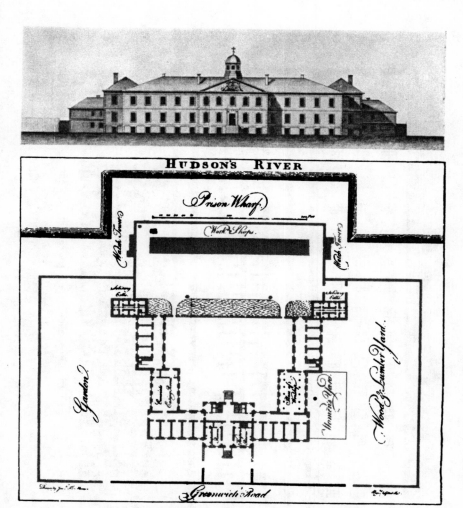

1. Front elevation and ground plan of Newgate, 1797. From an engraving by Gilbert Fox from originals by Joseph F. Mangin, architect, in [Thomas Eddy], *An Account of the State Prison . . . in the City of New-York* (New York, 1801). Reprinted by courtesy of the New-York Historical Society.

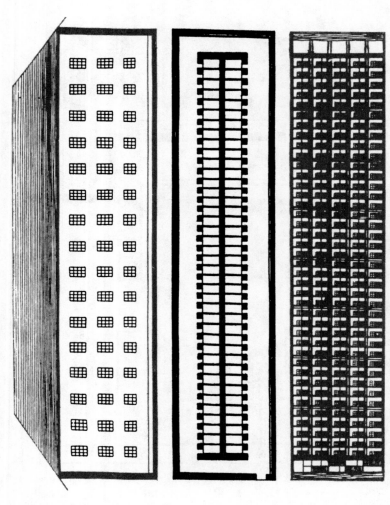

2. The north wing at Auburn prison, showing exterior elevation, floor plan, and breastwork of solitary cells. From *Report of Gershom Powers, Agent and Keeper of the State Prison at Auburn Made to the Legislature Jan. 7, 1828* (Albany, 1828). Reprinted by courtesy of the New-York Historical Society.

society should subject the criminal to no more pain than was necessary to preserve the safety of the community from his future depredations and to deter others from following his example. They believed that the certainty of punishment was far more important than severity for the purpose of preventing crime. Because theories of revenge and expiation were subjective, metaphysical, or emotional, they could furnish no scientific basis for human justice, and rationalists wanted them to be discarded. Such reform doctrines were stated most succinctly in the writings of the Italian theorist Cesare Beccaria, whose *Dei delitti e delle pene (An Essay on Crimes and Punishments)* was first published in 1764. They were popularized most effectively by Voltaire, who admired Beccaria warmly and contributed nearly a score of works to the cause of ameliorating penal laws. They were systematized most comprehensively by Jeremy Bentham, who devised an elaborate set of criteria for punishments and designed a model prison called the "Panopticon," a circular structure in which each cell was subject to surveillance from a central vantage point.[41]

In calling attention to serious evils and abuses, and in setting up standards by which the desirability of various new penal methods could be gauged, rationalists played an indispensable role in helping to pave the way for modern prison reform. The impact of their thinking was great both in England and in America. Sir William Blackstone's monumental *Commentaries on the Laws of England* showed the influence of Montesquieu, for example, in rejecting all expiatory theories of punishment and in espousing clearly definable goals of reformation, deterrence, and the security of society.[42] William Eden's *Principles of Penal Law* accepted the doctrine that criminals should be given the smallest penalties compatible

[41] See especially Phillipson, *Three Criminal Law Reformers, passim;* McCloy, *The Humanitarian Movement in Eighteenth-Century France,* pp. 182–185; Marcello T. Maestro, *Voltaire and Beccaria as Reformers of the Criminal Law* (New York, 1942), *passim.* Bentham's "Panopticon" influenced the design of the original Virginia penitentiary at Richmond, the first Western State Penitentiary at Allegheny, Pennsylvania, and the Illinois prison at Joliet, among others. Barnes and Teeters, *New Horizons in Criminology,* pp. 484–485.

[42] Blackstone, *Commentaries,* IV, 11–12.

with the safety of the group and contended that the very word "punishment" was applied to human institutions only "from an abuse in language," for "vengeance belongeth not to man." [43] The influence of Beccaria's ideas in America was shown in such measures as Thomas Jefferson's proposed bill for proportioning crimes and punishments in Virginia in the late 1770's,[44] as well as in the subsequent activities of various prison reformers.

Rationalist ideas on penal policy were carried to an extreme by such writers as the English radical William Godwin. Denying the existence of free will, Godwin argued that punishment was an anomaly because the whole concept of culpability was false. Coercion was justifiable only in extreme instances when "suffering the offender to be at large shall be notoriously injurious to the public security." Even when such restraint was necessary, it should be used only to keep the felon from harming others and to force him to submit to curative treatment. Godwin believed, however, that such treatment would actually have a deterrent effect, because it would be painful:

Few men would enter upon a course of violence with the certainty of being obliged by a slow and patient process to amputate their errors. It is the uncertainty of punishment under the existing forms that multiplies crimes. Remove this uncertainty, and it would be as unreasonable to expect that a man would wilfully break his leg, for the sake of being cured by a skilful surgeon. Whatever gentleness the intellectual physician may display, it is not to be believed that men can part with rooted habits of injustice and vice without the sensation of considerable pain. [45]

Such passages indicate that Godwin believed in some type of protracted institutional care, but this was not advocated by all rationalists. Beccaria was content to have prisons retain their time-

[43] Eden, *Principles of Penal Law,* pp. 6, 14, 52, 330.
[44] Dumas Malone, *Jefferson the Virginian* (Boston, 1948), pp. 269–271.
[45] William Godwin, *An Enquiry Concerning Political Justice* (Dublin, 1793), II, 231–235, 285–293, 297.

honored functions as places of detention for those awaiting trial. Voltaire saw no danger in continuing to use corporal punishments, although he objected to cruel and unusual inflictions. Eden was initially very critical of imprisonment as a penal method, asserting that "it sinks useful subjects into burthens on the community, and has always a bad effect upon their morals: nor can it communicate the benefit of example, being in its nature secluded from the eye of the people." If corporal punishments did not disfigure or mutilate, Eden did not oppose them; indeed, he displayed a predilection for penalties that involved public shame and ignominy. In America, Thomas Jefferson, like early Philadelphia reformers, was for a time in favor of public labor as the best alternative to sanguinary measures.[46]

One reason why rationalists did not quickly seize upon imprisonment as a satisfactory correctional method was a humanitarian consideration typified by Eden's remark that "jailers are in general a merciless race of men." [47] Although some workhouses were managed with an eye to neatness and efficiency—partly because this was necessary to achieve economic success in their operation—the usual European or American jail was a horrible place which generally discharged its inmates in far worse condition than they had been upon admission. That such men as Blackstone, Eden, and Bentham ultimately accepted imprisonment as a standard penal technique was chiefly due to the work of certain English reformers, most of them actuated by religious motives, who not only exposed miserable jail conditions but also tried to prove that a prison did not have to exemplify everything that was loathsome and terrible.

There had been an awareness of the need for remedying bad prison conditions in England as early as the period of Cromwell's

[46] Cesare Beccaria, *An Essay on Crimes and Punishments,* trans. Edward D. Ingraham (reprinted ed.; Stanford, Calif., 1953), pp. 109–111; Maestro, *Voltaire and Beccaria,* pp. 91–92; Eden, *Principles of Penal Law,* pp. 50, 57, 59–63; Malone, *Jefferson the Virginian,* pp. 272–273.

[47] Eden, *Principles of Penal Law,* p. 54.

Protectorate.[48] Moses Pitt's quaint but graphic treatise *The Cry of the Oppressed*, published in 1691, revealed shocking miseries prevailing in debtors' prisons throughout the realm.[49] A noted Anglican divine, Thomas Bray, reported on wretched jail conditions to the Society for Promoting Christian Knowledge at the turn of the eighteenth century. Finding that intermingling of the sexes, indiscriminate use of alcoholic beverages, corruption among the keepers, and other evils existed in British prisons, Bray recommended various methods that might make such institutions fit places of detention. Among these measures were official inspections; the prohibition of liquor and wine; the abolition of such old customs as garnish and chummage, under which incoming inmates were compelled to part with either their money or their clothing; segregation of the sexes; the separation of old from young offenders; systematic labor; and the promulgation of specific prison rules. Bray also suggested that inmates who behaved well should be aided in finding employment after release.[50]

Although these ideas were too much in advance of their time to be adopted, Bray's work was carried on by his friend and associate James Edward Oglethorpe, who headed a parliamentary committee which exposed vile conditions existing in various debtors' prisons in 1729 and 1730. Revealing that "the sale of offices, breaches of trust, enormous extortions, oppression, intimidation, gross brutalities, and the highest crimes and misdemeanours" were prevalent in the management of such prisons as the Fleet, Marshalsea, and Westminster, the report of this committee led to a sensational series of trials involving four wardens, including the notorious Thomas

[48] Auguste Jorns, *The Quakers as Pioneers in Social Work*, trans. Thomas K. Brown, Jr. (New York, 1931), pp. 166–167.

[49] Moses Pitt, *The Cry of the Oppressed: Being a True and Tragical Account of the Unparallel'd Sufferings of Multitudes of Poor Imprisoned Debtors, In Most of the Gaols in England* (London, 1691), *passim*.

[50] The text of Bray's report is included in Hepworth Dixon, *John Howard and the Prison-World of Europe*, 1st ed. only (London, 1849), pp. 10–18, and in William O. B. Allen and Edmund McClure, *Two Hundred Years: The History of the Society for Promoting Christian Knowledge, 1698–1898* (London, 1898), pp. 54–57.

Bambridge. The concern of Bray and Oglethorpe for imprisoned debtors also helped lead to the establishment of the American colony of Georgia in 1732.[51]

As the work of Bray and Oglethorpe shows, the shortcomings of English prisons troubled an occasional Anglican churchman. Of more importance for British and American penal reform, however, were the efforts of various reformers who belonged to the Society of Friends. Like William Penn, who was imprisoned three times prior to the founding of Pennsylvania, many Quakers had learned at first hand the terrors of confinement in typical English jails. Their belief in the doctrine of the "inner light" led them to seek not only to better prison conditions but also to convince their contemporaries that the aim of penal treatment should be to reform rather than to punish.[52]

A good example of an early Quaker prison reformer was John Bellers, a cloth merchant. Bellers traveled throughout England interviewing officials in an attempt to secure better conditions for incarcerated Friends, and was also interested in the workhouse movement. An opponent of capital punishment, he believed that many men became criminals because of adverse economic, environmental, or educational circumstances over which they had no control. Such people, he contended, were really children of the state, and the authorities should be as reluctant to put them to death as a loving father would be to kill his own offspring. Instead, they should be given curative treatment. Bellers knew, however, that confinement in British jails merely confirmed most offenders in vice and depravity. He therefore advocated strict regulation of prisons, suitable employment for inmates, restrictions upon the selling of intoxicating drinks in jails, and an end to the practice of allowing wealthy prisoners to buy special indulgences. He also

[51] Amos A. Ettinger, *James Edward Oglethorpe: Imperial Idealist* (Oxford, 1936), pp. 89–95; Verner W. Crane, "Dr. Thomas Bray and the Charitable Colony Project, 1730," *William and Mary Quarterly*, 3rd Ser., XIX (January, 1962), 49–63.

[52] Jorns, *The Quakers as Pioneers in Social Work*, pp. 163–166; William I. Hull, *William Penn: A Topical Biography* (London, 1937), pp. 181–196.

believed that inducing felons to get married might be a good way to steady and reform them. In view of the significant Pennsylvania penal code of 1682, it is interesting to note that Bellers knew William Penn and probably had a direct influence upon the Proprietor's thinking.[53]

Because their concern about penal policy helped lead to important correctional experiments in Pennsylvania, New York, and elsewhere, the Quakers played a key role in the development of American penology. The greatest single influence upon English and American prison reform in the late eighteenth century, however, was that of John Howard. A pious Dissenter who anticipated such later humanitarians as Dorothea Dix and Horace Mann in the utter abandon with which he poured his energies into an ameliorative cause, Howard threw himself into the work of prison inspection from 1773 onward. Visiting jails, dungeons, workhouses, bridewells, and other penal institutions throughout the length and breadth of Europe, he carefully collected facts on existing conditions, reported them to the public, proposed needed corrections, checked to see how these improvements worked if he could secure their adoption, and then reported to his readers again, all in a relatively cold and unemotional manner. Such techniques proved very effective, and set a precedent which was important not only in the development of penology but also in the evolution of social work in general. "It was Howard," states one modern scholar, "who first applied to the field of social distress the empirical method of collecting and comparing personal experience."[54]

Howard's importance rests not only upon the fact that he exposed bad jail conditions, but also upon his success in convincing influential men that prisons could be improved, could be made relatively humane, could serve as basic weapons with which to

[53] A. Ruth Fry, *John Bellers, 1654–1725: Quaker, Economist and Social Reformer. His Writings Reprinted, with a Memoir* (London, 1937), pp. 5–9, 14, 18, 75–77, 161–164. On the probability of Bellers having influenced Penn, see also Fitzroy, "Punishment of Crime in Provincial Pennsylvania," p. 245.
[54] Max Grünhut, *Penal Reform: A Comparative Study* (Oxford, 1948), p. 35.

fight crime and attempt the reformation of delinquents. Such reformers as Bellers and Bray had tried to do this, but Howard was the first person to do so with lasting results. Thus he effectively supplemented the work of rationalists who demonstrated the need for more scientific penal codes but who, with the possible exception of Bentham, did not have equal success in devising appropriate methods of correction. Rejecting the idea that jails were necessarily places of idleness and dissipation, Howard urged his countrymen to copy some of the techniques which had been worked out in various Dutch and Flemish workhouses he had visited. In his closely factual and logical way he proposed definite plans for prison construction, with provision for the solitary confinement of inmates at night; separation of the sexes; segregation of felons from lesser offenders; the maintenance of infirmaries, sickwards, and chapels; the hiring of qualified surgeons, chaplains, and inspectors; the prohibition of liquors and harmful practices; and the promulgation of fixed rules governing food, cleanliness, bedding, and conduct.[55]

The time was ripe for such suggestions, for the American Revolution had deprived Great Britain, at least temporarily, of a place to which clergyable and other types of offenders could be transported. The establishment of a penitentiary system such as Howard proposed appealed to reflective Englishmen as a possible alternative to deportation. William Eden overcame his previous objections to prisons and became a convert to Howard's ideas, as did Sir William Blackstone. Together these two men drafted comprehensive legislation authorizing the construction of national penitentiaries, the use of hard labor within them, the provision of proper food and clothing for inmates, and the maintenance of strict institutional discipline. Passed by Parliament in 1779, the "Hard Labour Act" seemed to indicate that a new era in criminal justice was at hand.[56]

Such promising prospects, however, did not materialize. A three-

[55] Howard, *The State of the Prisons*, pp. 42–68, 145.
[56] S. and B. Webb, *English Prisons under Local Government*, pp. 38–39.

man committee including Howard himself was appointed to implement the legislation, but the members could not agree upon sites
for the new penitentiaries, and Howard resigned in disgust in January, 1781. By this time, the death of Blackstone had removed one
of the act's strongest champions.[57] The new measure also aroused
opposition from a number of persons who pointed out that it permitted convicts to work together during the daytime and thus gave
them a chance to corrupt one another. Thus was provided a preliminary airing of an issue which split nineteenth-century prison
reformers into opposing camps and provided the basis for the
bitter disputes which took place between adherents of the Auburn
and Pennsylvania systems.

Well before the passage of the "Hard Labour Act," actual observation of the way in which English jails corrupted their occupants had prompted some individuals to recommend the separate
confinement of inmates. In a sermon preached in 1740, an Anglican prelate named Joseph Butler advocated a plan "to exclude all
sorts of revel-mirth from places where offenders are confined, to
separate the young from the old, and to force them both, in solitude with labour and low diet, to make the experiment how far
their natural strength of mind can support them under guilt or
shame and poverty." Three decades later, a published letter to Sir
Robert Ladbroke attempted "to show the good effects to be expected from the confinement of criminals in separate apartments." [58] Howard had read both of these documents, and believed
that it was necessary to separate convicts at night. He was nevertheless willing to allow group employment by day, possibly because
he thought that adequate techniques of supervision could be
devised and believed that joint labor would be economically
advantageous.[59]

One exponent of unmitigated solitary confinement was dead
by the time the "Hard Labour Act" was passed, but exerted some

[57] Dixon, *John Howard and the Prison-World of Europe*, pp. 285–290.
[58] Quoted in Grünhut, *Prison Reform*, pp. 30–31.
[59] Howard, *The State of the Prisons*, pp. 43, 60.

posthumous influence through his poetical work *Thoughts in Prison*. The Rev. William Dodd, a critic of too frequent capital punishments, had himself been convicted of forgery and sentenced to die. Making use of a period of solitary confinement preceding his execution, he publicly repented of his misdeeds and extolled the regenerative powers of being imprisoned in his lonely cell:

> Devotion's parent, Recollection's nurse,
> Source of Repentance true; of the Mind's wounds
> The deepest prober, but the safest cure!

> Hail, sacred SOLITUDE! These are thy works,
> True source of good supreme! Thy blest effects
> Already on my Mind's delighted eye
> Open beneficent.[60]

Another champion of utter solitude was Sir George Paul, later to become a significant penal administrator and pioneer in the building and management of Gloucester Penitentiary. Paul believed in the reformability of criminals, but held that this was best accomplished by preventing any contact between prisoners.[61]

The most prominent advocate of strict solitary confinement, however, was probably Jonas Hanway, a reformer and writer whose extensive work for the betterment of prison conditions has been virtually eclipsed by the fame of his contemporary, Howard. Though he admitted that for a time solitude could be "nauseous to the taste" and "terrible to the imagination," Hanway shared Dodd's mystical faith in its regenerative power, even in cases where it was used only for a few days.[62] In 1776, three years before the passage of the "Hard Labour Act," Hanway laid down a plan for a model institution which would ensure the complete isolation of its inmates. Here, about fifty years before the building of the

[60] William Dodd, *Thoughts in Prison* (London, 1777), p. 87.

[61] William Crawford, *Report . . . on the Penitentiaries of the United States* (n.p., 1834), p. 28.

[62] Jonas Hanway, *Solitude in Imprisonment* (London, 1776), *passim*, especially pp. 42, 75.

Eastern State Penitentiary in Philadelphia, was a vision of how to implement what later became famous as the Pennsylvania system.

A building of large dimensions, Hanway's prison was to accommodate over two hundred inmates in cells twenty-four feet deep by twenty feet wide by fourteen feet high. Each of these compartments was to be connected to a central chapel by an individual enclosed passageway terminating in a separate barred closet from which the inmate could see church services but not observe his fellow convicts. Walled gardens were provided for the physical exercise of sick and convalescent prisoners, or for the recreation of well-behaved inmates, and were to be reached by means of passageways similar to those leading to the chapel. Breaches of discipline were to be punished by confinement in a dungeon on a diet of bread and water. Tracts and printed sermons were to be distributed to the convicts, whose educational and religious needs were to take precedence over any considerations of potential gain which might accrue to the state from inmate labor. Anonymity was to pervade the institution to the highest possible degree; the prisoners were to be completely unknown to outsiders and even to the turnkeys except by number. Only the head warden, the clerk, and proper official visitors or religious advisers were to know them by name.[63]

It is not surprising that Hanway was strident in his opposition to the legislation passed in 1779. His tract *Distributive Justice and Mercy*, published in 1781, was an extended attack upon the new law. In 1784, Jeremy Bentham joined the exponents of isolation, believing that solitude prevented escape plots and the mutual contamination of prisoners. He later changed his mind, however, claiming that the close inspection possible under his Panopticon system would eliminate the need for keeping offenders apart at all times.[64]

The extent to which the opposition of such men as Hanway contributed to the failure of the "Hard Labour Act" is only con-

[63] *Ibid.*, pp. 111–124.
[64] Halévy, *The Growth of Philosophic Radicalism,* pp. 82–84.

jectural. Doubtless the dissension that prevailed in the committee charged with executing the law was partly responsible for the fact that the statute was not effectively implemented. While reformers quarreled, the government sidestepped the controversy and resorted to such expedients as brutalizing and pestilential prison ships or to the old remedy of deportation, this time to Australia. A second penitentiary act was passed in 1791, but its provisions were permissive and it could not be enforced.[65] Three years later, Parliament endorsed Bentham's Panopticon system, but difficulties involving the selection of a site and the purchasing of land wrecked the project and made it one of the most disappointing episodes of the utilitarian philosopher's career. Further action to establish a penitentiary system was not taken until after the end of the Napoleonic Wars, when construction was begun on Millbank prison.[66]

In France, events followed a similar course. After the outbreak of the Revolution, the National Assembly decreed in 1791 that felons should be confined separately from those awaiting trial, and set up regulations providing for decent food, sanitary quarters, and humane treatment. Plans were made to build new prisons, and supplementary decrees were issued in 1794, but the tangible results were disappointing. Because of the overcrowding of jails, especially during the Reign of Terror, conditions in many institutions became progressively worse instead of better. Like the British "Hard Labour Act," the French law of 1791 passed into oblivion; the vicissitudes of war and revolution provided an inhospitable atmosphere for prison reform.[67] Even in Ghent, discipline deteriorated at the celebrated Maison de Force, and the practice of keeping inmates separated at night was discontinued.[68]

In looking back over the evolution of penal methods in Europe,

[65] S. and B. Webb, *English Prisons under Local Government*, pp. 40–41.

[66] Phillipson, *Three Criminal Law Reformers*, pp. 129–130.

[67] McCloy, *The Humanitarian Movement in Eighteenth-Century France*, pp. 150–171; John H. Cary, "France Looks to Pennsylvania: The Eastern Penitentiary as a Symbol of Reform," *Pennsylvania Magazine of History and Biography*, LXXXII (April, 1958), 187–188.

[68] Lucas, *Du Système Pénitentiaire*, II, 259–260, 262.

therefore, it becomes clear that the United States was less the originator of the penitentiary system than the recipient of a long tradition which European countries carried to the point of climax but failed to culminate. While the Napoleonic Wars raged in the Old World, leadership in correctional matters passed to America more or less by default. But this in no way diminishes the importance of what was achieved in the United States. In building upon European precedents, making a pragmatic test of theories originally conceived across the Atlantic, and from time to time adding new ideas and techniques of their own, American reformers made a noteworthy contribution to the development of modern penology. With the construction of Newgate prison under way in 1796, Thomas Eddy and his fellow New Yorkers took their place beside Pennsylvania humanitarians in the vanguard of this significant effort.

# Chapter II

# The First Experiment

THE legislation which Thomas Eddy secured in 1796 provided for two state penitentiaries. One of these was to be built at Albany under the supervision of a committee which included Philip Schuyler. The other was to be constructed in New York City by Eddy and his associates.[1] Less than a year later, however, the Albany plan was abandoned, possibly because it was believed that the number of convicts from upstate areas would be small and that one prison would therefore suffice.[2] "Newgate," which rose in Greenwich Village on the east bank of the Hudson about a mile and a half from City Hall, was for nearly two decades to be the only institution receiving felons convicted under the new penal code. This penitentiary, prophesied Eddy in 1801, would "become a durable monument of the wisdom, justice, and humanity of its legislators, more glorious than the most splendid achievements of conquerors or kings; and be remembered when the magnificent structures of folly and pride, with their founders, are alike exterminated and

[1] *Laws of the State of New York Passed at the Sessions of the Legislature Held in the Years, 1789, 1790, 1791, 1792, 1793, 1794, 1795, and 1796, Inclusive* (Albany, 1887), III, 671–672.

[2] *Laws . . . 1797, 1798, 1799, 1800, Inclusive* (Albany, 1887), IV, 11; Thomas Eddy to Philip Schuyler, Aug. 22, 1796, Schuyler Papers, New York Public Library. In this letter Eddy estimated that the number of convicts at the proposed Albany prison would not exceed thirty or forty "for several years to come."

forgotten." [3] Thus began the history of an institution which became within a generation an object of derision among well-informed citizens.

As could be expected, Eddy leaned heavily on the experience of Pennsylvania in constructing New York's first penitentiary. In April, 1796, he wrote for advice to Caleb Lownes, a Quaker iron-merchant who was an inspector of the Walnut Street Jail. Lownes responded with a long letter giving his views on penal discipline and containing detailed information about improvements being contemplated at the Philadelphia prison. In July, he made a personal visit to New York to assist in drawing up plans for Newgate, making suggestions which, according to Eddy, saved the Empire State "an expense of Ten Thousand pounds." [4]

It is not surprising, therefore, that Newgate when completed showed a considerable similarity to the Walnut Street Jail. In each institution, two wings containing quarters for inmates extended backward from a central structure housing administrative offices. At the New York prison, solitary cells for the worst offenders were placed in the rear portions of the wings; at Philadelphia, they were put in a separate building altogether. At both institutions, workshops were erected behind the main prison complex. In some important respects, however, Newgate was different from its Pennsylvania prototype. Unlike the Walnut Street Jail, which contained accommodations for vagrants, suspects, and debtors, Eddy's penitentiary was from the beginning designed and constructed for felons only. It was also provided with a large room for public worship, whereas the Philadelphia establishment had been built before it was thought advisable to hold religious exercises among criminals. [5]

[3] [Thomas Eddy], *An Account of the State Prison or Penitentiary House, in the City of New-York* (New York, 1801), p. 70.

[4] Caleb Lownes to Eddy, April 19, 1796, and Eddy to Schuyler, July 14, 1796, Schuyler Papers.

[5] A plan and description of the Walnut Street Jail is provided in Harry Elmer Barnes and Negley K. Teeters, *New Horizons in Criminology* (1st ed.; New York, 1943), pp. 494–495. See also Negley K. Teeters, *The Cradle of the*

Eddy's correspondence makes it clear that he consulted Howard's writings on prisons while supervising the construction of New-gate.[6] Nevertheless, he disregarded Howard's idea that it was necessary to keep convicts in solitary confinement at night, much to his later regret. His decision to allow inmates to mingle even during sleeping hours was probably influenced by the confidence which Lownes expressed in the state of discipline at the Walnut Street Jail, where nighttime separation did not occur except among the most hardened or refractory prisoners. At the completed New York institution, most convicts were housed in fifty-four apartments with dimensions of twelve by eighteen feet, designed to accommodate eight occupants each.[7]

Eddy not only designed Newgate, but also became its first agent, a position roughly corresponding to that of today's warden. He brought to his new assignment a philosophy which was both stern and humanitarian. An unsentimental man, he believed that the prison administrator had to consider his charges as "wicked and depraved, capable of every atrocity, and ever plotting some means of violence and escape." [8] On the other hand, he held that no two inmates were alike, and that it would be a mistake to treat convicts as if they had been formed in one common mold. Along with Caleb Lownes, he believed that inmates fell into three broad cate-

Penitentiary: The Walnut Street Jail at Philadelphia, 1773–1835 (n.p., 1955), pp. 70, 93, 100, 129–132. In addition to the plan of Newgate appearing in this book (Fig. 1, following p. 16), see the pictures of the institution in Clifford M. Young, Women's Prisons Past and Present and Other New York State Prison History (Elmira, 1932), p. vii, and in W. David Lewis, "Newgate of New-York: A Case History (1796–1828) of Early American Prison Reform," New-York Historical Society Quarterly, XLVII (April, 1963), 144, 169.

[6] Eddy to Schuyler, Aug. 22, 1796, Schuyler Papers.

[7] [Eddy], Account of the State Prison, p. 18. Several years before, Lownes had written an enthusiastic description of the discipline prevailing at the Walnut Street Jail (see his "An Account of the Alteration and Present State of the Penal Laws of Pennsylvania" in William Bradford, An Enquiry How Far the Punishment of Death Is Necessary in Pennsylvania [Philadelphia, 1793], pp. 73–93), and he expressed similar optimism in his correspondence with Eddy in 1796 (see Lownes to Eddy, April 19, 1796, Schuyler Papers).

[8] [Eddy], Account of the State Prison, p. 25.

gories: hardened offenders; criminals who, though depraved, still retained some sense of virtue; and young persons convicted for the first time. The existence of such varied types called for individualized treatment.[9]

To Eddy's mind, the reformation of the offender was the chief end of punishment. Although he believed in the possibility of deterrence, he regarded this as "momentary and uncertain." Restitution might also be obtained through correctional procedures, but the primary goal was "eradicating the evil passions and corrupt habits which are the sources of guilt." In order to promote rehabilitation he encouraged religious worship and established a night school. In the latter, he restricted the classes to the well-behaved as an incentive to good deportment, and charged the students four shillings' worth of extra labor to inculcate thrift. He was disinclined to rely on fear and severity, and approved warmly of provisions in the law of 1796 which prohibited corporal punishment at Newgate. His chief disciplinary weapon was solitary confinement on stinted rations, and he forbade his keepers, who were unarmed, to strike convicts. He allowed well-behaved inmates to have a supervised visit with their wives and relatives once every three months, and saw that his charges were given a coarse but ample diet.[10]

Despite his emphasis upon humanitarian treatment, Eddy stripped the regime at Newgate of anything resembling frills or self-indulgence. As soon as an incoming inmate had been bathed, provisioned, and interrogated, he was assigned to a prison shop and made to realize that his convict life would be one of hard work. It took two years to complete enough shops to provide full employment, but under Eddy's frugal and efficient management the penitentiary soon became a relatively prosperous industrial unit. Shoemaking was the first trade to be inaugurated, followed

[9] Cf. Samuel L. Knapp, *The Life of Thomas Eddy* (New York, 1834), pp. 60–61, and Lownes to Eddy, April 19, 1796, Schuyler Papers.

[10] Knapp, *Life of Thomas Eddy*, pp. 11, 59; [Eddy], *Account of the State Prison*, pp. 27, 29, 32, 53–54.

by the production of nails, barrels, linen and woolen cloth, wearing apparel, and woodenware. The program had two goals: to promote reformation through inculcating "habits of industry and sobriety," and to make possible an "indemnity to the community for the expense of the conviction and maintenance of the offender." By 1803, the profits of the Newgate shops actually yielded a tiny surplus after the prison's expenses had been paid.[11]

It is a tribute to Eddy's skill in handling men that he was able to employ a working force consisting of many who were "hardened, desperate, and refractory, and many ignorant, or incapacitated through infirmity and disease," and achieve satisfactory results. He did this, interestingly enough, without imposing the harsh and unmitigated slavery which later came to characterize penal labor under the Auburn system. Each convict at Newgate was charged a set amount upon the prison books for his clothes and maintenance, and accounts were kept of the proceeds from his labor. If he compiled a good behavior record, he was given upon release a share of the profits he had helped to earn. Inmates who demonstrated capacity and skill were used as superintendents and foremen in the shops. Indeed, the inauguration of shoemaking was made possible by a convict who had been a cobbler and who instructed his fellow prisoners in the trade.[12]

Despite the incentives which Eddy held out to those who conformed, it was not easy to maintain order. In 1799, guards were forced to open fire when fifty or sixty men revolted and seized their keepers. Several felons were wounded before the mutiny was quelled.[13] In 1800, the assistance of the military was necessary to break up a riot. A local newspaper reported that three or four ringleaders were injured, and it was also rumored that a keeper had

[11] Knapp, *Life of Thomas Eddy*, pp. 31, 64–65; [Eddy], *Account of the State Prison*, pp. 33–34; *Journal of the Assembly of the State of New-York* [hereafter cited JA], 27th Session (1804), p. 87.

[12] Knapp, *Life of Thomas Eddy*, p. 64; [Eddy], *Account of the State Prison*, pp. 33, 35–36.

[13] See Orlando F. Lewis, *The Development of American Prisons and Prison Customs, 1776–1845* (n.p., 1922), p. 56.

been knifed in the face.[14] On April 4, 1803, twenty inmates tried to scale the walls in an effort to escape. After ordering them to desist without avail, prison guards opened fire and killed four convicts, one of whom was an innocent bystander.[15]

The need to meet force with force on such occasions must have been distasteful to the Quaker warden, but his correspondence did not betray any lack of confidence in the Newgate experiment. In 1802, he wrote to the English police reformer Patrick Colquhoun that the progress of the institution fulfilled his "most sanguine expectation." Feeling that he was no longer needed, he intended to resign in a short time. The bloodshed that occurred in April, 1803, did not appear to shake his faith. His aims as a prison reformer, he told Colquhoun a month afterward, were "now so far accomplished, and put into a train of successful experiment," that he would be able to spend some of his time attending to other matters. A letter sent to the British reformer in July expressed continued optimism.[16]

Eddy's expectations were too sanguine. Some new inspectors were appointed in 1803, and he found himself unable to get along with them. The root of the difficulty is not entirely clear, but it appears that the Jeffersonians wrested control of the prison from the Federalists. Since Eddy belonged to the latter party, political differences may have contributed to the dissension. The Quaker agent also differed with his associates over economic matters, and it is likely that the introduction of a contract labor system in the shoemaking shop aroused his displeasure. By January, 1804, the situation had become so unpleasant that he resigned.[17] "I devoted seven years in endeavoring to establish this excellent institution,"

[14] *Prisoner of Hope* (New York City), June 7, 1800.

[15] JA, 27th Session (1804), p. 87.

[16] Eddy to Colquhoun, June 5, 1802; May 22, 1803; and July 15, 1803, in Knapp, *Life of Thomas Eddy*, pp. 181, 199, 203.

[17] See especially Cadwallader D. Colden to David Hosack, June 23, 1833, and Eddy to Colquhoun, June 20, 1804, in *ibid.*, pp. 19, 207; JA, 26th Session (1803), p. 96, and 27th Session (1804), p. 86; Blake McKelvey, *American Prisons: A Study in American Social History Prior to 1915* (Chicago, 1936), p. 7.

he wrote plaintively to Colquhoun, "and am not a little mortified, that there is some reason to apprehend all my labours are like to be lost." [18] Late in 1805, he indicated once more that developments at the penitentiary were not to his liking. Despite the existence there of cleanliness and good order, he disapproved of the severity of the discipline, and pointed out that industrial profits had declined since the days when he had been in office.[19]

In subsequent years Newgate became more and more of a disappointment to the state, and Eddy's pessimism was vindicated. One can speculate that the absence of the Quaker reformer from the management of the institution he founded may have had something to do with this, but the real causes went far deeper. From the very beginning there were defects in the situation at Newgate which would have jeopardized the prison's success under any administrator, even Eddy. To say this is not to detract from Eddy's stature as a prison reformer, nor unduly to criticize those who had helped him to establish the penitentiary, but rather to affirm that these men were not omniscient. Some things had to be learned from experience.

One of Newgate's handicaps probably reflected the esteem in which the principle of checks and balances was held by New Yorkers in the post-Revolutionary period. Responsibility for the government of the prison was divided among a great number of public officials. Over-all authority was in the hands of a group of seven inspectors and all the justices of the state supreme court. Regulations for the internal management of the institution were made by the inspectors; the justices, or any two of them; the mayor and recorder of New York City; and the state attorney-general and assistant attorney-general. The inspectors appointed an agent, whose primary concern was the financial and industrial operation of the prison, and a principal keeper, who was the chief disci-

[18] Eddy to Colquhoun, June 20, 1804, in Knapp, *Life of Thomas Eddy*, p. 207. A major riot had occurred at the prison in May, and Eddy blamed this on the neglect of keepers who had been appointed since his departure.

[19] Eddy to Colquhoun, Sept. 27, 1805, in *ibid.*, p. 215.

plinary official. The agent was paid twice as much as the principal keeper, but the two men were theoretically independent of one another. This hodge-podge of administrative responsibility was further complicated in 1801 by the creation of a military prison guard under the sole direction of the mayor of New York City.[20]

It was possible to detect certain advantages in this complicated system. Eddy, for example, pointed out that giving judges a role to play in penal administration enabled them to see how convicts really lived and thus to dispense justice more intelligently. He also argued that division of authority decreased the chances for corruption and abuse of power. Furthermore, some degree of consolidation was provided in the early years when, for reasons of economy, the agent was customarily made an inspector.[21] Eddy thus held both positions concurrently and exerted a strong influence upon disciplinary as well as financial matters. Finally, not all of the officials empowered to administer the prison performed their duties energetically, and this inertia probably benefited institutional management.[22]

Despite such mitigating circumstances, however, the administrative framework was definitely unwieldy. The anomaly of a prison guard force which was unaccountable to those who carried the main burden of responsibility was particularly irksome to penitentiary officials. In 1811, the inspectors urged that the commander of the guard be demoted and placed under the control of the principal keeper, but this brought a protest from the commander, an aged and crippled veteran of the Revolution. It also caused some heart-searching among legislators who had scruples about demoting a man who had bled for his country's independence.[23] In the end, little was done. An act embodying most of the suggestions which the inspectors had made was finally passed in 1817,

[20] *Laws . . . 1796*, p. 672; [Eddy], *Account of the State Prison*, pp. 21–29; Anonymous, "A View of the New-York State Prison," in William Roscoe, *Observations on Penal Jurisprudence* (London, 1819), Appendix, pp. 34–43.

[21] [Eddy], *Account of the State Prison*, pp. 22–23.

[22] Anonymous, "A View of the New-York State Prison," p. 34.

[23] JA, 34th Session (1811), pp. 105–106, 185, 245.

but appears to have been imperfectly carried out. Another law directed to the same end was passed in 1820, but with similar results. By 1822, the controversial guard force was still under the direction of the mayor, although the inspectors had gained some authority in making rules for its conduct.[24] The whole affair was symptomatic of the bickering and confusion which was possible under the prison's loose administrative system.

Equally unfortunate was the speed with which offices at Newgate became political posts. Eddy's resignation in 1804 was but one example of the unsettling influence of partisan forces, for throughout the prison's history the political pressures which affected staff positions produced undesirable results. "In the first place, there being no assurance of permanency, in the enjoyment of these stations, good men have been constrained to decline them," reported an investigating group in 1822; "and in the second place, where they have accepted them, the precarious tenure with which they are held, destroyed that ambition, and extinguished that hope of reform, that would otherwise have been cherished."[25]

Another obstacle to orderly administration lay in the fact that there were at least four different types of offenders among the inmates at Newgate: adult male felons, female criminals, juvenile delinquents, and the criminally insane. Observers noted frequently and with disapproval the presence of young boys and girls among the convicts.[26] The females could never be satisfactorily integrated into the life of the institution, despite the provision of separate quarters and exercise facilities for them. Refractory and economically unprofitable, they disturbed routine by enticing male convicts

[24] *Ibid.*, 41st Session (1818), p. 416; 44th Session (1820), pp. 216–217; and 45th Session (1822), pp. 99–100; *Laws . . . Commencing January 1816, and Ending April 1818* (Albany, 1818), IV, 313.

[25] Society for the Prevention of Pauperism in the City of New-York, *Report on the Penitentiary System of the United States* (New York, 1822), pp. 41–42.

[26] [W. A. Coffey], *Inside Out, or An Interior View of the New-York State Prison* (New York, 1823), pp. 55, 57, 60; Charles G. Sommers, *Memoir of the Rev. John Stanford*, D.D. (New York, 1835), p. 273; John Stanford, Petition of Jan. 21, 1812, Stanford Papers, New-York Historical Society; Society for the Prevention of Pauperism, *Report on the Penitentiary System*, p. 43.

and trying to form liaisons with them. "The utmost vulgarity, obscenity, and wantonness, characterizes their language, their habits and their manners," reported a disgusted ex-inmate. "Their beastial salacity, in their visual amours, is agonizing to every fibre of delicacy and virtue." [27] Doubtless there were many felons who found these tactics tempting rather than repulsive. When a Swedish nobleman named Axel Klinkowström visited the prison in 1819, he was told that the forty women confined there caused more problems than the rest of the inmates put together.[28] The insane were chronically difficult to manage. There was always a small group of felons who were clearly deranged, such as a maniac who thought he had occasioned the dethronement of Napoleon, won the victories of Perry and Macdonough, and fought for revolutionary causes in Latin America. "Poor creature!" observed a fellow convict, "his history would fill an octavo." [29]

Good penal care is a costly item, and Newgate's administrators frequently found legislative appropriations grossly inadequate. This was reflected in the low salaries paid to staff members. An ex-convict who wrote an exposé of conditions at the penitentiary in 1823 admitted that some keepers set a good example for the inmates, but alleged that many of them were small-minded, intoxicated with their power, vulgar, and occasionally cruel. On the other hand, he argued, it was hard to expect a capable man to lead the life of a turnkey for $500 per year, especially when he had to stay inside the stockade almost constantly and was permitted to visit his family and friends only once every two weeks.[30]

A scarcity of funds prevented Newgate from having an adequate

[27] [Coffey], *Inside Out*, p. 61.
[28] Franklin D. Scott, trans. and ed., *Baron Klinkowström's America, 1818–1820* (Evanston, Ill., 1952), p. 99.
[29] [Coffey], *Inside Out*, p. 69.
[30] *Ibid.*, pp. 42–51. Some of the statements of this ex-inmate must be used with caution. Newgate's inspectors branded *Inside Out* as "a book . . . written with a revengeful and malignant spirit, and for the purpose of bringing the prison into disrepute and to excite mutiny within its walls." (JA, 47th Session [1824], p. 249.) This, however, is an extreme statement. Most of Coffey's claims are entirely consonant with material that can be found in other sources pertaining to the prison.

reformatory program despite the efforts of Eddy and those who shared his desire for curative treatment. The limited program it did possess was largely owing to the selfless labors of John Stanford, an elderly clergyman who took up part-time duties at the prison about 1807. Stanford served for little or no pay and without a definite appointment until 1812, when the legislature formally authorized the institution to have a part-time chaplain. The main burden of his work involved preaching, private exhortation, and visits to the sick and dying. He managed, however, to carry on a series of night classes for the inmates, teaching such subjects as Latin and mathematics in addition to the three R's. Oral examinations were held before the inspectors whenever Stanford believed the convicts were ready for them. Inmate teachers were used whenever possible.[31] A circulating library was also established, but this was quashed by the inspectors after some of the books were returned soiled, torn, or dog-eared.[32] Stanford suffered another disappointment when the inspectors ordered the abandonment of singing classes he had arranged in an effort to make public worship more meaningful and attractive to the felons.[33] Valuable though his labors were, his part-time status alone prevented him from taking adequate care of Newgate's needs. His services were spread thinly, for New York City hired him to be chaplain for the municipal penitentiary, the bridewell, the debtors' prison, the public almshouse, and the city hospital.[34]

To the financial problems that prevented Newgate from hiring an adequate and fully competent staff were added various difficulties encountered by agents who attempted to administer the penal labor system. As a rule, the state furnished all raw materials, supervised all manufacturing processes, and assumed full responsibility for marketing prison-made goods, either in filling custom orders or

---

[31] Sommers, *Memoir of John Stanford,* pp. 117, 163, 176, 188, 218; JA, 43rd Session (1820), p. 239.

[32] [Coffey], *Inside Out,* pp. 29–30.

[33] Draft reports of 1819 and 1823, Stanford Papers.

[34] Charles Lucas, *Du Système Pénitentiaire en Europe et aux États-Unis* (Paris, 1828–1830), II, 53. Lucas estimated that Stanford had the care of from 2,100 to 3,500 inmates, not counting a variable number of imprisoned debtors.

in displaying products at the prison storehouse for the benefit of prospective buyers.[35] Under this system the agent had many problems. If he did not estimate market conditions correctly he was liable to get caught with a large inventory of merchandise which merely deteriorated in storage. By 1815, the penitentiary had accumulated over $106,000 worth of goods which provided a tempting target for inmate incendiaries. By the end of 1816, one vexed agent asked the legislature for permission to clear off these stocks at auction for whatever they would bring, or to ship them out "to some southern or foreign port"—in brief, to any place where Newgate would be rid of them.[36]

One basic industrial problem stemmed from the substandard talent of most inmate workers. The few capable and experienced hands were likely to be pardoned and replaced by new men who were wholly unfamiliar with their tasks. Some convicts were so old and infirm that they had to be given such relatively unprofitable work as oakum picking, in which old ropes were unraveled and saturated with tar for use in ship-caulking. The shops were also in constant danger of fires set by refractory inmates, and some prisoners deliberately spoiled their work if they thought they could escape detection.[37] At other times, products were ruined through sheer incompetency. Workers in the weave shop, for example, dyed cloth hastily and sometimes burned it with unnecessarily powerful acids.[38]

Agents were continually harassed by the unsystematic way in which Newgate was supplied with money. Almost from the beginning the state expected it to pay as many of its expenses as possible out of its industrial earnings. If these were insufficient, emergency appropriations could be requested. The prison there-

[35] See especially *Laws . . . 1796 Inclusive*, p. 673, and E. T. Hiller, "Development of the Systems of Control of Convict Labor in the United States," *Journal of Criminal Law and Criminology*, V (July, 1914), 246–247.

[36] JA, 38th Session (1814), p. 215; 39th Session (1816), p. 125; and 40th Session (1816–1817), p. 285.

[37] *Ibid.*, 39th Session (1816), pp. 124, 128; 40th Session (1816–1817), pp. 284–285; and 48th Session (1825), p. 273.

[38] [Coffey], *Inside Out*, pp. 137–138.

fore had no dependable supply of ready cash if sales were slow or business conditions depressed. As early as 1804, the inspectors complained that chronic shortages of money made it impossible for them to buy supplies when they could secure the cheapest rates, and stated that they had already borrowed $4,000 for institutional use on their own private security. In 1811, they again reported that the agent often lacked cash with which to purchase raw materials and other necessities, and asked that he be empowered to borrow up to fifteen or twenty thousand dollars annually from New York City banks. In 1815, the agent protested that he was constantly in debt, and that annual appropriations merely sufficed to pay off the obligations of the preceding year.[39]

However bad its financial and industrial problems, Newgate's greatest difficulty was overcrowding. It had been designed for less than four hundred and fifty inmates, and as New York's population increased it could not possibly accommodate the large numbers of new convicts who were forced upon it. The situation was met in two ways: by packing prisoners into facilities designed for half their number, and by preserving a rough balance between intake and outgo, if possible, by frequent use of the pardoning power. Both expedients were demoralizing in their effect upon discipline and morale.

European penal theorists had believed that pardons would be virtually unnecessary under well-regulated criminal codes, and had condemned their use on other grounds. "To show mankind that crimes are sometimes pardoned, and that punishment is not the necessary consequence," contended Beccaria, "is to nourish the flattering hope of impunity." William Godwin echoed this argument and stated that any system placing men under the capricious benevolence of public functionaries smacked of slavery.[40] New York reformers sympathized with these beliefs; Thomas Eddy, for

---

[39] JA, 27th Session (1804), pp. 86–87; 34th Session (1811), p. 106; and 39th Session (1816), p. 129.

[40] Cesare Beccaria, *An Essay on Crimes and Punishments*, trans. Edward D. Ingraham (reprinted ed.; Stanford, California, 1953), pp. 158–159; William Godwin, *An Enquiry Concerning Political Justice* (Dublin, 1793), II, 320–321.

example, asserted that clemency should be extended only upon unequivocal evidence of reformation, the achievement of an extremely good behavior record, or the finding of mitigating facts not known before the trial.[41] Bitter and inescapable reality, however, made virtually indiscriminate pardoning a necessity; the unwelcome remedy became an avowed means of keeping the prison population within bounds by approximately 1807–1808. By the end of 1821, when there were actually 817 inmates at Newgate, it was estimated that there would have been over two thousand without the use of clemency.[42] Even so, the institution was still overcrowded.

The liberal use of pardons was not only harmful to prison discipline, but also dangerous to the public safety. Since almost ten times as many inmates were discharged by pardon as through expiration of sentence, no criminal at Newgate expected to serve out his term. Most commonly, he expected to fulfill about half his sentence. Convicts were outraged if detained beyond this extent, and for some time after the semiannual pardoning seasons the prison was in an unsettled condition. Disappointed felons were unwilling to work and ready to gain revenge upon the state through sabotage.[43] The practice of having regular seasons for the exercise of clemency also resulted in the release of forty or fifty convicts on the same day, causing mass disruption of the prison industries and a time of intense anxiety for citizens living near the penitentiary.[44] The business of securing pardons became a semi-illicit activity. Pettifogging lawyers hung about the doors of the prison, bargaining with inmates, circulating false petitions, importuning the

[41] [Eddy], *Account of the State Prison*, p. 67; "Remarks on present state of our Prisons by Thomas Eddy," Nov. 17, 1818, DeWitt Clinton Papers, Vol. XXIV, Columbia University Library.

[42] *Journal of the Senate of New-York* [hereafter cited JS], 45th Session (1822), pp. 154–157.

[43] JA, 45th Session (1822), p. 88. In the five years prior to 1817, 740 inmates were pardoned and 77 released upon expiration of sentence. (JS, 40th Session [1816–1817], p. 167.)

[44] JA, 37th Session (1814), pp. 197–198.

Governor with dubious evidences of reformation, and securing the liberty of men who were in many cases unfit to return to freedom.[45] Clever felons attempted to gain medical pardons by resorting to all sorts of ruses. One convict was said to have procured his release from a life sentence after four years by eating a mixture containing Castile soap.[46]

In view of its many shortcomings, it is not surprising that Newgate failed to realize the prospects envisioned by Thomas Eddy in 1801. There was a brief surge of economic prosperity during the embargo period and the War of 1812, however, probably because of the increased demand for domestic manufactures during the years of nonimportation and conflict. Production at Newgate leaped considerably; by 1815, the prison was turning out brushes, spinning wheels, clothespins, bobbins, spools, butter churns, washtubs, pails, hoops, wheelbarrows, machinery, cabinets, whips, and a variety of woven goods. At least seventy looms were in operation, and the agent was considering the introduction of steam power. Markets were sought not only in the New York City area but also in New Haven, Hartford, Providence, and Newport. An anonymous staff member who wrote a description of Newgate in this period was optimistic about its future. He conceded that the institution was not perfect, but believed that each passing year would "add to its improvement." [47] In 1813, prison administrators hailed a temporary slackening in the pace of congestion as "a decisive proof of the efficacy of the system, and highly consolatory to the patriot and philanthropist." [48]

These promising conditions did not last. A crime wave, related at least in part to difficulties facing returning soldiers seeking employment, occurred after the War of 1812, and there was a great increase in the number of offenders sentenced to Newgate. The

[45] *Ibid.*, 48th Session (1825), p. 128; Edward Livingston, "Introductory Report to the Code of Reform and Prison Discipline," *The Complete Works of Edward Livingston* (New York, 1873), I, 570.
[46] [Coffey], *Inside Out*, pp. 167–169.
[47] Anonymous, "A View of the New-York State Prison," pp. 36–37, 46–48, 58.
[48] *Laws of the State of New-York ... 1814* (Albany, 1814), Appendix, p. 293.

pardoning power could not be used frequently enough to keep the prison population in bounds, despite a wholesale use of the prerogative in 1816.[49] The inspectors' report for that year sounded a note of panic. Convicts were "literally crammed into their rooms at night," and could scarcely move in the crowded apartments. Authorities feared that a sudden epidemic of sickness might decimate the ranks of the inmates, and wondered whether or not a return to the sanguinary system of the days before 1796 would occur if conditions were not rectified. The unsettled commercial conditions after the war hurt the institution financially, and made it difficult to calculate safely in buying raw materials and manufacturing goods.[50] By 1816, the prison was deeply in debt and burdened with heavy inventories of unsold merchandise.[51]

Under the pressure of these conditions the legislature embarked upon a series of efforts to remove some of the defects in the penal system. In 1816, it authorized the construction at Auburn of a new prison which was destined to become one of the most famous institutions of its kind in the world. In 1817, it revamped the prison industries. In order to reduce state risks as much as possible, the lawmakers required convicts to work only on raw materials brought to the penitentiaries by private entrepreneurs who agreed to pay a fixed labor charge to have them made into manufactured goods. If the prison population exceeded 450, the governor was authorized to permit the employment of any number of inmates in such ways as he deemed proper. Permission was granted to allow felons to be used in canal construction, provided the entrepreneurs who contracted for them were willing to bear the burden of their expense and upkeep while on the job. Inventories of

---

[49] On the crime wave that erupted in both Europe and America in 1815, see Gustave de Beaumont and Alexis de Tocqueville, *On the Penitentiary System in the United States,* trans. Francis Lieber (Philadelphia, 1833), pp. 65, 262, as well as Georg Rusche and Otto Kirchheimer, *Punishment and Social Structure* (New York, 1939), p. 97. The number of convictions to Newgate increased from 295 in 1815 to 436 in 1816. (JA, 48th Session [1825], p. 127.)

[50] JS, 40th Session (1816–1817), pp. 6–7, 168.

[51] *Ibid.,* 39th Session (1816), p. 107; JA, 40th Session (1816–1817), p. 285.

prison-made goods which had accumulated over the years were to be sold at auction for whatever they would bring.[52]

At the same time, the legislators attempted to mitigate over-crowding and bring some order into the pardoning situation. Out of 419 men sentenced to Newgate for grand larceny, half had stolen less than $25 each; any theft of this amount or less was therefore redefined as petty larceny, punishable by fine or imprisonment in a county jail instead of consignment to the state penitentiary. The chaotic pardoning system was altered by allowing the prison inspectors to abridge an inmate's term by one-quarter for good behavior and a satisfactory production record. As a further in-centive to diligence, it was provided that 20 per cent of all convict earnings over and above the cost of support were to be set aside for the prisoner or his family upon release.[53]

A more momentous step was soon taken in an attempt to ensure better discipline. Throughout Newgate's history the usual punish-ment for infractions of prison rules had been solitary confinement on shortened rations, and the use of corporal inflictions had been prohibited. The increasing congestion after the war, however, had produced a number of disciplinary problems. In 1816, the agent and the inspectors complained that the threat of ordinary punish-ments was insufficient to deter convicts from plotting arson. The following year, the legislature prescribed the death penalty for any inmate who committed arson or assaulted an officer with intent to kill, but even this failed to improve the situation. In June, 1818, unrest among the prisoners culminated in a severe riot. According to the inspectors, "a large majority of the convicts were concerned, and the institution was literally threatened with total destruction." Military force had to be summoned before the violence subsided, and even after about one hundred ringleaders had been placed in solitary or restricted confinement their conduct became so out-

[52] *Laws ... Commencing January 1816, and Ending April 1818* (Albany, 1818), IV, 79–80, 310–311, 315–316.

[53] *Ibid.*, pp. 311–312, 315; JS, 40th Session (1816–1817), pp. 170–171; JA, 45th Session (1822), p. 219.

rageous that the sentinels patrolling the walls were told to fire among them.[54]

The legislature responded to such troubles with an act in April, 1819, legalizing flogging at both Auburn and Newgate. No more than thirty-nine blows were to be inflicted upon one occasion, and then only by the principal keepers under the direction and supervision of two inspectors. The use of stocks and irons was also permitted.[55]

This was a highly significant enactment. It in effect constituted an admission by the lawmakers that the penitentiary system was now deemed unworkable unless certain relics of the sanguinary era were superimposed upon it. Paradoxically, the new law actually made it possible for criminals to be punished more inhumanely than would have been the case under the old penal code. Whereas a thief might have been given thirty-nine lashes under the old system and then set free, he could now be sentenced to a long prison term and flogged repeatedly if he did not conform to certain rules under confinement. Although the act of 1819 was clearly worded to guard the exercise of the chastising power from abuse, its provisions were not always scrupulously obeyed, and in time practices came into being which might have astonished the legislators who enacted it. For better or worse, the New York prison system had acquired one of its most controversial features.

The lawmakers were not content to rely upon sheer force, however, and attempted to cope with some of the disciplinary problems facing the prisons by inaugurating a system of classification. Penal administrators were required "to separate and keep alone and apart from the other convicts, those prisoners who have been convicted of the higher crimes, those who have been twice, or oftener, imprisoned, those who are young, those who are old, those who are healthy, and those who are unhealthy." [56] Although this provision

---

[54] JA, 39th Session (1816), pp. 124, 128; *Laws . . . Commencing January 1816, and Ending April 1818*, p. 315; JA, 42nd Session (1819), p. 338.

[55] *Laws of the State of New-York . . . 1819* (Albany, 1819), p. 87.

[56] *Ibid.*, pp. 87–88.

was significant in that it anticipated later correctional developments, it was difficult to impose upon institutions which had not been designed for such a degree of separation. Officials at Newgate implemented it to some extent by placing various types of offenders in different sleeping rooms at night, but it was still possible for divergent groups to mingle in the daytime.[57] John Stanford went beyond this by advocating the establishment of an "honor group" of inmates who had good behavior records and likely prospects of rehabilitation, but this was not carried out.[58]

Even considering that it sanctioned flogging, the body of prison legislation passed in the period 1816–1819 represented a well-reasoned attempt to rectify New York's penal difficulties. The lawmakers had tried to come to grips with the problem of overcrowding, to give the inmates various incentives for good behavior, and to provide effective disciplinary alternatives if such conduct was not forthcoming. Other events calculated to ease pressures at Newgate occurred in 1824, when a House of Refuge was provided for juvenile delinquents, and in 1825, when a law was passed permitting insane convicts to be transferred to the Bloomingdale asylum in New York City.[59] Unfortunately, however, the hoped-for results never materialized, and the prison for which Eddy had once envisioned so great a future instead went down as a failure.

Continuing economic difficulty was one feature of this disappointing outcome. Although the contract system decreed by the act of 1817 was not completely strange, having been briefly used at Newgate some years before in the manufacture of shoes and nails, the prison did not satisfactorily adjust to the new legislation. In 1818, its profits sagged to $16,000, not nearly sufficient to defray costs of $58,000 for food and maintenance alone. The inspectors complained that it was difficult to make contracts, and urged a temporary return to state accounts. The auction sale of goods

---

[57] JA, 43rd Session (1820), p. 244.

[58] Draft of report to inspectors, 1821, Stanford Papers.

[59] Bradford K. Peirce, *A Half Century with Juvenile Delinquents* (New York, 1869), pp. 32–74; JA, 48th Session (1825), Appendix C, p. 22.

which had piled up in storage did not help very much, for these wares had deteriorated into a condition of virtual unsalability.[60] The prison economy had barely begun to recover from the effects of the contract law when it was staggered by the Panic of 1819. The failure of the shoemaking contractor threw many inmates out of work for over three months until a new agreement was signed specifying rates 40 per cent lower than those prevailing before. Prisoners engaged in sawing marble were also idle for a time. The fact that such conditions were bad for disciplinary as well as financial reasons probably explains various evasions of the law of 1817. By 1821, less than half of Newgate's industries were running on a contract basis, legislative pronouncements notwithstanding.[61]

Economic conditions gradually improved at the prison, and in 1821 the agent indicated that the worst was over. All able-bodied convicts were employed, and labor was securing a better return. By dint of rigid economy a better balance was achieved between intake and outgo, and in 1826 the institution's financial progress elicited praise from Governor DeWitt Clinton.[62] Nevertheless, the goal of self-support remained elusive, and enemies of the prison derived satisfaction from pointing to the large sums which the state had expended for its upkeep over the years since its founding.[63] Whatever economic headway the penitentiary made came too late to save it from its critics, and was more than counterbalanced by the chronically poor state of its discipline.

Although continued overcrowding and an inability to prevent plotting by separating inmates were circumstances which officials could do little to alter, many of Newgate's disciplinary short-comings were traceable to ineffective administration. The inspectors, for example, held wide discretionary powers under the

[60] JA, 41st Session (1818), pp. 274–275, 602. For previous usage of the contract system at Newgate, see *ibid.*, 26th Session (1803), p. 96, and 27th Session (1804), p. 86.

[61] *Ibid.*, 43rd Session (1820), p. 240, and 48th Session (1825), p. 273.

[62] *Ibid.*, 44th Session (1820–1821), p. 215; 45th Session (1822), p. 90; and 47th Session (1824), p. 248; *The Message from the Governor to the Legislature . . . January 3, 1826* (Albany, 1826), p. 13.

[63] See for example Prison Discipline Society, *Second Report* (1827), p. 65.

*Elam Lynds*

3. Elam Lynds, 1784–1855. From Charles R. Henderson, ed., *Correction and Prevention: Prison Reform and Criminal Law* (New York, 1910). Reprinted by permission of the publisher, the Russell Sage Foundation.

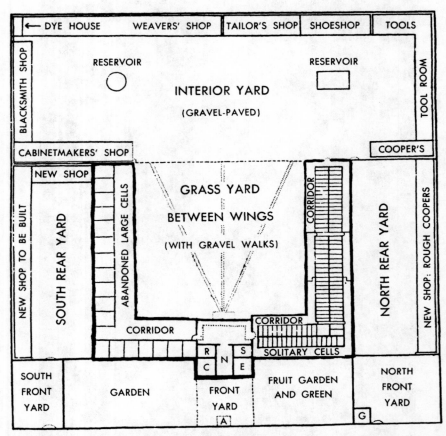

4. Ground plan of Auburn prison, c. 1828. A: eastern front gate; G: guardhouse; N: main hall; C, R, E, S: offices and adjoining apartments of clerk, keeper, and inspector. Adapted from *Report of Gershom Powers, Agent and Keeper of the State Prison at Auburn Made to the Legislature Jan. 7, 1828* (Albany, 1828). Reprinted by courtesy of the New-York Historical Society.

penal act of 1796 to regulate the admission of visitors, but failed to make good use of them. It became customary to permit any-body—even a child—to enter the prison grounds upon paying a small fee; visitors became so accustomed to regarding their entrance as a right that they threatened lawsuits if excluded, and penitentiary officials timidly bowed to such pressure. Many visitors brought the felons such items of contraband as rum, tools, money, and unauthorized messages.[64] In addition, alcohol and other forbidden items were smuggled into the institution by contractors, who used them as bribes to secure better work from inmates.[65]

Supervision of convict life was generally lax. Indiscriminate jostling and confusion was allowed to prevail in the yard; on Sundays in particular the felons milled about freely, sang obscene songs, wrestled with one another, and carried on petty gambling.[66] An investigating commission from the state legislature reported in 1825 that the inmates were insolent, that idleness was widespread, that one convict was actually sleeping at his work, and that another had sabotaged his stock of materials without being punished for it.[67] Sanitation was evidently poor, for one visitor stated in 1826 that Newgate's prisoners were in a filthier condition than any he had ever seen, with the exception of those confined in the notorious city jail at Washington, D.C.[68] Possession of knives among convicts, difficult to prevent at any prison, was widespread; such weapons were used either to damage industrial goods or to gain revenge upon informers.[69] In a vain attempt to induce better behavior the inspectors placed large placards at various places bearing such inscriptions as, "He that will not work shall not eat," "The way

---

[64] *Laws . . . 1796 Inclusive,* p. 675; JA, 48th Session (1825), pp. 106–107; [Coffey], *Inside Out,* p. 194. The admission fee in 1825 was 12½ cents per person (James Hardie, *The Description of the City of New-York* [New York, 1827], p. 194).

[65] JA, 47th Session (1824), p. 251.

[66] [Coffey], *Inside Out,* p. 106.

[67] JA, 48th Session (1825), pp. 104–107.

[68] Prison Discipline Society, *Third Report* (1828), p. 17.

[69] JA, 42nd Session (1819), p. 341; 48th Session (1825), p. 106; and 50th Session (1827), p. 81.

of the transgressor is hard," and "He that walketh uprightly walketh surely, but he that perverteth his ways shall be known," but as one hostile critic pointed out, these were poor substitutes for effective discipline.[70] Under such circumstances the fact that officials managed to avoid a repetition of the ugly riot of 1818 must be attributed as much to luck as to superior management. In 1823, when news arrived that a prison had been burned in Virginia, a portending insurrection at Newgate was quashed only with the aid of informers and other loyal inmates.[71]

Prominent citizens recognized that many of Newgate's troubles could have been averted under fully competent leadership.[72] On the other hand, they reasoned that the basic design of the penitentiary was deficient, especially in that it permitted convicts to corrupt one another and pool their knowledge about ways of committing crime. Typical was the comment of a committee of well-known New York reformers and philanthropists who reported on the penitentiary situation in 1822:

Convicts of all ages, and all degrees of turpitude, have been placed together, and all the evil and fatal consequences of vicious communications have been exhibited. . . . Your Committee need to appeal to no documents, to shew the total want of a proper division of convicts in our Penitentiary. The defect is well known to the whole community, and is as obvious to the eye, as the prison itself. Culprits come out far more depraved and desperate, than they were when they received their sentence. The young are advanced in the paths of guilt; the old, confirmed in their baseness; morals, instead of being improved, are broken down; conscience, instead of being restored to a reproof, is blunted and banished. No statement of ours can be too strong on this point. The fact stands complete and conclusive.[73]

[70] Stephen Allen, *Observations on Penitentiary Discipline, Addressed to William Roscoe, Esq. of Liverpool, England* (New York, 1827), p. 18.

[71] JA, 47th Session (1824), p. 249.

[72] *Ibid.*, 41st Session (1818), p. 13, showing views of DeWitt Clinton, and 48th Session (1825), p. 104, containing the observations of a legislative investigating commission.

[73] Society for the Prevention of Pauperism, *Report on the Penitentiary System*, p. 30.

Thomas Eddy himself condemned the design of the institution he had built only two decades before. He confessed to Peter Jay in 1816 that "a most striking error" had been committed in his plan, which should have provided for five hundred solitary sleeping rooms.[74] In 1818 he made the same admission in a memorandum to DeWitt Clinton.[75] "*No* benefit, as it regards *reformation,* ever has been, *nor ever will be* produced," he told an English penal reformer a year later, "unless our prisons are calculated to have separate rooms . . . so that every man can be lodged by *himself.*" [76]

One possible way of rectifying matters that occurred to citizens was to remodel Newgate. A legislative committee recommended in 1822 that old floors and partitions be torn out in the prison and two hundred solitary cells be built.[77] This, however, was bound to be expensive, and would not begin to provide single accommodations for all the inmates. Thomas Eddy himself came out against such an approach, arguing that Newgate was "so badly contrived that it can never be successfully used as a Penitentiary." [78] Such men as Eddy advocated abandoning the old prison altogether and building another where new techniques could be used in facilities designed expressly for the purpose, an idea that seemed especially cogent after the development at Auburn of an ingenious system featuring solitary confinement at night and group labor in silence by day. One attractive possibility was the construction of a new penitentiary near large marble deposits at Sing Sing in Westchester County which could be quarried by inmates.[79]

After considerable agitation and deliberation this idea pre-

[74] Eddy to Jay, Feb. 14, 1816, in Knapp, *Life of Thomas Eddy*, p. 244.

[75] "Remarks on present state of our Prisons by Thomas Eddy," Nov. 17, 1818, DeWitt Clinton Papers, Vol. XXIV.

[76] Eddy to Samuel Hoare, Jr., Nov. 15, 1819, in Knapp, *Life of Thomas Eddy*, p. 299. Italics are Eddy's.

[77] Society for the Prevention of Pauperism, *Report on the Penitentiary System*, Appendix, pp. 102–103.

[78] Eddy to George Tibbits, Stephen Allen, and Samuel M. Hopkins, Jan. 7, 1825, in Knapp, *Life of Thomas Eddy*, p. 88.

[79] This prospect had been investigated as early as 1821 (JA, 44th Session [1820–1821], pp. 250–252), but the legislators conducting the inquiry at this time favored the renovation of Newgate rather than its abandonment.

vailed. On March 7, 1825, the legislature authorized the building of a new prison, which commissioners shortly thereafter placed at Sing Sing "on account of its marble-beds, its accessibility by water and its salubrity." [80] The Common Council of New York City purchased Newgate for use as a debtor's prison and bridewell, and when the new penitentiary was completed in 1828 the state abandoned the old institution altogether.[81] Officials at Newgate fought against this series of events, arguing the superior rehabilitative value of diversified penal industries as opposed to marble quarrying and criticizing the harsh treatment of the convicts who were building the prison at Sing Sing, but it was of no use.[82] New York's first experiment in penitentiary management had come to an end.

At Newgate, prison reformers encountered a problem which still faces the twentieth-century penal administrator. Finding the quick, cheap, and often brutal methods of the past distasteful or lacking in deterrent effect, the post-Revolutionary generation had taken culprits out of free society, in which most people were law-abiding, and thrown them together in a milieu in which nearly every individual was a felon. However bad his previous environment had been, the offender was now in one which was potentially worse. In such a situation, what was to prevent the inmate from becoming even more deeply corrupted than he had been when originally convicted, more unmanageable under confinement, and more dangerous to society after release? This question was one of special gravity with regard to such an institution as Newgate, where overcrowding was chronic, administration frequently poor, and rehabilitative efforts continually underfinanced.

[80] *Laws of the State of New-York . . . 1825* (Albany, 1825), pp. 16–17; George J. Fisher, "Ossining," in J. Thomas Scharf, ed., *History of Westchester County, New York* (Philadelphia, 1886), II, 349; JA, 49th Session (1826), pp. 304–305. Fisher errs in stating that the act was passed in 1824.

[81] Hardie, *Description of the City of New-York*, p. 191; Sidney I. Pomerantz, *New York: An American City, 1783–1803* (New York, 1938), p. 322.

[82] See especially JA, 49th Session (1826), p. 198, and 51st Session (1828), p. 269.

Faced with such a problem, New York prison reformers groped for an answer throughout the decade which followed the War of 1812. Experimenting with ideas that had originated in Europe and were being implemented in Pennsylvania, which was experiencing penal difficulties at the same time, prison administrators in the Empire State eventually devised a system which, for all its borrowings from outside sources, possessed a high degree of originality.

The keynote of the new approach was isolation. John Howard had advocated separating convicts at night, and such reformers as Jonas Hanway had championed complete solitary confinement. American prison leaders now turned to these ideas, reasoning that the way to correct the evils arising in a society limited to criminals was to prevent any meaningful society from being formed in the first place. At such new penitentiaries as those at Auburn and Sing Sing, the convict was to be so completely cut off from his fellows as to be incapable of corrupting them or of being the recipient of evil influences. At the same time, he was to be subjected to such constant surveillance and coercion that he would have no choice but to conform to the rules established by those who had control over him.

Such treatment would surely punish; would it also reform? Would it stimulate the mind to reflect upon better things and induce repentance, or would it stupefy the prisoner's intellect and make him even less fit for normal social life? Would it work in practice? These were some of the questions that confronted penal reformers in New York as the search for an effective penitentiary system shifted from old and discredited Newgate to grim new institutions which rose on the banks of the Owasco Inlet in Cayuga County and the Hudson River at Sing Sing.

# Chapter III

# The Setting
# for a New Order

OVERCROWDED conditions at Newgate had occasioned talk of building a new penitentiary in New York as early as 1809 and 1810; the great increase of convictions which came after the War of 1812 made such a step imperative. Assuming that the needs of the New York City area could still be met by the facilities at Newgate, it was logical that a western community should be selected as the site of the new institution. The village of Auburn was chosen mainly for political reasons. It was a former Federalist stronghold which had turned Jeffersonian, a consideration which prompted Republican leaders at Albany to reward it with the hope of solidifying party support in a marginal district. It also possessed an outstanding political figure in John H. Beach, at the time one of the most powerful assemblymen in the state. Beach was well aware of the economic growth which the establishment of a large penal institution could stimulate in the Auburn area, and by April, 1816, he had succeeded in guiding through the legislature an act that accomplished his aims. Securing a place on the commission appointed to execute the new law, he joined two other Auburn landowners in offering the state a tract along the Owasco Inlet which provided water power for potential prison industries. On June 28, 1816, the foundation was laid for what

54

was to become one of the most famous penitentiaries in the world. By the winter of 1817 the new institution was ready for the reception of criminals.[1]

The area in which this prison was built was much different from the localities in which Newgate and the Walnut Street Jail were placed. Its heritage was that of Calvinist New England, and it lacked the Quaker influence represented by such men as Thomas Eddy and Caleb Lownes. It had been settled only since the Revolution, and in 1816 it lacked many of the refinements of large eastern centers. At first glance, it would seem to have been a proper scene for the working of the "frontier spirit" with reference to correctional matters. Was it not at Auburn that new penal administrators broke dramatically from eastern models and methods in the mid-1820's? Is it not conceivable that a rude western environment in this case proved inhospitable to transplanted institutions which had been based upon European precedents, and that a citizenry which had been liberalized by frontier conditions modified these institutions along distinctively American lines?

Such an analysis, however tempting, would be misleading. The great outpouring of New Englanders who settled western New York began in the 1780's, and "Genesee fever" was raging by 1790. By 1810, there were almost 200,000 people in western New York; by 1820, over 500,000. The beginnings of the prison at Auburn thus came late in the first generation of settlement; furthermore, the new institution was located in one of the more heavily populated parts of the area. The emigrants who settled in this region represented a sober, middle-class agricultural stock which had been pushed out of New England by adverse economic conditions. Bringing with them a desire for civilization, refinement, law, and order, they sought to establish the churches, schools, and other

[1] Ralph S. Herre, "A History of Auburn Prison from the Beginning to about 1867" (unpublished D.Ed. dissertation, Pennsylvania State University, 1950), p. 34; *Laws of the State of New York ... Commencing January 1816, and Ending April 1818* (Albany, 1818), IV, 78–80; D. Morris Kurtz, *Auburn, N. Y.: Its Facilities and Resources* (Auburn, 1884), pp. 23, 25; Henry Hall, *The History of Auburn* (Auburn, 1869), pp. 130–131.

institutions which would help to nourish a stable culture. The fact that the Auburn district had been a Federalist baliwick prior to the War of 1812 in itself indicates a conservative outlook. Finally, it should be remembered that the founding of Auburn prison and the birth of the Auburn system were not one and the same development. The latter did not occur until the mid-1820's, by which time the Erie Canal was bringing a booming prosperity and an ever greater influx of population to the counties through which it passed.[2]

What happened at Auburn reveals a determination to conserve established institutions, including the penitentiary, and not an impulse to originate something new and different. Eventually it proved necessary to innovate in order to conserve, but from the beginning the founders of the new prison showed no inclination to break away from established penal methods. For several years, the techniques used at the Auburn institution were copied closely from those employed at Newgate. These methods proved defective in actual practice, just as they did at the New York City establishment and at the Walnut Street Jail. As this happened, citizens became disillusioned with the penitentiary experiment; new policies were advocated; and, in some quarters, the very idea of institutional treatment was called into question. Following the example of Pennsylvania, which was turning to solitary confinement as a tentative answer to mounting penal problems, New York conducted an experiment with this type of discipline at Auburn. When this failed dismally, the future of the penitentiary hung in the balance so far as the Empire State was concerned.

It was at this point that officials from Auburn and other parts of the state established a new system, harsh but reasonably effective, which not only kept the penitentiary experiment alive but also

[2] See Chard P. Smith, *Yankees and God* (New York, 1954), pp. 298–304; David M. Ellis, "The Yankee Invasion of New York, 1783–1850," *New York History*, XXXII (January, 1951), 9; Whitney R. Cross, *The Burned-over District: The Social and Intellectual History of Enthusiastic Religion in Western New York, 1800–1850* (Ithaca, N. Y., 1950), pp. 57, 59, 77. Cross classifies the Auburn area as "economically mature" by 1820.

seemed to offer some hope of stopping a mounting crime wave. This system was devised at a time when there was widespread concern in both New England and New York about whether or not established institutions could survive transplantation to western areas, and also when American life was caught up in a state of rapid political, economic, and social flux. Although such older reformers as Thomas Eddy retained a measure of influence in penal matters, effective leadership passed to men who represented the attitudes of what one scholar has called "Greater New England." [3] Instead of reflecting the Quaker doctrine of the "inner light," the Auburn system exemplified the Calvinist belief in the depravity of man. Significantly, the new order found its most ardent defender in the head of a benevolent society formed not in New York City or Philadelphia, but in Boston.

Various analysts have noted that the original builders of Auburn prison had no idea of making radical changes from the standard models of the past. As Orlando F. Lewis has observed, the penitentiary "did not start as an iconoclastic, insurgent institution. It was no deviation, at first, from the conventional construction of the times." [4] Beaumont and Tocqueville asserted that when the new prison was built it was believed that Newgate's troubles had stemmed primarily from overcrowding, and that only more space was necessary for the ever growing number of felons. [5] One of the reasons for legislative willingness to sanction the establishment of a completely new institution was the feeling that the relative cheapness of building costs in western New York would make the project no more expensive than the alternative of merely expanding Newgate. [6]

At the time the Auburn establishment was constructed, responsible New York officials still regarded the Walnut Street Jail

[3] Smith, *Yankees and God*, pp. 4–5.

[4] Orlando F. Lewis, *The Development of American Prisons and Prison Customs, 1776–1845* (n.p., 1922), p. 79.

[5] Gustave de Beaumont and Alexis de Tocqueville, *On the Penitentiary System in the United States*, trans. Francis Lieber (Philadelphia, 1833), p. 4.

[6] JS, 39th Session (1816), p. 106.

as the model penitentiary. Philadelphia was at this time the cultural leader among American cities, and its institutions were widely copied throughout the period 1790–1830, especially in western areas.[7] Its prison had set the pattern not only for Newgate but also for penitentiaries in Virginia, Massachusetts, Vermont, Maryland, New Hampshire, Ohio, New Jersey, Tennessee, and Kentucky.[8] When municipal leaders in New York City wished in 1811 to gather some new ideas which might help them to reform conditions at Newgate, it was only natural that they sent John Stanford and Joseph Price to Philadelphia to take notes on the Walnut Street Jail.[9] In 1817, a committee from the New York Senate reported in glowing terms a visit to the Philadelphia prison. "It is conducted in a manner highly honorable to those entrusted with its management," they stated, "and, as it is the oldest establishment of its kind in the country, it is also believed to be as well organized and governed, and as creditable to those who projected it, as any that has hitherto been founded." [10]

It is therefore not surprising that the first prison structures built at Auburn were little different from those at Newgate or the Walnut Street Jail. The earliest quarters for felons were provided in what later came to be the institution's south wing, and consisted of sixty-one cells for two convicts each and twenty-eight apartments for eight to twelve men apiece. "This plan," reported a legislative group a few years later, "seems to have been adopted, in pursuance of the system at the New-York [i.e., Newgate] prison." [11] Auburn administrators also copied Newgate's industrial methods, setting up the same prison trades despite a feeling among the inspectors that the new penitentiary was peculiarly well-situated for the production of iron and nails. Even in minor

[7] Richard C. Wade, "Urban Life in Western America, 1790–1830," *American Historical Review*, LXIV (October, 1958), 21.

[8] Francis C. Gray, *Prison Discipline in America* (London, 1848), p. 26.

[9] Charles G. Sommers, *Memoir of the Rev. John Stanford*, D.D. (New York, 1835), pp. 141–142.

[10] JS, 40th Session (1816–1817), p. 169.

[11] JA, 44th Session (1820–1821), p. 903.

details the influence of the New York City institution was observable. As at Newgate, Auburn's convicts were allowed to go out of the prison into the village and surrounding area on errands, accompanied by a turnkey. The custom of using inmates as waiters and servants in the keeper's house was also borrowed from the older penitentiary.[12]

Administratively, the state demonstrated that it had learned some lessons from previous experience by the time the new prison was established. Five inspectors were responsible for its supervision, and the inclusion of court justices, attorneys-general, and other public functionaries in its government was avoided.[13] The offices of agent and principal keeper were united in one man. Although this was not a perfect arrangement—especially in that it required a person of considerable versatility to meet the requirements of a combined financial and disciplinary position—it may justly be said that responsibility for leadership was much more effectively allocated at Auburn than at Newgate.[14]

Financially, however, conditions had not improved much. Irregular methods of legislative appropriation resulted in frequent embarrassment. As early as 1821, the agent was paying bills in scrip which could be redeemed only when money came from Albany. A familiar note was sounded in 1825 when the inspectors revealed that they had been forced to advance "considerable sums from their private funds, to meet the indispensable demands of the prison," and had recently been obliged to raise $6,000 in a personal loan from an Albany bank.[15] Low salaries again made it

[12] *Ibid.,* 42nd Session (1819), p. 326, and 44th Session (1820–1821), p. 907.

[13] In Beaumont and Tocqueville, *On the Penitentiary System,* p. 27, footnote, it is stated that there were five inspectors until 1820 and three thereafter. This, however, is not corroborated by other sources. See especially Gershom Powers, *A Brief Account of . . . the New-York State Prison at Auburn* (Auburn, 1826), p. 1.

[14] JA, 43rd Session (1820), p. 96; Powers, *Brief Account,* p. 23; *Documents of the Assembly of the State of New York* [hereafter cited DA], 64th Session (1841), Vol. II, No. 28, p. 3.

[15] JA, 44th Session (1820–1821), p. 908, and 49th Session (1826), p 427.

difficult to hire an adequate staff. Often the prison had to rely upon men who had been thrown out of work elsewhere and were willing to accept jobs at the penitentiary temporarily until they could find something better.[16] In addition, staff positions were subject to political pressures, just as at Newgate.

The tendency of Auburn officials to imitate methods worked out at Newgate and the Walnut Street Jail, however, did not last long. By 1819, it was becoming clear that the postwar reform laws had not produced any significant improvement at the New York City prison, and the situation at Auburn was scarcely more encouraging. Inmates employed in building the new institution were allowed to work in company with civilian artisans, and in time a regular trade sprang up in which felons bartered articles manufactured in the prison shops for such items as tobacco, alcohol, or cash. Even guards participated in this illicit business. The inspectors reported that the convicts were becoming increasingly refractory. Attempts were made to set fire to the penitentiary, culminating at one point in a conflagration after which inmates had to be forced back into their cells at bayonet point. Prison officers asserted that more stringent methods were needed, and frightened citizens hastily organized a military force which met weekly for training in riot control.[17]

The act which legalized flogging in 1819 offered one means of meeting insubordination, but there were obstacles impeding its execution at Auburn. Some keepers had tender feelings about whipping the inmates; in addition, some of the civilian laborers who worked with the convicts sympathized with their plight and obstructed the enforcement of discipline. In 1821, several officers declined to flog some unruly felons, and an artisan named Thompson volunteered to do so. When Thompson came out of the prison that evening after inflicting the punishment, he was met by a mob of enraged laborers who gave him a coating of tar and feathers and

[16] Powers, *Brief Account,* p. 71; JA, 49th Session (1826), p. 428.
[17] JA, 42nd Session (1819), p. 235, and 44th Session (1820–1821), pp. 440–441, 903–904; Herre, "History of Auburn Prison," pp. 52–53.

rode him through the streets of Auburn on a rail.[18] In 1822, the inspectors' report to the legislature expressed grave concern about the deterioration of discipline and the effects this had upon the objects of imprisonment.[19]

With a similarly discouraging situation prevailing at Newgate, the Empire State had reached a crisis in prison management. Rumblings of disillusionment with the whole penitentiary idea had been evident even as the legislature pieced together the reform acts of 1816–1819. Newgate's inspectors, writing in 1816, advocated the establishment of a federal penal colony somewhere in the Pacific Northwest. If this could not be done, they suggested that New York set up a dumping-ground of its own in some remote area of the state.[20] A variant of this idea appealed to a legislator who advised that felons be employed on wilderness roads leading to such distant outposts as Chateaugay and Ogdensburg.[21] Racial bias was evident in suggestions made to DeWitt Clinton in 1817 that Negro convicts, whether slave or free, might be pardoned on condition that they be sent to one of the southwestern states or territories for agricultural labor.[22] A special committee recommended in 1818 that all ex-inmates be banished from the state upon release from prison and subjected to heavy fines if they returned.[23] All these proposals clearly reflected a lack of faith in the penitentiary and its potentialities for reforming offenders. A

[18] See varying accounts of this in Hall, *History of Auburn*, p. 133; Kurtz, *Auburn*, p. 43; and Herre, "History of Auburn Prison," pp. 54–55.

[19] JA, 45th Session (1822), p. 216.

[20] JS, 40th Session (1816–1817), p. 7.

[21] JA, 40th Session (1816–1817), p. 691.

[22] See DeWitt Clinton to Inspectors of the State Prison, New York, and to Robert Browne, John Murray, Jr., and Thomas Eddy, Sept. 6, 1817, DeWitt Clinton Letterbooks, Vol. III, Columbia University Library. Clinton rejected the proposal on the grounds that state law permitted slaves to be carried out of New York only after a ten-year ownership, that pardons should be bestowed on an individual rather than on a group basis, that no guarantee could be given for the good treatment of the deportees, and that New York would resent similar action by southern states.

[23] JA, 41st Session (1818), p. 601.

New York lawyer named John Bristed indicated such skepticism in 1818 when he wrote:

Our favourite scheme of substituting a state prison for the gallows is a most prolific mother of crime. During the severity of the winter season, its lodgings and accommodations are better than those of many of our paupers, who are thereby incited to crime in order to mend their condition. And the pernicious custom of *pardoning* the most atrocious criminals, after a short residence in the state prison, is continually augmenting our flying squadrons of murderers, housebreakers, footpads, forgers, highway robbers, and swindlers of all sorts. The effect of Mr. Bentham's plan of a penitentiary, with its panorama, and whispering gallery, is not known, because it has never been tried in this country; but, beyond all peradventure, our state prisons, as at present constituted, are grand demoralizers of our people.[24]

The difficulty of making prisons self-supporting added to popular disillusionment. In 1820, the chairman of a legislative committee argued that it might be a good idea to place these institutions under the direction of private entrepreneurs. In line with this suggestion he submitted a bid by William Pye of Albany to take over Newgate for at least five years. The state would continue to maintain all custodial and rehabilitative services, pay for all repairs, and refrain from taxing the profits of the establishment. In addition, Pye was to receive a state loan of $40,000 for fourteen years upon his promise to fulfill his own side of the bargain for only five. If after fourteen years he had brought the penitentiary to a point at which it was self-supporting, the repayment of the loan was not to be exacted. At the same time, an Albany group proposed to take over and complete Auburn prison in return for grants from the state totaling $160,000, plus whatever profits the

---

[24] John Bristed, *The Resources of the United States of America* (New York, 1818), p. 436. Italics are Bristed's. The allegation concerning Bentham's Panopticon is only partially true, for it is possible to discern the influence of this plan upon the Virginia State Prison at Richmond, a crescent-shaped structure built in 1800. New York officials debated the Panopticon idea in 1811 and rejected it. See Harry Elmer Barnes and Negley K. Teeters, *New Horizons in Criminology* (1st ed.; New York, 1943), p. 485.

firm might make in running the institutional industries. The Auburn agent, interestingly, had estimated that the completion of the penitentiary would cost only slightly over $113,000.[25] The effrontery of these proposals was worthy of the spirit of the "great barbecue" which was to follow the Civil War two generations later. Only sheer desperation on the part of a legislature faced with a chaotic penal situation could have caused them to be seriously considered.

This desperation was accompanied by a steadily hardening official attitude toward the criminal. In 1817, the agent at Newgate recommended that penal techniques be adopted which would convince the offender that the penitentiary "is not to be a mere place of good living and light punishment, but a place of dread and terror, and that his turpitude will receive the punishment it merits." [26] The legalization of stocks, irons, and flogging at the prisons in 1819 reflected the trend toward harshness. As the demand for severe and painful treatment of the felon gained strength, the deterrent theory of punishment was stressed at the expense of the reformative idea. "The great end and design of criminal law, is the prevention of crimes, through fear of punishment; the reformation of offenders being a minor consideration," stated the inspectors of Auburn prison in 1822. "The fear of punishment operates on a whole community; the means of reformation on a few individuals, and privation and suffering are best adapted to the attainment of both these objects." [27] At about the same time, a legislative commission emphasized the necessity of suffering and terror as preventive forces, and declared that the public should be inspired with "a salutary horror of the consequences of criminality." [28] Governor DeWitt Clinton wondered if society, in its desire to reform criminals, had neglected the superior importance

[25] JA, 43rd Session (1820), pp. 726, 811–812.

[26] Ibid., 41st Session (1818), p. 278.

[27] Ibid., 45th Session (1822), p. 218.

[28] Quoted in Society for the Prevention of Pauperism in the City of New-York, Report on the Penitentiary System in the United States (New York, 1822), Appendix, p. 99.

of intimidating would-be delinquents. "The end of punishment is the prevention of crime, by the infliction of pain, and the operation of fear," he asserted.[29] "What aspect should our Penitentiary present?" asked a group of prominent New York philanthropists. "A place where everything conspires to punish the guilty." According to these men, prisons should be "places which are dreaded by convicts," and "the anticipation of being immured within their walls" should be "generally productive of terror."[30] "It had become the common remark in the community," stated a penitentiary official a few years later, "that there had ceased to be any terror, suffering, or efficacy in prison punishments."[31]

The trend toward a harsh and punitive philosophy was matched by a corresponding transfer of sympathy from the offender, whatever his lot, to those who were affected by his crimes. "However much we lament over the sufferings of the guilty," stated the inspectors at Auburn, "the interest and safety of the innocent should not be forgotten."[32] Hard though the convict's life might be, it was often maintained, he fared better than many an honest laborer.[33] Fears of mounting crime led to increased emphasis upon the dangers to which the community was subjected by outlaws and the condign treatment which such creatures deserved. In the words of a prominent member of a legislative investigating committee in 1822:

Our newspapers teem with relations of crimes of every dye. Our cities, villages, and manufactories are frequently in flames. . . . It is understood that connected bands of horse stealers and counterfeiters extend from Canada, through several parts of the Union. The mails of the

---

[29] JS, 45th Session (1822), p. 13.

[30] Society for the Prevention of Pauperism, *Report on the Penitentiary System*, pp. 23, 66.

[31] Gershom Powers, *A Letter . . . in Answer to a Letter of the Hon. Edward Livingston* (Albany, 1829), p. 20.

[32] JA, 45th Session (1822), p. 219.

[33] See Powers, *Brief Account*, p. 66; Beaumont and Tocqueville, *On the Penitentiary System*, p. 163, footnote; DA, 58th Session (1835), Vol. II, No. 135, Part 2, p. 11, and Vol. IV, No. 330, p. 11.

United States no longer afford security. Felonies that affect the stability of our monied institutions are becoming common. . . .

The committee hesitate not to state their opinion, that a government which fails to repress such a course of criminality, fails also in its highest duty—that of protection. They are equally clear in the opinion, that after having for twenty-five years employed our sympathies and resources for the comfort of the criminal part of society, it is now our duty to look to the innocent; and that the industrious classes preyed upon by the convicts who are out of prison, and taxed for the support of those who are within, and suffering from the insecurity of all their means and savings, are now fit objects of our care.[34]

Faced by the impending breakdown of discipline at Auburn and Newgate, and imbued with a growing spirit of harshness, New Yorkers for the final time turned to Pennsylvania for help in correctional matters. Despite the enthusiastic reports which legislative investigators had brought back to Albany in 1817, the Walnut Street Jail was actually experiencing the same difficulties that were evident in the prisons of New York. Its labor system was breaking down by 1815, and internal tumults, overcrowding, and escapes characterized the years that followed. In 1817, a Philadelphia grand jury reported that there were from thirty to forty convicts lodged in rooms eighteen feet square, and that the prison had begun to assume the aspect of "a seminary for every vice." Serious riots occurred at the institution in 1817, 1819, 1820, and 1821.[35] Alarmed officials urged the construction of a new prison in which felons could be placed in strict solitary confinement, and in March, 1818, the Pennsylvania legislature approved the establishment of such a penitentiary at Allegheny, near Pittsburgh.[36]

[34] Remarks of Samuel M. Hopkins, quoted in JS, 44th Session (1822), p. 157.

[35] LeRoy B. DePuy, "The Walnut Street Prison: Pennsylvania's First Penitentiary," *Pennsylvania History*, XVIII (April, 1951), 141–142; Anonymous, "A Statistical View of the Operation of the Penal Code of Pennsylvania," in William Roscoe, *Observations on Penal Jurisprudence* (London, 1819), Appendix, p. 23.

[36] Eugene E. Doll, "Trial and Error at Allegheny: The Western State Penitentiary, 1818–1838," *Pennsylvania Magazine of History and Biography*, LXXXI (January, 1957), 7.

It is not surprising that New York, which had looked to the Keystone State for guidance in penal affairs so often in the past, soon undertook a similar experiment, especially since some of its own citizens had long advocated solitary confinement for certain types of delinquents. As early as 1803, Thomas Eddy had urged the erection of a municipal penitentiary in New York City where minor offenders could be imprisoned in complete solitude for short periods of time on restricted rations. By 1816, he was convinced that some solitary confinement would be good for all prisoners.[37] The spread of the idea that one of the worst features of inmate life at Newgate and Auburn was the tendency of criminals to corrupt one another resulted in added support for enforced solitude. There was some question about whether or not such treatment should exclude labor, but even one ex-convict was willing to sanction this for short-term offenders.[38]

By the early 1820's, some reformers regarded solitary confinement with the same type of quasi-mystical faith that Jonas Hanway and William Dodd had manifested in eighteenth-century England. One group of enthusiasts believed that six months of solitude would leave a greater impression on the mind of an offender and constitute a more effective safeguard against crime than ten years of confinement in penitentiaries as they were customarily managed. These reformers recommended that work be allowed in some cases and not in others.[39] A similar proposal was made by a legislative group which suggested that henceforth only felons serving life sentences should have their punishment alleviated by being allowed the diversion of labor.[40] The widespread existence

[37] The 1803 suggestion was actually embodied in an enactment of the legislature, but the law was permissive and its provisions were never executed. See Samuel L. Knapp, *The Life of Thomas Eddy* (New York, 1834), pp. 202–203, and Society for the Prevention of Pauperism, *Report on the Penitentiary System*, p. 16. The latter mistakenly places these developments in 1804.

[38] [W. A. Coffey], *Inside Out, or An Interior View of the New-York State Prison* (New York, 1823), pp. 126–127.

[39] Society for the Prevention of Pauperism, *Report on the Penitentiary System*, pp. 51–53.

[40] JS, 45th Session (1822), pp. 160–161.

of such ideas, the disillusionment which grew out of the apparent failure of previous methods, and the shift to a more stringent and vindictive philosophy of penal treatment formed the background for a nearly disastrous experiment with solitary confinement which began at Auburn in 1821.

In 1819, William Brittin, the first agent at Auburn, had started the construction of a north wing which was to contain facilities for solitary confinement. This move was calculated at least in part to enable the prison to conform to the classification requirements imposed by the legislature that year.[41] He had completed between one and two hundred cells in this new wing by 1820, but most of these were destroyed in a fire set by inmate incendiaries. Undaunted, Brittin rebuilt and completed what was to become one of the most frequently copied prison structures in the world. In the center of the new wing was an island of cells which was five tiers high and surrounded on all four sides by a vacant area eleven feet wide. The individual cells were seven feet long by three and one-half feet wide by seven feet high, and each tier consisted of two rows of these cubicles placed back to back. Enclosing the island and the area around it was an outer shell pierced by small windows affording some degree of illumination. Here was the famous Auburn-style cellblock, which was to be imitated in one penitentiary after another, even into the twentieth century. It was a prison within a prison. Even should a convict manage to break out of it—this was extremely unlikely—he would still have to get past the wall surrounding the entire institution in order to escape.[42]

[41] See *Laws of the State of New-York . . . 1819* (Albany, 1819), pp. 87–88, as cited above, p. 46.

[42] See especially Powers, *Letter*, p. 6, and Barnes and Teeters, *New Horizons in Criminology*, p. 519. For a plan of Auburn prison which shows the layout of the north wing and that of the old south wing side by side, indicating graphically the difference between the two, see Fig. 2, following p. 16. I have found no conclusive evidence to indicate that Brittin was influenced by the similar design of the Maison de Force in Ghent when he built the Auburn north wing, but inasmuch as a plan of the Flemish institution could be found in Howard's works there is a distinct possibility that such a connection existed.

On March 13, 1821, a legislative commission which had studied New York's growing penal problems recommended that Auburn's inmates be divided into three classes. The first category of convicts, consisting of the most hardened offenders, would be placed in constant solitary confinement as soon as the north wing was ready for occupancy. A less dangerous grade of prisoners would be kept in solitude part of the time and permitted to work in groups when not so confined. Finally, the "least guilty and depraved" were regularly to be allowed to work together in the daytime but to be separated at night.[43] On April 2, 1821, the experiment was authorized by law. "At this period," stated a prison official later, "the legislature and public at large had become so dissatisfied and discouraged with the existing mode of penitentiary punishments, that it was generally believed, that unless a severer system was adopted, the old sanguinary criminal code must be restored." [44]

On Christmas Day, 1821, eighty hardened criminals were placed in solitary confinement in the cells of the north wing. They were allowed no work, were forbidden to lie down in the daytime, and were condemned to remain in this situation until their sentences should expire.[45] For at least a time, prison officials entertained no doubts about the efficacy or defensibility of the new program. "One who would expect gentle means, with advice and admonition, to produce a change of moral character in convicts, should not forget that such means have been tried in vain upon them in society," stated the Auburn inspectors in 1822, "and he will find that no radical change can be effected until their stubborn spirits are subdued, and their depraved hearts softened, by mental suffering." [46] It was not possible to preserve the penitentiary system and prevent a return to the sanguinary code, asserted the same officials in 1823, "unless the convicts are made to endure great suffering, and that applied, as much as possible, to the mind."

[43] JA, 44th Session (1820–1821), p. 904.

[44] Powers, *Brief Account*, p. 32.

[45] *Ibid*. The prohibition of lying down in the daytime was in all likelihood an attempt to retard muscular atrophy.

[46] JA, 45th Session (1822), p. 218.

The demands of nature must indeed be complied with; their bodies must be fed and clothed. . . . But they ought to be deprived of every enjoyment arising from social or kindred feelings and affections; of all knowledge of each other, the world, and their connections with it. Force them to reflection, and let self-tormenting guilt harrow up the tortures of accusing conscience, keener than scorpion stings; until the intensity of their sufferings subdues their stubborn spirits, and humbles them to a realizing sense of the enormity of their crimes and their obligation to reform.[47]

Despite high hopes at the official level, however, it quickly became obvious that the experiment was little short of catastrophic to its victims, many of whom were unable to submit to it without going insane. One became so desperate that he sprang out of his cell when his door was opened and jumped from the fourth tier, narrowly averting death when a stove pipe broke the force of his fall. Another tried to commit suicide by cutting his veins with a piece of tin. Yet another "beat and mangled his head against the walls of his cell, until he destroyed one of his eyes." The condition of the unfortunate wretches by 1823 prompted Governor Yates to visit the prison and conduct a personal investigation. As a result of his findings he decided to pardon most of them, and by the close of the year the greater number had been released.[48]

It was revealed later that over half the deaths in the prison in 1823 occurred among the solitary inmates; that these men seemed to acquire a peculiar susceptibility to consumption under such treatment; and that some complained of "numbness and swellings of their limbs, which they described as paralyzed or frequently falling asleep." Others suffered from general weakness and debility.[49] Those who placed implicit faith in solitude received another shock when it was discovered that the deterrent effect of the treatment upon the unfortunate convicts had proved to be negligible. One of the pardoned criminals committed a burglary

[47] Quoted in Powers, *Brief Account*, p. 35.
[48] JA, 51st Session (1828), Appendix A, p. 45; Powers, *Brief Account*, pp. 32–36.
[49] JA, 47th Session (1824), p. 126, and 48th Session (1825), p. 122.

on the very first night after his release, and twelve of them were eventually reconvicted.[50] In 1825, the majority of a special commission voted for the discontinuance of solitary confinement except as a possible device for punishing breaches of prison discipline. By the end of the year, the experiment begun in 1821 had come to an end.[51]

New York had thus encountered another setback in its search for an effective penal policy. Now that solitary confinement had failed so miserably, what alternatives were left? The answer came from a small group of legislators and prison officials and was based upon techniques worked out among the two groups of inmates not subjected to complete solitude after 1821. The new program, featuring solitary confinement at night and group activity in absolute silence by day, became famous in penal history as the Auburn system.

Before analyzing this system in actual operation, it is desirable to understand the broader social situation within which it was spawned. To state that previous penal methods had failed, that convicts had become increasingly hard to manage, and that the resulting public disillusionment had been accompanied by a steadily hardening attitude toward the criminal does not explain the full significance of the new order. The birth of the Auburn system did not take place in a vacuum in which only penological considerations mattered. It was part of a larger picture, and it seems peculiarly fitting in retrospect that the institution from which it took its name was located in western New York.

The period that followed the War of 1812 in the United States was one of rapid and profound change. Politically, the trend toward universal manhood suffrage was slowly paving the way for the great Jacksonian triumph of 1828 and giving previously disfranchised groups a feeling of power. Economically, the nation was in the throes of industrialization and was experiencing all the dislocations which this entailed in a society which had been, and

[50] Powers, *Brief Account*, p. 36.
[51] JA, 48th Session (1825), pp. 123–126; Elliot G. Storke and James H. Smith, *History of Cayuga County, New York* (Syracuse, 1879), p. 155.

still was, overwhelmingly agricultural. In rapid succession the country's commercial and manufacturing interests witnessed the deluge of foreign-made goods following the end of the conflict with Britain, the rise of feverish speculative activity in newly opened areas, a severe financial panic in 1819, and then another round of supercharged internal development highlighted by the large-scale digging of canals. Socially, class conflict began to appear as industrial workers struggled to exist on low wages and united to form nascent trade unions. Finally, the attention of citizens everywhere was directed to pressing domestic, rather than international, problems, and a great surge of humanity began migrating westward into areas which, if not in a primitive frontier state, at least lacked some of the civilizing institutions which had given life a certain degree of stability in the old, settled areas.[52]

How could the old agrarian virtues survive in a nation plunging into the era of modern capitalism?[53] Could public morality and order endure in a rapidly changing society which was allowing more and more economic and political freedom to its members? If not, the American experiment itself might result in failure. Such portentous considerations were especially relevant in recently settled areas where burgeoning populations existed without the restraining influence of deeply rooted institutions. Here was a battleground upon which mighty issues were to be decided, and reformers imbued with a sense of what Clifford S. Griffin has called

[52] In an even broader international perspective, it is pertinent to note that these developments took place in a period of reaction in the Western world following the downfall of Napoleon. On the significance of this insofar as reform movements are concerned, see especially Charles I. Foster, *An Errand of Mercy: The Evangelical United Front, 1790–1837* (Chapel Hill, N.C., 1960), *passim*.

[53] This question emerges as a key to the whole Jacksonian period in Marvin Meyers' brilliant work, *The Jacksonian Persuasion* (Stanford, Calif., 1957). Other books which have influenced my thinking on the conservative impulse to reform during this period are John R. Bodo, *The Protestant Clergy and Public Issues, 1812–1848* (Princeton, 1954); Charles C. Cole, Jr., *The Social Ideas of the Northern Evangelists, 1826–1860* (New York, 1954); Foster, *An Errand of Mercy*, cited above; and Clifford S. Griffin, *Their Brothers' Keepers: Moral Stewardship in the United States, 1800–1865* (New Brunswick, N.J., 1960).

"moral stewardship" were determined that the conflict must not be lost. Although he was at the time chiefly concerned about an imaginary Roman Catholic menace, Lyman Beecher was manifesting anxieties that had plagued his contemporaries for two decades or more when in 1835 he maintained that "the religious and political destiny of our nation is to be decided in the West," and that population in that area was "rushing in like the waters of the flood, demanding for its moral preservation the immediate and universal action of those institutions which discipline the mind and arm the conscience and the heart." [54]

How could the battle be won? First, by transplanting those institutions which nourished a stable culture: churches, schools, courts of law. The energy with which emigrants from New England erected academies and houses of worship in young western communities is too well known to require further comment. Mere institutions, however, were not enough; they had to be supplemented by a powerful effort to develop within the individual person strong inner controls which would compensate for the wide economic and political freedoms which had been granted him and guarantee that conformity without which no orderly society could exist. Here, as cultural historians have realized, was a key to the proliferation of home missionary societies and revival campaigns in the era of such stalwart evangelists as Charles Grandison Finney. Finally, if all these influences did not succeed in keeping potential backsliders, dissipators, and lawbreakers in tow, citizens could turn to what one scholar has called "a distinctive feature of Puritanism: the regulation of the morals and actions of those whom the regulators deemed dangerous to society because they were unable to take care of themselves." [55]

[54] See Smith, *Yankees and God*, p. 309, quoting from Lyman Beecher, *Plea for the West* (Cincinnati, 1835).

[55] Marcus L. Hansen, *The Immigrant in American History*, ed. Arthur M. Schlesinger (Cambridge, Mass., 1940), p. 111. I have been influenced by Chapter V of this work, which approaches some of the problems I have just described within the context of immigration history. See also Emil Oberholzer, Jr., *Delinquent Saints: Disciplinary Action in the Early Congregational Churches of Massachusetts* (New York, 1956), p. 245.

This last alternative was somewhat extreme, amounting to a denial of individual liberty. Because of this, reformers realized that it was preferable, where possible, to develop inner controls through the use of revivals, temperance societies, organizations to preserve the sanctity of the Sabbath, and Sunday schools. If these did not accomplish the desired results, however, defenders of public order were prepared to use more forcible methods. Sabbatarians demonstrated this, for example, by attempting to outlaw Sunday mail deliveries and by boycotting managers of public conveyances which ran on the sacred day. Later, temperance advocates showed the same tendency in their fight for legal prohibition of alcoholic beverages. The velvet glove of persuasion contained the iron fist of coercion. Significantly, some of the strongest protagonists of temperance and Sabbath-keeping were believers in an Old Testament type of theocracy who had no strong faith in democracy anyway.[56]

This willingness to suppress nonconformity and individualism, if necessary, played an important role in prison reform after the War of 1812. It could be vented with full force upon the criminal, who was not only a more serious threat to order and social stability than the drunkard or the Sabbath-breaker but who had also been a traditional target of coercive tactics from time immemorial. If the would-be reformer of other men's morals found it advisable to use voluntary measures so far as was practicable when dealing with the ordinary free citizen, he need feel no such scruples with regard to the felon. At the very least, the convicted criminal might be made to display an outward conformity under a properly stringent regime, and it was not inconceivable that inner controls could be developed within him once submission had been achieved. Stripped of every vestige of personal freedom, the convict could be forced to abstain from alcohol and other stimulants,

[56] Cross, *Burned-over District*, pp. 131–135; John A. Krout, *The Origins of Prohibition* (New York, 1925), *passim*. The theocratic attitude which I have touched upon here is explored at length in Bodo, *The Protestant Clergy and Public Issues*, previously cited. For a good illustration of the type of reformer who possessed the coercive mentality described above, see Frank L. Byrne, *Prophet of Prohibition: Neal Dow and His Crusade* (Madison, Wis., 1961).

compelled to attend church services, and given his choice between reading religious literature or none at all.

It would be difficult to find a better example of a society struggling with the fears and forces which have just been surveyed than the area in which the Auburn system was devised. The tide of emigration from New England, so important in various western regions, had started earlier in upstate New York by virtue of sheer geographical proximity. Since the opening of the Phelps and Gorham tracts in the late 1780's there had been a steady outpouring of humanity into the Empire State; according to one estimate, 800,000 people either settled in New York or passed through it on their way to other habitations in the period between 1790 and 1820.[57] This trend was accentuated with the opening of the Erie Canal. "During the twenties," states one scholar, "population grew more rapidly here than in any other part of the country. Albany gained 96 per cent, Utica 183, Syracuse 282, Buffalo 314, and Rochester 512. The entire five counties surrounding the western half of the canal increased 135 per cent in the decade."[58]

This battleground for the forces of civilization and social upheaval quickly became the target of home missionary societies largely organized in New England or inspired by leaders in that section. Revivals occurred with such regularity and effect that western New York became known as the "Burned-over District." It was only natural that crusades against drunkenness, Sabbath-breaking, and other disturbing influences flourished in the area. In the words of Whitney R. Cross:

Four benevolent movements experienced such sudden growth in western New York during the twenties and generated such controversies that they seem collectively to merit consideration as a major portent of the era to come. These were not complete innovations but had long roots in the past. They were not unique in this locality, for they claimed national scope. Yet the campaigns to circulate Bibles, to found Sunday

[57] Smith, *Yankees and God*, pp. 301–302, citing Ellis, "The Yankee Invasion of New York," pp. 3–7.

[58] Cross, *Burned-over District*, p. 56.

schools, to encourage temperance, and to enforce Sabbath observance all spurted so suddenly here and so intensified and broadened their appeals in this region that they became in their proportions veritable peculiarities of this time and place in American History.[59]

These crusades reached intensity only after an initial "boom period" had been succeeded by a comparative degree of maturity in which citizens could contemplate the problems which had arisen and the need for stabilizing influences. Sabbatarianism, for example, reached a climax in the late 1820's. The prevention of crime, however, was such a pressing matter that action occurred more quickly to deal effectively with the lawless. To the statewide pressure which accompanied the deterioration of discipline at Auburn and Newgate was added the force of local events taking place throughout western New York. The influx of construction workers and boatmen which accompanied the Erie Canal was a particularly unsettling influence. Some of these indulged in various immoralities; in addition, it became common for many laborers to turn to thievery in the long winters when the waterway froze over and work was not available. Detailed statistics of the incidence of crime in canal districts are not available for the 1820's, but a later survey covering a six-year period in the 1840's disclosed that the rate of offenses per capita in the eighteen counties bordering the waterway was more than twice as high as that which prevailed in the counties south of the artery but not adjacent to it.[60] There is little reason to suppose that the situation was much different twenty years before, or that the incidence of crime would have alarmed sober and God-fearing men less than such evils as illiteracy, inebriety, or indifference to the Lord's Day.

It is instructive to study the personal antecedents of some leading pioneers of the Auburn system against the distinctive social

[59] *Ibid.,* p. 126.

[60] *Ibid.,* pp. 132 and *passim;* DA, 72nd Session (1849), Vol. VI, No. 243, pp. 77, 85–87. The relative incidences were 1 to 1,276 for the canal counties and 1 to 2,676 in counties south of the waterway. On the wintertime thievery common among "canal boys," see DA, 69th Session (1846), Vol. IV, No. 93, p. 2, and the *Northern Christian Advocate* (Auburn), Jan. 21, 1846.

and moral background of the Burned-over District. One of these men was Gershom Powers, an intensely religious individual who had come from New Hampshire to teach school in the Cayuga County hamlet of Sempronius before going on to a career as frontier judge, Jacksonian congressman, and prison agent. Samuel M. Hopkins, another early exponent of the Auburn system, was a farmer-lawyer who emigrated from Connecticut, spent years on the New York frontier, and had some sort of a religious experience shortly before plunging into prison reform. Elam Lynds, a lash-wielding warden who came to epitomize the discipline worked out at Auburn, was a native of Connecticut who lacked the religious impulses of Powers or Hopkins but possessed a desire for order as intense as theirs, if not more so.[61] It was hardly accidental that the activities of these men attracted the enthusiastic support of such New England reformers as Louis Dwight, a former Andover Seminary student and agent of the American Bible Society who wanted not only to spread the benefits of the Auburn system to criminals but also to see some of its principles adopted in colleges, academies, and even in private homes.[62] Nor is it surprising that the Prison Discipline Society, founded in Boston by Dwight and dedicated to the spread of the Auburn system, attracted the support of such Sabbatarians and temperance advocates as Jeremiah Evarts, Josiah Bissell, Arthur and John Tappan, Edward Delavan, and Gerrit Smith, all of whom were high officers, "Life Directors," or "Life Members."[63] In short, the development of the Auburn system was part of a larger pattern of conservative reform activities flourishing at the same time.

The new penal order which arose in New York also reflected the contemporary milieu in other ways. In the era following the War of 1812 the United States experienced an expansion of nationalistic feeling, marked by a strong conviction that the country had a great

[61] More extended treatments of these men, with documentation, will be provided in Chapter IV.

[62] See William Jenks, *A Memoir of the Rev. Louis Dwight* (Boston, 1856), *passim;* Prison Discipline Society, *Eighth Report* (1833), p. 6.

[63] Prison Discipline Society, *Third Report* (1828), pp. 83–84.

mission to perform in spreading its superior republican institutions to the rest of mankind. It was easy to forget America's cultural debts to the Old World, to portray monarchical Europe as the center of all that was corrupt and decadent. Surely the young nation need not look to such a source for lessons in the framing of public policies and the management of social institutions; it was rather its task to enlighten, to teach, to play the role of standard-bearer.[64]

This spirit was present in the development of the Auburn system. Thomas Eddy, as we have seen, had been influenced by European theorists and kept up a correspondence with reformers in the Old World. His close friend John Griscom eventually managed to take a trip abroad, inspect various penal and charitable institutions, and seek out such humanitarian leaders as Elizabeth Fry.[65] The maintenance of such foreign contacts was nothing unusual among American reformers who had grown up in the eighteenth century.[66] A survey of the mass of official reports and other writings of those who were most important in the development of the Auburn system, however, discloses a different picture. Here one will hunt with little or no success for an acknowledgment of indebtedness to European pioneers or precedents, or for so much as an indication of interest in what was happening in the prisons of the Old World. Although it may be assumed that these American correctional leaders knew something about the work of such European reformers as Beccaria or Howard, it would be difficult to prove it. To be sure, they were eager to impress visitors from foreign countries, and willing to advise them if

[64] For an extended analysis of the American sense of "mission," see Ralph H. Gabriel, *The Course of American Democratic Thought* (1st ed.; New York, 1940), pp. 22–25. For a particularly stimulating analysis of the idea of European decadence in this period, emphasizing in this case the role of agrarian values, see John William Ward, *Andrew Jackson, Symbol for an Age* (New York, 1955), pp. 31–36.

[65] John Griscom, *A Year in Europe* (New York, 1823), Vols. I and II *passim*.

[66] Michael Kraus, "Eighteenth Century Humanitarianism: Collaboration Between Europe and America," *Pennsylvania Magazine of History and Biography*, LX (July, 1936), 270–286.

asked to do so. Elam Lynds could meet Tocqueville and Beaumont in a Syracuse hardware store and tell them how prisons should be administered.[67] Stephen Allen, another devotee of the Auburn system, could write a tract to set William Roscoe of Liverpool straight on matters of penitentiary policy.[68] A steady stream of European visitors could come to the prisons of New York to see how things were done. The exchange of ideas in these situations, however, was basically a one-way proposition. The function of those who developed the new order was to expound, to court approval rather than to seek advice. Their system, they believed, was the best on earth.[69]

Another attitude prevalent in Jacksonian America was a veneration for "common sense" and intuitive wisdom as opposed to book learning and intellectual discipline.[70] Here, too, the pioneers of the Auburn system shared the spirit of the times. There had been a healthy respect for intellectual pursuits in the circles in which Thomas Eddy and his fellow humanitarians had moved. John Griscom was not only a reformer but also a pioneer American chemist. David Hosack, another friend of Eddy's, was a prominent surgeon, writer on medical subjects, owner of a large library, and founder of the New York Botanical Garden. DeWitt Clinton, who shared Eddy's humanitarian and economic interests, pursued recondite learning with such zeal that political opponents ridiculed

[67] George Wilson Pierson, *Tocqueville and Beaumont in America* (New York, 1938), pp. 206–212.

[68] Stephen Allen, *Observations on Penitentiary Discipline, Addressed to William Roscoe, Esq. of Liverpool, England* (New York, 1827).

[69] See DS, 59th Session (1835), Vol. I, No. 13, p. 3. By way of contrast, Philadelphia prison reformers maintained contact with European experts. The Society for Alleviating the Miseries of Public Prisons listed such corresponding members as Thomas Folwell Buxton, Basil Montagu, Samuel Woods, William Roscoe, Joseph John Gurney, Charles Lucas of France, and Prince Gallitzin of Russia. (*Constitution of the Philadelphia Society for Alleviating the Miseries of Public Prisons* [Philadelphia, 1830], p. 10.) Perhaps the pronounced tendency for Quakers to maintain contact with one another through correspondence and travel accounted in part for the way in which the practices of penal reformers in Pennsylvania differed from those in New York.

[70] See Ward, *Andrew Jackson,* pp. 46–78.

him on this score.[71] At Newgate, a keeper once impressed the Swedish visitor Axel Klinkowström by taking a volume of Howard's writings off his bookshelf and expounding the English reformer's ideas.[72]

Far different was the attitude of those who pioneered the Auburn system. Of these, only Samuel M. Hopkins had clearly defined intellectual interests, and these were apparently strongest at the turn of the nineteenth century.[73] Elam Lynds had a positive scorn for philosophical reflection. In a stinging rejoinder to the criticisms of the English reformer William Roscoe, Stephen Allen asserted that he had never despaired of the penitentiary idea; his only fear had been that "the enthusiasm of theorists, and those who have only studied the world of mankind in their closets, might so far prevail, as to perfect their object, and have their schemes of conversion and reformation, again put on trial." [74]

The same attitude was reflected in a report on penal matters submitted to the New York legislature in 1827 by Samuel M. Hopkins and a fellow prison reformer, George Tibbits. After referring sarcastically to the musings of "recluse and studious men about the virtues of felons," Hopkins and Tibbits brought up the failure of William Goodell, an agent who tried unsuccessfully to reverse the trend toward harshness at Auburn in the mid-1820's. Goodell's troubles, they averred, stemmed from infection by the ideas of "well meaning men" who knew little of criminals in actual life but did not let this stop them from propounding penal theories.[75]

[71] Edgar F. Smith, "Griscom, John," *Dictionary of American Biography*, VIII, 7; John W. Francis, *Old New York* (New York, 1858), pp. 84–85; William W. Campbell, *The Life and Writings of DeWitt Clinton* (New York, 1849), pp. xxv–xxvi, xxxii, and *passim;* Dixon R. Fox, *The Decline of Aristocracy in the Politics of New York* (New York, 1919), pp. 202–204.

[72] Franklin D. Scott, trans. and ed., *Baron Klinkowström's America, 1818–1820* (Evanston, Ill., 1952), p. 96.

[73] Samuel M. Hopkins, *Sketch of the Public and Private Life of Samuel M. Hopkins* (Rochester, N.Y., 1898), pp. 12, 23, 28.

[74] Allen, *Observations on Penitentiary Discipline*, p. 65.

[75] JA, 50th Session (1827), Appendix A, pp. 8, 30.

In sum, the representative exponent of the Auburn system was a nationalistic man of action who had no use for recondite studies. Not until phrenologists began applying the ideas of such theorists as Gall, Spurzheim, and Combe at Sing Sing in the 1840's was a speculative tendency to appear in the prisons of the Empire State. Even then, the trend did not last long before the phrenologists were thrown out. A legislative commission which warmly approved of this result asserted that common sense and "mother wit, sharpened by a knowledge of men as we meet them in our daily walks of life, are the best qualifications for a keeper. . . . We trust that the old fashioned wisdom, founded on the word of God, may soon take the place of the sublime 'physical truths' of phrenology." [76]

Distinctly related to its age, the Auburn system was run by tough-minded men who literally put their charges through the school of hard knocks. With the collapse of the venture in complete solitary confinement in 1825, the stage was set for a new order, and a state that had already conducted two major penological experiments now embarked upon another.

[76] DS, 70th Session (1847), Vol. IV, No. 153, pp. 5–6.

# Chapter IV

# The Auburn System
# and Its Champions

THE dismal failure of absolute solitary confinement at Auburn prison marked a turning point in the tactics of New York penal reformers. Thenceforth, these men no longer looked to Pennsylvania for guidance. While the experiment with utter solitude was in progress, administrators at Auburn had devised a new system for the convicts who were not being subjected to complete isolation. This regime, which became world-famous, was now imposed upon all inmates without deviation.

The most distinctive feature of this system was that it rejected solitary confinement except at night, and yet attempted to prevent convicts from communicating with one another at any time. In order to accomplish this goal, it was necessary for prison officials to devise elaborate techniques for constant surveillance and to make unsparing use of coercion and intimidation. To gather hundreds of dangerous and sometimes desperate men together within the confines of an institution no larger than a city block and attempt to enforce absolute silence despite allowing them to mingle with one another was a daring enterprise. That it succeeded as well as it did was partly due to the inventiveness and sheer determination of those who carried it out.

Three of the leaders who championed the new order constituted a legislative team which investigated prison conditions and eventually supervised the building of the penitentiary at Sing Sing. One of these men, George Tibbits, was a merchant and politician who demonstrated considerable ability in financial matters but achieved no lasting significance as a prison reformer.[1] Much more important in this regard were his colleagues, Stephen Allen and Samuel M. Hopkins. Both of these men agreed upon three basic principles: that convicts had not been treated with sufficient severity; that too much faith had been placed in their reformability; and that drastic changes would have to be made if the penitentiary idea were to succeed.

Allen was a merchant and Tammany-connected politician who became mayor of New York City, a member of the state legislature, and a holder of various offices under the Jacksonians. The drift of his penological thinking is revealed in the fact that during his mayoralty he was instrumental in having the treadmill adopted at the city prison. His later activities as president of the Society for the Reformation of Juvenile Delinquents and administrator of the New York House of Refuge indicated that he had a certain amount of sympathy for youthful misdemeanants, but his attitude toward adult offenders was exceedingly dour. Although the House of Refuge received state aid for educational and rehabilitative work, Allen believed that the separation of church and state forbade the use of public money for the religious or moral training of mature felons, and that educational efforts in prisons were unwise because they took time away from the inmates' labor. Holding that criminals "had not the same claim upon our commiseration, that the honest and unfortunate part of our species have," he believed "that the reformatory plan, or the system of attention, kindness, and forbearance, has failed, and will fail, wherever, or whenever it is put into operation." He even admired Connecti-

[1] Tibbits helped to formulate the plan used to raise funds for the building of the Erie Canal. For a short sketch of his career, see James G. Wilson and John Fiske, eds., *Appletons' Cyclopaedia of American Biography* (New York, 1887–1889), VI, 110.

cut's Simsbury copper mines, where convicts were immured in slimy dungeons fifty feet or more below the surface of the earth.[2]

Samuel M. Hopkins, a former federal congressman, was an influential member of the state legislature during the 1820's and exerted strong pressure for changes in penal discipline. A native of Connecticut who fluctuated between law, farming, and politics, his career was characterized by rootlessness and scarred by financial disappointment. A religious experience in 1821, previously alluded to, may have influenced his subsequent efforts in penal reform.[3] In 1822, he took part in an intensive investigation of the penitentiary problem and presented a lengthy committee report to the legislature on this subject.[4] One prison reformer later remembered having heard Hopkins deliver "an able and vehement speech" at Albany in which he contended that inmate life had not been sufficiently severe and should produce more terror and suffering.[5]

Men like Allen and Hopkins played an essential role in the development of the Auburn system, giving new and more stringent methods of discipline support at the legislative level and helping to mold public opinion in favor of harsh policies. More important

[2] See James Hardie, *The History of the Tread-mill* (New York, 1824), pp. 15–16; Bradford K. Peirce, *A Half Century with Juvenile Delinquents* (New York, 1869), p. 151; Stephen Allen, *Observations on Penitentiary Discipline, Addressed to William Roscoe, Esq. of Liverpool, England* (New York, 1827), pp. 7, 35, 44, 46. A biographical account of Allen is contained in Freeman Hunt, *Lives of American Merchants* (New York, 1856–1858), II, 169–200. For descriptions of the Simsbury mines, see Orlando F. Lewis, *The Development of American Prisons and Prison Customs 1776–1845* (n.p., 1922), pp. 64–67, and Richard H. Phelps, *Newgate of Connecticut: Its Origin and Early History* (Hartford, 1876), *passim*.

[3] Samuel M. Hopkins, *Sketch of the Public and Private Life of Samuel Miles Hopkins* (Rochester, N.Y., 1898), pp. 3–39, 44–46.

[4] Society for the Prevention of Pauperism in the City of New-York, *Report on the Penitentiary System of the United States* (New York, 1822), Appendix, pp. 90–107.

[5] Gershom Powers, *A Letter ... in Answer to a Letter of the Hon. Edward Livingston* (Albany, 1829), p. 20.

in devising and implementing such methods, however, were actual prison administrators. These men were imbued with a belief that their most important task was to break the convict's spirit and bring him into a state of utter submission. This was the only way, they reasoned, to keep an inmate in line and make sure that he would conform to the unnatural discipline demanded under the Auburn system. Once this state of subjection had been achieved, however, exponents of the system divided into two schools of thought about subsequent policy. One group was content to reduce the prisoner to an automaton and derive maximum benefit from his labor in the penitentiary shops. Defenders of this approach insisted that reformation was a chimera and believed that deterrence was the primary goal of punishment. Other reformers, however, held that an educational and religious rebuilding process should follow the breaking of the inmate, who might ultimately return to free society not merely a chastened but actually a better man.

Ordinarily it is not difficult to divide the most prominent exponents of the Auburn system into one or the other of these groups. Elam Lynds was the representative par excellence of the first, and Gershom Powers and Louis Dwight typified the second. Robert Wiltse, Lynds's deputy and eventual successor as warden at Sing Sing, followed his mentor's example in espousing policies based upon sheer coercion and deterrence; Stephen Allen also had obvious affinities with this school of thought. Samuel M. Hopkins was an exponent of Lyndsian methods in the mid-1820's but clearly became disillusioned with them by the end of the decade. Certain figures, however, are more difficult to categorize because of insufficient data on their careers. Of these, the most important was John D. Cray.

It was rumored about Auburn in later years that Cray, as a minor officer in the British army in Canada during the War of 1812, deserted his post.[6] He apparently made his way into New York after the conflict, settling in the Auburn area and encounter-

6 DA, 75th Session (1852), Vol. I, No. 20, p. 77.

ing financial difficulties which made him only too happy to accept the position of deputy keeper at the new prison.[7] The sketchiness of details about Cray's background and career is particularly unfortunate because he was probably the man who devised most of the elaborate techniques which were necessary to maintain the silent system, such as the lockstep, various seating and working arrangements, and the undeviating routine which inmates followed from dawn to dark.[8] According to available descriptions, he was a person of unusual firmness and vigilance, "possessed of vast intellectual resources, and endowed with that energy and decision of character which eminently fitted him to be the founder of a new system."[9]

Cray's willingness to place the convict under a stern and coercive regime was typical of the founders of the Auburn system. On the other hand, he was more than an exponent of sheer force, for he started a small school at the prison for young inmates who did not know how to read or write. This incurred the displeasure of his immediate superior, Elam Lynds, who insisted that such instruction would only make the prisoners "more capable villains" after they had been released. In retrospect, therefore, Cray appears to have been an early exponent of the ideas held by such men as Gershom Powers, who became warden at Auburn in 1826 and

[7] Powers, *Letter*, p. 7.

[8] After studying the available evidence I concur here with Blake McKelvey, *American Prisons: A Study in American Social History Prior to 1915* (Chicago, 1936), p. 8, in concluding that Cray, rather than Lynds, was probably responsible for most features of the Auburn routine. Powers' *Letter*, previously cited, contains considerable sworn testimony of officers who had been on the prison staff during the formative period and makes a case for Cray in a convincing manner despite its transparent bias against Lynds. In support of Lynds's claim to be the "father of the Auburn system," see especially Gustave de Beaumont and Alexis de Tocqueville, *On the Penitentiary System in the United States*, trans. Francis Lieber (Philadelphia, 1833), pp. 6, 291, and George Combe, *Notes on the United States of North America during a Phrenological Visit in 1838-9-40* (Philadelphia, 1841), II, 74.

[9] Auburn *Weekly American*, April 1, 1857. See also Powers, *Letter*, *passim*, and Nicolaus H. Julius, *Nordamerikas sittliche Zustände, Nach eigenen Anschauungen in den Jahren 1834, 1835, und 1836* (Leipzig, 1839), II, 142.

wrote a pamphlet building up the case for Cray rather than Lynds as the chief architect of the system for which the institution was becoming famous. By this time, Cray himself was gone from the scene, for he had found his position under Lynds too difficult to endure and resigned in 1823.[10] According to one source, he emigrated westward and eventually became a municipal official in Detroit.[11]

Cray's departure left the prison temporarily under the firm control of Lynds, who had been appointed agent and principal keeper after the death of William Brittin in 1821.[12] This grim and unrelenting administrator was the supreme exponent of harshness and severity in dealing with convicts. Possessed of the same "indomitable will" and "inflexibility of purpose" which was popularly attributed to Old Hickory of Tennessee, of whose party the warden became a member, Lynds was an authentic Jacksonian "man of iron." [13] A ceaselessly vigilant person with an ever ready whip, he combined a salty sense of humor with an apparent insensitivity to the pain which he inflicted upon others. All in all, he is one of the most fascinating figures in the history of American penology.

Like Samuel M. Hopkins, Lynds came to New York from Connecticut. Born in Litchfield in 1784, he moved to Troy as a youth and learned the hatter's trade. He found military affairs more to his liking, however, and became an active participant in the state militia. After the outbreak of war in 1812 he entered federal service and became an infantry captain. It is significant, in view of the rigid discipline imposed upon convicts under the Auburn system, that Lynds had a military background, and that

---

[10] Powers, *Letter, passim.*

[11] Julius, *Nordamerikas sittliche Zustände*, II, 142. I have attempted to verify this, but without success.

[12] Powers, *Letter*, p. 6.

[13] The parallel is drawn with reference to John William Ward, *Andrew Jackson, Symbol for an Age* (New York, 1955), pp. 153–165. Although Lynds is not mentioned in this work, I believe he typifies the "man of iron" theme that Ward develops.

Cray is reputed to have had one. The marching maneuvers performed by the inmates, and even the punishments inflicted upon them for breaches of prison rules, may well have been adapted in part from army practices.[14]

The end of the war created drab prospects for Lynds. He was unenthusiastic about re-entering the hat business, but seems to have had no alternative. Settling in Auburn, he resumed his trade but soon found a more congenial opportunity with the opening of the new penitentiary. Joining the staff sometime in 1817, he entered upon the area of his major life's work.[15]

Lynds became one of the most bitterly controversial prison administrators of his day, and it is difficult to avoid concluding that cruelty was part of his makeup. Nevertheless, he must be viewed against the background of his time and understood rather than castigated. He believed, like other exponents of the Auburn system, that it was necessary to break the spirit of the convict. To this fundamental tenet he added a personal twist; the head of a prison, he told Beaumont and Tocqueville, "must be thoroughly convinced, as I always have been, that a dishonest man is ever a coward. This conviction, which the prisoners will soon perceive, gives him an irresistible ascendancy, and will make a number of things easy, which, at first glance, may appear hazardous." [16] Ruling through fear and intimidation, he held that the least offense against prison discipline should be punished by flogging just as quickly as thunder succeeded lightning in a storm.[17] Doubting that an adult criminal could ever be reformed, he viewed the prison as a place of punishment and a terror to potential offenders.

---

[14] On other possible military influences upon the Auburn discipline, see Ralph S. Herre, "A History of Auburn Prison from the Beginning to About 1867" (unpublished D.Ed. dissertation, Pennsylvania State University, 1950), p. 108.

[15] On these and other biographical details, see *ibid.*, p. 44, and Thorsten Sellin, "Lynds, Elam," *Dictionary of American Biography*, XI, 527.

[16] Beaumont and Tocqueville, *On the Penitentiary System*, p. 203.

[17] John Luckey, *Life in Sing Sing Prison, as Seen in a Twelve Years' Chaplaincy* (New York, 1860), p. 111.

The ultimate aim of his tactics was to reduce the inmate to "a silent and insulated working machine." [18]

For those who objected that his methods were brutal or misguided, Lynds had nothing but withering scorn. When a subordinate officer in the Auburn stone shops remonstrated on one occasion that it was wrong to force convicts to work in freezing winter temperatures without drawers, the warden replied laconically that the inmates "would want ruffle shirts next." [19] When a chaplain, John Luckey, interceded for milder treatment on behalf of a prisoner whom he believed to be insane, Lynds turned on him with bitter sarcasm. "Your opinion of that hypocritical scoundrel's case reminds me of the decision of one of your benevolent dupes on a similar case in the Wethersfield prison," he declared. "This fool would insist upon it that a certain unruly convict was deranged. The Warden asked him how he had ascertained that said convict was insane; the old granny replied that he had opened the bosom of the convict's shirt and smelt of his breast, and thereby became convinced of the fact. Perhaps you have done the same." Mortified, Luckey never interceded again.[20]

This stern and unyielding figure became a legend within his own lifetime. Stories about him form part of the folklore of penology, and even when assessing contemporary testimony one must be wary of exaggeration. A minority member of an investigating committee stated, for example, that on a certain night some keepers had difficulty determining the identity of inmates who were making noises in their cells, and that Lynds had advised them to "take out fifteen, twenty or twenty-five and flog them all, and you will be sure to get the right one." This, as well as a similar charge, Lynds denied under oath.[21] One of the most famous tales involving the warden related to the plan of an inmate barber to murder him by cutting his throat. Learning of this, Lynds went

[18] DS, 69th Session (1846), Vol. IV, No. 20, p. 6.
[19] *Ibid.*, 63rd Session (1840), Vol. II, No. 48, p. 50.
[20] Luckey, *Life in Sing Sing Prison*, p. 181.
[21] DS, 63rd Session (1840), Vol. II, No. 38, p. 9, and No. 48, p. 35.

to the barber, seated himself in the chair, and demanded to be shaved. When the prisoner had complied with the order without carrying out the plot, Lynds is supposed to have told him, "I am stronger without a weapon than you are when armed." [22] The same story, however, was told about Amos Pilsbury, warden of the Wethersfield prison in Connecticut. Such tales probably shed more light upon popular stereotypes than upon the actual conduct of the wardens themselves. [23]

Although Lynds never lacked critics, he was for a time one of the most admired men in New York. Thomas Eddy disapproved of his mania for whipping, but otherwise admired him unreservedly. "He is a complete enthusiast in favour of the penitentiary system," Eddy told one English reformer, "and has those peculiar qualifications, that will enable him to carry it to a degree of perfection that it has never yet attained." [24] Edward Livingston believed that some of Lynds's methods were "liable to strong objections," but praised his firmness, courage, and knowledge of human nature. [25] Such astute observers as Beaumont and Tocqueville were "profoundly impressed" by Lynds, and asserted that his "practical abilities are admitted by everyone, including his enemies." [26] Persuasive both in preachment and in performance, he won complete

[22] See Harry Elmer Barnes and Negley K. Teeters, *New Horizons in Criminology* (1st ed.; New York, 1943), p. 522.

[23] Zebulon R. Brockway, *Fifty Years of Prison Service* (New York, 1912), pp. 35–36. One historian of American prisons discovered several variants of the Pilsbury story, as well as a Sing Sing version (Lewis, *Development of American Prisons,* pp. 177–178). These stories blend well with the "man of iron" theme described in Ward, *Andrew Jackson,* pp. 153–165. Such behavior in the barber chair has much the same spirit of courage and determination which caught the public fancy with regard to Jackson's famous duel with Charles Dickinson.

[24] Eddy to William Roscoe, Dec. 15, 1825, in Samuel L. Knapp, *The Life of Thomas Eddy* (New York, 1834), pp. 317–318.

[25] Edward Livingston, "Introductory Report to the Code of Reform and Prison Discipline," *The Complete Works of Edward Livingston* (New York, 1873), I, 520.

[26] George W. Pierson, *Tocqueville and Beaumont in America* (New York, 1938), p. 210; Alexis de Tocqueville, *Journey to America,* ed. J. P. Mayer (New Haven, Conn., 1960), p. 23.

acquiescence in his ideas from Allen, Tibbits, and Hopkins when the three legislators visited Auburn in 1824 on an official tour of inspection.[27] The prison's board of inspectors exhibited the same confidence by giving him unqualified power to direct discipline in whatever ways he should deem fit.[28]

Even with such plenary authority, running a penitentiary on the Auburn system was a difficult task requiring constant watchfulness and attention to small details. The collapse of the experiment with complete solitude in no way diminished the conviction that prisoners must be isolated from one another both to ensure order and to prevent moral contamination. Even though all inmates were now allowed to work together in a state of close physical proximity, their separation was to be as complete as if each were surrounded by an invisible wall.

In order to achieve this goal it was necessary to devise an unchanging routine that functioned with machinelike regularity. This could not be done if inmates were treated like individuals, or even if they were divided into different classifications; henceforth convicts were to be handled *en masse*. This attitude took hold as the Auburn system spread throughout the country, and by 1833 Beaumont and Tocqueville could remark that the "uselessness of classifications" was "well established in the United States." [29] Under such administrators as Lynds, all prisoners underwent exactly the same treatment with as little variation as was possible.

This was true regardless of an inmate's behavior record; no amount of exemplary deportment was to win him any special considerations or privileges. Nor was it to heighten his hopes for

---

[27] Lewis, *Development of American Prisons*, p. 95; Powers, *Letter*, pp. 4–5.
[28] JA, 48th Session (1825), p. 103.
[29] Beaumont and Tocqueville, *On the Penitentiary System*, p. 155, footnote. The idea that all convicts should be treated in exactly the same manner, which became almost an obsession with exponents of the Auburn system, may also have been related to the spirit of egalitarianism that was so broadly prevalent in the Jacksonian period and that Tocqueville analyzed so perceptively in his famous treatise, *Democracy in America*.

executive clemency. Pardons, declared the Auburn board of inspectors in 1824, made "a mockery of public justice." [30] It took time for this idea to win acceptance in actual practice, for until 1828 the number of pardons annually exceeded that of releases through expiration of sentence. From 1829 onward, however, the latter outnumbered the former by wide margins.[31] According to prison officials, an inmate's behavior was a poor index with regard to his real nature anyway, for in general "men of the most artful, desperate, and dangerous character, are the most orderly, submissive, and industrious, when confined." [32] Elam Lynds used this argument to convince Beaumont and Tocqueville that "one should never give a prisoner remission because of his good conduct in prison," and the French investigators echoed his sentiments in their work on American penitentiaries.[33]

Invariability of routine and treatment helped Auburn officials to establish a workable system, but it also made certain problems inevitable from the outset. If no convict was to be given special privileges or rewards, it was impossible to use deprivation of these as a disciplinary device or to stimulate inmate cooperation by means of positive incentives. Instead, administrators attempted to reduce their charges to a state of physical and psychological helplessness, adapting for this purpose some methods previously used at Newgate and adding various new techniques of their own invention.

From the moment a convict entered the prison at Auburn he was subjected to a process of calculated humiliation, in which every attempt was made to strip away whatever pride and self-respect he possessed. At Newgate, prisoners had been obliged to wear different types of uniforms, depending upon how many con-

---

[30] Quoted in Gershom Powers, *A Brief Account of ... The New-York State Prison at Auburn* (Auburn, 1826), p. 49.

[31] See tables of pardons and releases in Frédéric-Auguste DeMetz, *Rapport sur les Pénitenciers des États-Unis* (Paris, 1837), p. 53.

[32] JA, 45th Session (1822), p. 218.

[33] Tocqueville, *Journey to America*, pp. 27–28; Beaumont and Tocqueville, *On the Penitentiary System*, pp. 33–34.

victions appeared on their records.[34] Under the Auburn system, all inmates wore black-and-white striped outfits which made them look grotesque and ridiculous. Although the convicts were forbidden visitors of their own, citizens who paid a fee could come to the prison and look at them much as if they were animals in a zoo. The word of an inmate was never to be taken. A convict was to use the most polite terminology when speaking or referring to prison officers, but to refrain from any titles or expressions of respect when talking about his fellows. In short, he was to be taught that he was an outcast who could expect no sympathy from the society which he had injured and offended.[35]

Humiliation was accompanied by isolation. The inmate was not permitted to write or receive letters, and was to know nothing of events taking place in the outside world. His reading material was limited to a Bible and, in certain instances, a prayer book.[36] He was never to communicate in any way with his fellow convicts. Officers at Newgate had attempted to keep inmates from talking to one another when at work in the shops, but the total suppression of conversation was prevented by overcrowded conditions and group sleeping quarters.[37] To enforce isolation and silence at Auburn, administrators relied upon a machinelike routine and special techniques designed to facilitate close surveillance, coupled with the ever present threat of immediate punishment for infrac-

[34] [Thomas Eddy], *An Account of the State Prison or Penitentiary House, in the City of New-York* (New York, 1801), p. 39; Lewis, *Development of American Prisons,* p. 58. The use of striped clothing at Newgate apparently did not begin until 1815.

[35] The various features of the Auburn discipline are described at length in Powers, *Guide, passim.* For a provocative discussion of analogous techniques employed in penal and other types of institutions today, see Erving Goffman, "On the Characteristics of Total Institutions: The Inmate World," in *The Prison: Studies in Institutional Organization and Change,* ed. Donald R. Cressey (New York, 1961), pp. 23–48.

[36] Although this was justified on a number of other grounds, I believe the prohibition of other reading matter reflected to some degree the anti-intellectualism described in the preceding chapter.

[37] See "Remarks on present state of our Prisons by Thomas Eddy," Nov. 17, 1818, DeWitt Clinton Papers, Vol. XXIV, Columbia University Library.

tions. One of the most famous of the innovations at Auburn was the lockstep, probably devised by Cray. As convicts marched in single file, each placed his right hand on the shoulder of the man in front of him. Maintaining an erect posture at all times, the felons kept their faces constantly inclined in the direction of keepers who stood alongside the column and watched for the slightest movement of lips. Any use of facial muscles that could possibly constitute a signal was also prohibited. When not in marching formation, the inmates were required to keep their eyes on the ground. At night, when they were in their cells, keepers noiselessly patrolled the ranges in their stocking feet, ready to report for punishment the slightest breach of discipline.

Such punishment invariably took the form of lashing, which became perhaps the most controversial feature of the entire system. Although the law of 1819 which had legalized flogging contained safeguards designed to prevent abuse, chiefly in allowing stripes to be laid on only by principal keepers under the supervision of prison inspectors, these provisions were evaded under the new order. Imbued with the increasingly harsh spirit of the times, administrators and legislative investigators alike quickly became dissatisfied with legal restrictions, and advocated broadening the flogging power by allowing any keeper or turnkey to chastise a convict as he saw fit. A select committee recommended this to the legislature in 1821, and in the following year proponents of the change again asked for recognition of "the power incident by common law to every keeper, to correct his prisoner within reasonable bounds, for misbehavior." [38] When Allen, Hopkins, and Tibbits visited Newgate in 1825 they were sickened by kangaroo courts in which inmates and keepers appeared before the inspectors to argue their respective cases before punishment was determined. "The men upon whom the responsibility of the safe keeping of the convicts rests, ought to possess the power to punish them," the three commissioners declared.[39]

[38] JA, 44th Session (1820–1821), p. 904; JS, 45th Session (1822), p. 162.
[39] JA, 48th Session (1825), p. 105.

The episode in which an Auburn laborer was tarred and feathered for flogging a convict in 1821 (cf. p. 60) indicates that restrictions upon the whipping power were not being scrupulously obeyed by prison authorities at that time. With the development of the Auburn system, and particularly after Lynds gained *carte blanche* authority to handle disciplinary matters, keepers and turn-keys were given wide latitude in the flogging of felons. The dubious legality of this practice, and the fact that there were some critics of harsh methods despite the prevailing sentiment in favor of severity, made it certain that sooner or later an issue would be made on the matter.

This state of affairs was reached early in 1826 after the death of a female convict named Rachel Welch. An Irish immigrant who had been admitted to the prison about a year before, she had become pregnant during her confinement, probably by an inmate who brought her meals while an inattentive keeper stood at the foot of the stairs leading to her cell. She was also violent and refractory, and her continued insubordination eventually earned her a flogging at the hands of an assistant keeper named Ebenezer Cobb on July 27, 1825. Ironically, by this time Lynds had left Auburn to supervise the building of the penitentiary at Sing Sing, and his place had been taken by Richard Goodell, a man who actually wanted to reduce the incidence of whipping. Shortly after the lashing, Miss Welch became sick and threatened to miscarry, but she finally managed to go full term and had her child on the fifth of December. She experienced a turn for the worse shortly afterward, however, and died on January 12, 1826. Although two other practitioners disagreed, the physician who had attended her during pregnancy insisted that the flogging had contributed to her death.[40]

Whatever the merits of this claim, the lashing of Rachel Welch

[40] JA, 6oth Session (1827), Appendix A, *passim*. A local minister who wrote a curious tract in biblical style in 1838 claimed that the father of the child was Elam Lynds himself, but no evidence is given to support this. See Ezra the Scribe [pseud. for Rev. Silas E. Shepard], *The Chronicles of Auburn* (Auburn, 1838), pp. 3–4.

was in flagrant violation of the law of 1819, which had expressly forbidden the whipping of female convicts under any circumstances.[41] It did not take long for a public outcry to develop, and popular resentment only increased when the inspectors appointed a new agent, Gershom Powers, who was known to approve of the flogging of inmates.[42] A grand jury was impaneled to investigate reports of cruelty at the penitentiary, and this body found that turnkeys had been given summary authority to inflict corporal punishment immediately after an infraction and without the supervision of higher officials. The jury maintained that such whippings directly contravened the law, called them "serious evils," and declared:

The absolute power of punishment is a dangerous authority to repose in the discretion of every petty officer who may chance to be appointed. . . . The inevitable tendency of the system is to abuse, oppression and cruelty; and the report to the keeper, *after the infliction of the punishment, is a miserable guaranty against* barbarity in the infliction of it. . . .

The Grand Jury also apprehend that this absolute committal of the destiny of the prisoners to the will of a turnkey is calculated to have an evil effect on the mind and disposition of the convict. Unreasonable, rash and cruel punishments can only render prisoners mad and desperate, and tend to anything else but reformation.[43]

Such protests were futile. Although Ebenezer Cobb was convicted for assault and battery by a local court and fined $25, his superiors retained him in his job.[44] A state investigating commission composed of George Tibbits and Samuel M. Hopkins came to Auburn in July, 1826, to take stock of the situation and decided that the law of 1819 "did not abrogate and take away the right to use the rod as to male convicts, in all circumstances and in all cases which may arise, in which it may become necessary to

[41] *Laws of the State of New-York,* 42nd Session (1819), p. 87.
[42] Auburn *Cayuga Free Press,* Feb. 1, Feb. 8, and March 29, 1826.
[43] *Ibid.,* March 15, 1826. Italics are as given.
[44] *Ibid.,* Jan. 25, 1826; William Crawford, *Report . . . on the Penitentiaries of the United States* (n.p., 1834), p. 18, footnote.

use it in the state prison; and that to check transgressions promptly in their incipient steps, and thereby to prevent and stop their further progress, is the preferable mode, and the power to do it a necessary power to be entrusted to the assistant keepers." In the view of the commissioners, "Whenever the offence is fresh and flagrant, . . . when it is in the face of other prisoners; when it is in the nature of a continuing act, and when the example is of a kind to be either infectious or to impair the authority of the officers by delay, we take it that instant chastisement ought to follow." [45] At the prison, subordinate officers continued to lash the convicts as before.

Outraged citizens were not yet ready to submit. Within a short time they secured an indictment against a turnkey for the caning of an inmate. Once more they suffered disappointment. The judge who heard the case delivered a long charge to the jury epitomizing the harsh penal philosophy which had come into vogue within the preceding decade. The legislators of 1819, he declared, had no way of foreseeing situations which might confront a keeper in attempting to maintain order among convicts. Occasions would inevitably arise in which prompt punishment was indispensable upon the spot. This was a "common law right," regardless of the act of 1819; "wretched and inefficient indeed, would be the system of government in such a prison, which would require the keepers, whenever their authority was resisted, to go into the village and call two of the Inspectors, before obedience to their lawful commands could be enforced." It was even proper, the judge asserted, for turnkeys to whip convicts and then bring them to trial before the inspectors, after which the inmates might receive more stripes for

[45] JA, 50th Session (1827), Appendix A, pp. 9–10. A reading of this document demonstrates the erroneousness of the statement sometimes made that Lynds was dismissed as keeper at Auburn because of the Welch episode (see, for example, Elliot G. Storke and James H. Smith, *History of Cayuga County, New York* [Syracuse, 1879], p. 155, and Herre, "History of Auburn Prison," p. 93). As we have seen, Lynds was not even in charge at Auburn when the lashing occurred, and was at that time supervising the construction of the new penitentiary at Sing Sing.

the same offenses. Felons, after all, were not ordinary men, but desperadoes who "should most deeply feel the awful degradation and misery, to which their vicious courses had reduced them." They must be made to realize "that the ordinary sympathies of our nature could not be extended to them, consistently with the welfare of society, and that they must not be indulged."[46]

The law of 1819 thus failed to prevent the whipping—or even the caning and clubbing—of convicts by any prison official who felt this to be necessary. Scattered protests arose from time to time, but the "common law right" to flog was not again seriously challenged for over a decade. Some penitentiary administrators, such as Gershom Powers, set up certain rules and regulations to govern the lashing of inmates, but wardens could not be omnipresent even if they wanted to keep the practice within bounds. A French investigator, Frédéric-Auguste DeMetz, was generally correct in asserting that the amount of chastisement which a turnkey could inflict was virtually unlimited.[47]

Defenders of flogging used a number of arguments in its favor. It was quick; it took only a small amount of the convict's time away from his labor; it could allegedly be more easily proportioned to the relative seriousness of offenses than could such punishments as solitary confinement.[48] Whipping was commonly used in the armed forces, which not only helps to explain its defensibility to such veterans as Lynds but also suggests why citizens who knew that floggings were administered to soldiers and sailors did not think it wrong to have them given to convicts.[49] The use of corporal punishment in schools was also cited to justify this type of treatment in penitentiaries.[50]

[46] Quoted in Powers, *Brief Account*, pp. 66–69.

[47] DeMetz, *Rapport sur les Pénitenciers des États-Unis*, p. 14.

[48] Prison Discipline Society, *First Report* (1826), pp. 17–18.

[49] See especially Mathew Carey, *Thoughts on Penitenciaries and Prison Discipline* (Philadelphia, 1831), p. 68. Carey was a vigorous exponent of the Auburn system in Pennsylvania, but failed to secure its adoption there.

[50] Powers, *Brief Account*, p. 61; Prison Discipline Society, *Eighth Report* (1833), p. 28; JA, 50th Session (1827), Appendix A, p. 5.

Taking into account the social tensions which prevailed when the Auburn system came into being, the widespread disillusionment with previous penal experiments, the premises upon which such administrators as Lynds and Powers operated, and the sheer difficulty of enforcing the silent system, it is not difficult to understand why lashing became a common occurrence in the prisons of New York. The susceptibility of this type of punishment to abuse, however, and the anomaly of permitting frequent floggings in prisons after rejecting the sanguinary methods of colonial days drew the fire of noted critics both at home and abroad.[51] Although accounts of whippings were sometimes exaggerated, especially by political enemies of penitentiary officials, it was all too clear that these punishments sometimes got out of hand and that they gave sadistic keepers abundant opportunities for psychological gratification.[52] The effects of a lashing could be devastating if the whip were skillfully applied. "An inexperienced keeper of but ordinary muscular power, when using the Sing Sing cat," stated a warden on one occasion, "would scarcely heighten the color of the skin by a dozen blows, while a vigorous practical keeper, by adopting a peculiar swing in raising the cat and a drawing motion in striking, can cut the skin at nearly every blow." [53]

Perhaps the most unfortunate aspect of flogging was its use in the handling of inmates who were suspected of feigning insanity in an attempt to shirk their duties. Popular theories of mental alienation, as Dorothea Dix later discovered, were very crude, and deranged convicts were sometimes subjected to appalling mistreatment. In general, as an investigator stated in 1840, penitentiary officers tended "to consider every manifestation of insanity as an attempt at deception, and punish it accordingly. This rule was not departed from in cases where the manifestations of insanity were

---

[51] See for example Livingston, "Introductory Report," pp. 518–519; Charles Lucas, *Du Système Pénitentiaire en Europe et aux États-Unis* (Paris, 1828–1830), I, 21.

[52] See especially DA, 70th Session (1847), Vol. VIII, No. 255, Part 2, p. 37.

[53] *Ibid.*, 69th Session (1846), Vol. IV, No. 138, p. 2.

so clear, that it would seem impossible to have mistaken, or over-looked them." [54] A prison physician once asserted that any staff member who even hinted that a convict might be deranged was met with "jeers and ridicule." [55]

The lash was used not only to subdue convicts but also to drive them to unsparing efforts in the prison shops. For a short time during the unsettled period following the War of 1812 some reformers advocated dispensing entirely with convict labor, and this was actually done with the inmates who endured the experiment with complete solitude. Some leaders condemned the attention which had previously been paid to industrial revenue, and contended that a contrary attitude might actually be economical in its results. In 1822, Samuel M. Hopkins advocated "the abandonment of labour as an engine of punishment," arguing that the state could thereby eliminate "a vast and expensive list of shops, implements, inventories of stock and bad debts, with the expenses of a guard." [56]

After the trial of strict solitary confinement collapsed, however, such opinions were rapidly changed. By 1825, it was the stipulated duty of prison agents "to cause all the expenses . . . of any kind, to be supported wholly, or as nearly as shall be practicable, by the labor of the prisoners." [57] Advocates of the Auburn system commonly believed that penitentiaries should not only bear the cost of their own food, clothing, medical expenses, and staff salaries, but also pay for the charges incurred in trying and convicting inmates and in transporting the felons from the point of sentence to

---

[54] DS, 63rd Session (1840), Vol. II, No. 38, pp. 9–10.

[55] DA, 75th Session (1852), Vol. I, No. 20, pp. 82–83. For a particularly flagrant case of mistreatment involving an insane convict named Patrick Mastison, see JA, 50th Session (1827), Appendix A, pp. 13–14 and Crawford, *Report*, p. 17, footnote. For other accounts of floggings and cruelty in the treatment of deranged inmates, see JA, 50th Session (1827), p. 80; DA, 58th Session (1835), Vol. II, No. 135, Part 2, p. 31; 70th Session (1847), Vol. VIII, No. 255, Part 2, pp. 14, 57–58; 75th Session (1852), Vol. I, No. 20, p. 76; and DS, 63rd Session (1840), Vol. II, No. 48, p. 68.

[56] Society for the Prevention of Pauperism, *Report on the Penitentiary System*, pp. 43–45, 75, and Appendix, p. 100.

[57] JA, 48th Session (1825), Appendix C, p. 30.

prison. Any profits remaining after these demands had been met could be used to maintain institutions for juvenile delinquents.[58] Under the implementation of such a philosophy the convict's life was one of hard, unrelenting toil.

In the busy shops of such prisons as Auburn and Sing Sing there were conflicting motives at work. Some administrators believed that steady labor made better men of the inmates and helped to fit them for employment after they had been released. Other officials merely concentrated on profits without any regard for human values. In either case, the policy of self-support was bound to please the taxpayer and harmonized well with the desire for frugal government that was very prevalent during the Jacksonian era.

Aside from the hypothetical acquisition of better habits and usable skills, the inmates gained nothing from their toil but the barest possible living accommodations. Just as exponents of the Auburn system did away with various positive incentives to induce convicts to conform to the new discipline of silence, so did they also dispense with financial means which had previously been used to stimulate inmate productivity. The new school of penal reformers frowned upon profit-sharing or payments for extra work on the grounds that such devices involved extra bookkeeping and might give convicts the means to purchase unnecessary indulgences. The sections of the prison law of 1817 which provided for monetary inducements and time off for good behavior died upon the statute books.[59]

Because of the emphasis upon squeezing the last possible cent of profit out of prisons and the unwillingness of administrators to

---

[58] See especially Prison Discipline Society, *Ninth Report* (1834), p. 55, and Anonymous, "Prison Discipline," *North American Review*, XLIX (July, 1839), 27–28. "It is surprising," commented the author of the latter article, "how little it costs to do good, if we really set ourselves to work in the right way."

[59] See especially Prison Discipline Society, *First Report* (1826), pp. 30–32. In their work *Punishment and Social Structure* (New York, 1939), p. 131, Georg Rusche and Otto Kirchheimer state that the law of 1817 was utilized at Auburn and that "prisoners were stimulated to work by the expectation of privileges and rewards, rather than through discipline. . . . The hope of commutation

make any distinctions between inmates regardless of past records or future prospects for amendment, little money was allocated for educational expenditures and the chances for effective rehabilitation were jeopardized from the outset. This was especially true under the leadership of a man like Lynds, who not only opposed such ventures as Cray's school for convicts but also objected to the appointment of a resident chaplain at Auburn. Without denying that an inmate might learn certain lessons of abtemiousness and industry under a severe regime, and become a law-abiding citizen after his release out of sheer terror at the prospect of being returned to prison, such leaders were extremely skeptical about the possibility of a radical change in a criminal's personality or attitude toward life.

The Lyndsian point of view in this regard was succinctly stated in a report written in 1834 by an officer at Sing Sing, probably Robert Wiltse. "Having been in habits of association with the most infamous and degraded of their species," stated this document, "they [convicts] can *feel* nothing but that which comes home to their bodily suffering. . . . The hope once entertained of producing a general and radical reformation of offenders through a penitentiary system, is abandoned by the most intelligent philanthropists, who now think its chief benefit is in the prevention of crime." [60] Stephen Allen, using capital letters to emphasize his beliefs, wrote that the reformation of a confirmed villain, however desirable, was "A FORLORN HOPE." "How can a man labour hard, and at the same time be taught lessons of morality and religion?" he expostulated. "It is not to be expected, because it is unreasonable." [61] Educational efforts were wasted on convicts; as Lynds told Alexis de Tocqueville, prisons were "full of boorish men" who

---

tended to reinforce discipline while serving as a substitute for money wages." This was certainly not true under the Auburn system. For correct evaluations, see McKelvey, *American Prisons*, p. 43, and Charles R. Henderson, ed., *Correction and Prevention: Prison Reform and Criminal Law* (New York, 1910), pp. 13–14.

[60] DS, 57th Session (1834), Vol. II, No. 92, pp. 38, 41. Italics are as given.

[61] Allen, *Observations on Penitentiary Discipline*, pp. 7, 33.

had "great difficulty grasping any idea or even any intellectual sensations." [62] In view of the widespread existence of this outlook, it was not strange that when the Prison Discipline Society sent Jared Curtis to Auburn to act as chaplain the state failed for years to contribute a single penny to his salary, which was borne by the Society alone.[63]

The doctrine of severity received perhaps its most thoroughgoing exposition in a report made to the state legislature in 1825 by Allen, Tibbits, and Hopkins. Breathing the spirit of Elam Lynds, this document dramatically revealed the difference between prevailing attitudes toward convicts and those which had been held by post-Revolutionary humanitarians. In a society which supported no other institution for the reformation of morals at public expense and which contained many virtuous but poor citizens, the three commissioners stated, the criminal must not expect kind treatment and special rehabilitative care. Thomas Eddy's generation had been mistaken in viewing felons as victims of adversity when in cold fact they were "desperately wicked." In that misguided period "there seems to have existed, in this and other countries, an almost universal sentiment of partial regard to criminals of all sorts, and to sturdy beggars; and generally in favor of all who get their living by inflicting distresses, and imposing burdens, in breach of the laws, upon the best of mankind." Far from meriting special treatment, such desperadoes deserved to be subjected to hard labor at the hands of a parsimonious state, and the commissioners filled their report with suggestions about how expenses could be trimmed by forcing convicts to wear wooden shoes, to sleep on mats made from the husks of Indian corn, and to eat food

[62] Tocqueville, *Journey to America*, p. 28.

[63] Prison Discipline Society, *Second Report* (1827), pp. 6, 11, 44–45, 72; JA, 51st Session (1828), Appendix A, p. 27. In 1842, the Society informed the New York legislature that it had paid $5,476.53 in chaplains' salaries in the Empire State between 1825 and 1835, and solicited reimbursement, but I have found no evidence that this request was ever granted (see DS, 65th Session [1842], Vol. II, No. 50, pp. 1–5). Curtis was probably the first full-time resident prison chaplain in America.

which would cost no more than three cents per ration. Paying periodic lip service to the idea that penal treatment should be reformative as well as preventive, and asserting that vengeance was not a proper object of justice, these officials nevertheless made it clear that they wanted intimidation far more than rehabilitation.[64]

Such ideas had important and vociferous critics, both at home and abroad. The English reformer William Roscoe was so alarmed by the harshness of the foregoing report that he appealed to Lafayette, then on a triumphal tour of America, to use his influence against the philosophy it represented. He also complained about the new outlook in his correspondence with Thomas Eddy, and prepared a tract on prison discipline for general distribution in the United States, inaugurating a spirited trans-Atlantic controversy with various upholders of coercive doctrine, especially Stephen Allen.[65] In New York City, the inspectors of Newgate prison were loud in disapproving the new tendencies in penal reform. "The criminal is destroyed, when his ignorance of good is sealed with cruelty, and the barrier to reformation is hedged in with whips and scorpions," they argued. "No man will act from an impulse received from counsel given by an enemy. The hand of friendship only can be extended to guide, and this only, will be received by the misguided wanderer." Unequivocally rejecting a basic tenet of the Auburn system, the Newgate officials maintained that "it is certainly more for the interest of society to reform a criminal than to subject him to punishment for the mere purpose of deterring others from the perpetration of offences."[66]

Thomas Eddy, who admired many aspects of the new order, was

[64] JA, 48th Session (1825), pp. 103–104, 108, 114, 117–118.

[65] Henry Roscoe, *The Life of William Roscoe, by his Son* (Boston, 1833), II, 175–179; William Roscoe to Eddy, March 31, 1825, and Thomas S. Traile, "Memoir of William Roscoe, Esq.," in Knapp, *Life of Thomas Eddy*, pp. 314, 366; Hopkins, *Sketch of the Public and Private Life of Samuel Miles Hopkins*, pp. 39–40; Allen, *Observations on Penitentiary Discipline, passim*. Roscoe's tract was entitled, *Remarks on the Report of the Commissioners Appointed by the Legislature of New York* (Liverpool, 1825).

[66] JA, 47th Session (1824), pp. 254–255, and 48th Session (1825), pp. 254–255.

far from sharing all the theories of such men as Allen, Tibbits, and Hopkins. "Those who assert . . . that to attempt to reform convicts, by exercising kind and conciliatory means, is chimerical and absurd," he remonstrated to the three commissioners, "certainly do not reflect, that to advise and admonish the most profligate and abandoned, is the usual practice of life, and is solemnly enjoined by the precepts of the Founder of our holy religion." Hopkins, Eddy informed Roscoe, was slowly becoming more enlightened as a prison reformer, but in the meantime he held "some very incorrect notions respecting the penitentiary system." Eventually, the Quaker predicted, whipping and severity would give way to more humane methods. "The public feeling, and the principles of common sense, will prevail, and do away the deep rooted prejudices of our public legislation—the work is slow but sure." [67]

Opposition to the Auburn system also arose in Pennsylvania, which faced a penal crisis of its own in the 1820's. As it became clear that the Allegheny prison near Pittsburgh was not well designed for the experiment in solitary confinement which was being carried on there, such influential leaders as Mathew Carey, Charles Shaler, Edward King, and Thomas J. Wharton launched a vigorous effort to secure the adoption of the methods which had been developed in New York. This group was defeated, however, through the exertions of such reformers as Roberts Vaux and John Sergeant, and Pennsylvania retained a system of strict solitary confinement, though with labor permitted as an alleviating and rehabilitative device. Put into operation in the Eastern State Penitentiary at Cherry Hill in Philadelphia, this plan became the chief alternative to the one used in the Empire State. [68]

Despite opposition from various reformers and failure to win favor in Pennsylvania, however, the Auburn system enlisted the

[67] Eddy to Tibbits, Allen, and Hopkins, Jan. 7, 1825, and to Roscoe, Dec. 15, 1825, in Knapp, *Life of Thomas Eddy*, pp. 91, 320.

[68] Eugene E. Doll, "Trial and Error at Allegheny: The Western State Penitentiary, 1818–1838," *Pennsylvania Magazine of History and Biography*, LXXXI (January, 1957), 8–15; Negley K. Teeters and John D. Shearer, *The Prison at Philadelphia: Cherry Hill* (New York, 1957), pp. 20–30.

support of able propagandists who won many more battles than they lost in spreading their ideas. One of the foremost of these was Gershom Powers. By studying law in his spare time, this young schoolmaster from New Hampshire secured admission to the Cayuga County bar and ultimately became the first judge of Auburn's Court of Common Pleas. The establishment of the prison stimulated his interest in penitentiary discipline, and he soon became a member of the board of inspectors.[69]

Unlike such men as Allen and Lynds, Powers was not an advocate of sheer coercion. This is especially significant because it was his interpretation of the Auburn system, as expressed in two widely circulated pamphlets, which acquainted many influential citizens throughout the United States with the workings and early history of this plan of discipline.[70] Like Louis Dwight, who as secretary of the Prison Discipline Society was by all odds the most effective propagandist for the Auburn system, Powers was an intensely religious individual who believed that after being thoroughly subdued an inmate could be reformed through spiritual and educational influences. Such an attitude was far more likely to win widespread support in a nation caught up in an era of evangelistic and revivalistic fervor than the utter harshness of the Lyndsian school of thought.

Powers' efforts to spread the Auburn system were limited largely to writing about it, especially since his time was taken up in actual prison administration and, later, in political activities. His essential moderation with regard to disciplinary matters was clearly revealed after he succeeded Richard Goodell as agent of the penitentiary at the peak of the Rachel Welch controversy. Although he approved of flogging, he attempted closely to regulate the use of the whip. He strictly prohibited the hitting of convicts with sticks,

[69] 81st Congress, 2nd Session, House Document No. 607, *Biographical Directory of the American Congress, 1774–1949* (Washington, 1950), p. 1699.
[70] These are the *Brief Account of ... the New-York State Prison at Auburn* (1826) and the *Letter ... in Answer to a Letter of the Hon. Edward Livingston* (1829), previously cited in this chapter.

canes, and fists, and stipulated that the head, face, eyes, and limbs of an inmate must not be endangered when the "cat" was administered.[71] He also permitted the opening of a school for illiterate and semiliterate prisoners, thereby vindicating the departed Cray.[72] His desire to have a chaplain in residence at the penitentiary was fulfilled when the Prison Discipline Society provided the services of Jared Curtis. "Though convicts," Powers stated in one of his pamphlets, "they are still accountable and immortal beings; and, deprived as they are, at such trying seasons, of the sympathies and kind offices of their parents, their wives, and their children, they need, in a peculiar manner, some benevolent and pious friend, to instruct and console them. Should they die, the reflection remains, that all was done that humanity and Christian charity demanded." [73] Stubbornly refusing to believe that many criminals could not be changed for the better, he kept in touch with local sheriffs and other officials to see how ex-inmates were doing after they had been released from Auburn. He also tried to find out how his charges had become involved in crime and to assess the effects of their imprisonment upon them, using preliminary interrogations before they began their sentences and parting interviews after they had served their time.[74]

Powers' career as a prison administrator and propagandist was comparatively short. His election to the national House of Representatives as a Jacksonian Democrat in 1828 temporarily removed him from the Cayuga County scene, and his return to Auburn as an inspector of the penitentiary in 1830 was followed by his death a year later.[75] Although his activities in helping to spread the Auburn system were of great importance, they were eclipsed by the efforts of Louis Dwight, the energetic leader of the Prison Discipline Society.

[71] Powers, *Brief Account*, pp. 60–61.
[72] Prison Discipline Society, *Second Report* (1827), pp. 44–46.
[73] Powers, *Brief Account*, pp. 18–19.
[74] JA, 50th Session (1827), pp. 79–104, and 51st Session (1828), pp. 55–85.
[75] *Biographical Directory of the American Congress*, p. 1699.

A New Englander of fervent religious convictions who had been nurtured in Hopkinsian theology, Dwight had originally aspired to be a preacher of the gospel. This ambition was thwarted by a lung injury which he incurred as a result of inhaling gases in a chemistry laboratory at Yale, and the young zealot spent several years in a nearly frantic effort to find a mission in life. He eventually became an agent of the American Bible Society and was assigned the task of distributing the Scriptures to convicts. Traveling southward and placing Bibles in prisons as far away as the Carolinas, Dwight found the mission he had so ardently desired, the reformation of penal conditions. Upon his return to Boston in 1825, he organized the Prison Discipline Society with the aid of a group of philanthropists and spent the rest of his life in a career so reminiscent of the activities of John Howard that it might well have been consciously or subconsciously modeled upon them. Visiting one jail or prison after another, driving himself mercilessly, accepting no social invitations, and enduring the most wretched conditions of travel, he became a crusader for proper penal conditions, which to him meant the Auburn system. Although he was supported in his work by a large societal membership drawn from various states, he virtually dictated the affairs of his organization. Samuel Gridley Howe, who became a bitter critic of Dwight's ideas and methods, declared him to be "*de facto* the Society. He acts for it, speaks for it, and directs its whole policy." [76]

For Auburn prison, Dwight had only unstinted praise. "It is not possible to describe the pleasure which we feel in contemplating this noble institution," he stated in the first annual report of his society, "after wading through the fraud, and material and moral filth of many Prisons. We regard it as a model worthy of the world's imitation." [77] Although he did not overtly take sides with regard to differences of opinion between the individual leaders who set up

[76] William Jenks, *A Memoir of the Rev. Louis Dwight* (Boston, 1856), *passim;* Samuel Gridley Howe, *An Essay on Separate and Congregate Systems of Prison Discipline* (Boston, 1846), p. 7.

[77] Prison Discipline Society, *First Report* (1826), p. 36.

and administered the system, his philosophy was clearly akin to
that of Gershom Powers. Convicts, he declared in 1833, "are creatures of the same glorious Creator with ourselves. . . . They have
souls like our own, in their nature mysterious, in their existence
immortal. . . . And they are objects of regard to the Son of God,
the Lord Jesus Christ. . . . They are capable of love; but generally, when committed to Prison, they are filled with malice.
. . . The very aggravation of their guilt is the loud call for your
pity and prayers, and efforts. And their case is not hopeless." [78]

Dwight's vision of what the Auburn system could accomplish
was not limited to the area of correctional matters. An ardent temperance advocate and Sabbatarian, he not only wanted to eliminate
all levity and vice from prisons but to use penal institutions as
object lessons for the rest of society. Sometimes he did this in a
negative way, as a warning to free citizens; in one report, for example, he reminded Sabbath-breakers that many convicts had
started on the path to the penitentiary by failing to observe the
Lord's Day. [79] At other times, however, he upheld the Auburn-
style prison as a veritable model for free institutions; indeed, it is
not too much to say that he wanted to convert individual American homes into miniature penal establishments. Believing that
such penitentiaries as the one at Auburn were "great observatories,
on great principles, touching the government, conduct, and reformation of men," he held that the principle of solitary quartering
at night "would be useful, in all establishments, where large numbers of youth of both sexes are assembled and exposed to youthful
lusts; and . . . it would greatly promote order, seriousness, and
purity in large families, male and female boarding schools, and
colleges." He recommended a plan for a Massachusetts school in
which individual night rooms would be so placed in galleries as
to be subject to close surveillance from a central location. In his
view, the "unceasing vigilance" which characterized the Auburn
system afforded "a principle of very extensive application to fam-

[78] Prison Discipline Society, *Eighth Report* (1833), pp. 35–38.
[79] *Ibid.,* p. 28.

ilies, schools, academies, colleges, factories, mechanics' shops." [80]

To spread the Auburn system and to combat the rival regime of utter solitude as practiced at Cherry Hill in Philadelphia became a consuming mission for Dwight. In his crusade for the New York method he was able to make effective use of one overpowering argument which constituted his principal trump card. "When a new prison is to be established," Samuel Gridley Howe once pointed out, "the edifice and the system of discipline are to be discussed and selected by a body of men who, however unfitted they may be for understanding any other merit of a system, can all appreciate that of economy." [81] It was possible to build an institution patterned on Auburn prison at a cost averaging $91 per cell; by contrast, the larger apartments which Pennsylvania reformers found necessary for inmates who were to be kept alone at all times cost about $1,650 per unit. Few legislators could resist the logic of such figures, especially when they realized that the congregate labor possible under the Auburn system had a much higher potential for profit than the individual craft methods that had to be used at Cherry Hill.[82] The techniques practiced in the Auburn shops were somewhat similar to those used in many factories; the methods employed at Philadelphia smacked of the past, of an industrial era that was dying. In addition, the penitentiary at Auburn had a head start on its Pennsylvania rival, which did not received its first inmate until October 25, 1829.[83]

With such advantages working in his favor, Dwight could point with satisfaction by 1833 to the establishment of Auburn-style prisons in Maine, New Hampshire, Vermont, Massachusetts, Connecticut, New York, the District of Columbia, Virginia, Tennessee,

[80] Prison Discipline Society, *Fourth Report* (1829), pp. 56–57, 61–63.

[81] Howe, *Essay on Separate and Congregate Systems,* p. 80.

[82] See estimates given in Carey, *Thoughts on Penitentiaries,* p. 37, and in Beaumont and Tocqueville, *On the Penitentiary System,* pp. 74, 277. For an example of the potency of these cost considerations, see E. Bruce Thompson, "Reforms in the Penal System of Tennessee," *Tennessee Historical Quarterly,* I (December, 1942), 300–301.

[83] Teeters and Shearer, *The Prison at Philadelphia,* pp. 83–84.

Louisiana, Missouri, Illinois, Ohio, and Upper Canada.[84] At this time only Pennsylvania, New Jersey, and Maryland were using the method of complete solitude.[85] Proud of the fame which their techniques had gained, officials at Auburn congratulated themselves in 1835 on having "the best system of prison discipline in the world." [86]

Disappointed in previous penal experiments, New Yorkers could now believe that they had found the solution which had previously eluded them. The fact that the new system worked much more satisfactorily than its predecessors and was gaining widespread acceptance outside the state augured well for its continued success. In the long run, however, a favorable outcome depended upon the answers to certain key questions. Would prison officers be able indefinitely to maintain the efficiency and vigilance which the proper functioning of the new system demanded? Would public opinion continue to support an experiment based in large measure upon a harsh attitude toward the offender? What would be the results of the Auburn system upon the inmates themselves, under either the Lyndsian program of sheer coercion or the somewhat milder and more positive approach favored by such men as Powers and Dwight? Time alone would provide the answers to these questions, as masters and convicts put them to the test of actual experience in the prisons of the Empire State.

[84] Prison Discipline Society, *Eighth Report* (1833), p. 6.
[85] See Teeters and Shearer, *The Prison at Philadelphia,* p. 201. Rhode Island finally adopted the Pennsylvania system in 1838, but gave it up in 1844. Maryland renounced the solitary method in 1838, and New Jersey abandoned it in 1858.
[86] DS, 58th Session (1835), Vol. I, No. 13, p. 3.

# Chapter V

# Portrait of an Institution

LIKE many other prisons before and since, the penitentiary at Auburn was surrounded by a high stone wall. Once he had been admitted beyond this, the visitor was confronted by a three-story administration building flanked on both sides by wings in which the cells were located. A somewhat bizarre effect was given to the central edifice by what an English traveler once called "an absurd nondescript set of pinnacles placed on top of the building, in the midst of which is a representation of a sentinel with a musket." The latter was a statue of a soldier which had been put in place in 1821. Made of wood and subject to the ravages of weather and worms, it was finally replaced in 1848 by a replica made of sheet copper and dubbed "Copper John" by inmates who longed to see the old veteran face to face, an act which could be done only from outside the wall. "Whether he is meant as a scare-crow to the prisoners or not," stated the Englishman, "I cannot tell; but I am sure that he and the litter of pinnacles around him are a grievous annoyance to the eye." [1] A puzzled French architect remarked that the style of the administration building was hard to define, but that the decorations on the roof reminded one of a mosque.[2]

[1] Anonymous, "Auburn Prison," Part I, *Correction*, XIV (May, 1949), 9–10; Charles A. Murray, *Travels in North America during the Years 1834, 1835, and 1836* (London, 1839), I, 78.

[2] Guillaume Blouet, *Rapport . . . sur les Pénitenciers des Etats-Unis* (Paris, 1837), p. 9.

An incoming convict was apt to be too apprehensive to speculate about such questions of style or taste. As a precaution against violence or escape, he was usually encumbered with manacles and irons. He had probably been confined before and after trial in a filthy county jail, where he had quite likely contracted one or another disease and become infested with vermin. He might also be drunk when he arrived at Auburn, for some sheriffs allowed felons to consume alcoholic beverages on their way to the penitentiary.[3]

The average inmate received at Auburn was fairly young. The Erie Canal, which passed within ten miles of the institution, provided work for up to five thousand youths every year, many of whom were orphans. When winter came and the artery was frozen over, swarms of homeless young vagabonds were thrown upon society in counties along its route. Quickly exhausting whatever funds they might have saved, suffering from exposure, and subject to various temptations and immoral influences, they turned to crime in order to exist, and frequently found themselves in prison before spring arrived. Such "canal boys" usually formed a large segment of Auburn's inmate body.[4]

The chances were good that the new arrival at the penitentiary had received a substandard education and had committed his crime under the influence of alcohol. In better than one case out of two, he had been convicted of some form of theft, usually grand larceny. Unlike his twentieth-century counterpart, he was rarely serving time for a sexual offense. In some cases he was a federal prisoner, for the national government had no penitentiaries of its own for civilians and farmed out persons convicted in its courts to state penal institutions. In about one of eleven cases the new convict was a Negro, and the chances were approximately one in six that

[3] See DS, 55th Session (1832), Vol. II, No. 18, pp. 1–2; 73rd Session (1850), Vol. I, No. 16, p. 151; and 81st Session (1858), Vol. I, No. 4, p. 22; Gershom Powers, *A Brief Account of . . . the New-York State Prison at Auburn* (Auburn, 1826), p. 5, footnote; DA, 56th Session (1833), Vol. III, No. 199, p. 29.

[4] DA, 69th Session (1846), Vol. IV, No. 93, p. 2; *Northern Christian Advocate* (Auburn), Jan. 21, 1846.

he had been born abroad. Although ante-bellum statistics on recidivism are apt to be inaccurate, he was probably beginning his first sentence. According to an analysis taken by the prison chaplain in 1836, only one convict in seventeen had been at Auburn before, although this survey probably missed inmates who had previously served time at Sing Sing or in out-of-state prisons.[5]

As soon as a new convict entered the penitentiary he was subjected to a thorough cleansing, and his hair was cropped short. This was likely to be a rough process. An inmate who went through the ordeal at Sing Sing was particularly bitter about the haircut, asserting that "the barber pleases his keeper best, when he makes the subject appear the worst; consequently, his head is often so much disfigured by clips and gashes in his hair, that he would hardly be known by an acquaintance."[6] When the preliminary ablutions were over, the convict received his ring-striped uniform. This was sometimes new, but was more often worn, patched, ill-fitting, and still smelling of the body odors of its previous possessor.[7] These circumstances, plus the possibility of infection if the last wearer had been afflicted with a transmittable skin disease, probably concerned the felon less than the psychological consequences of his grotesque and humiliating garb. Critics of the Auburn system protested against this corrosion of human dignity. "The old convict or the shameless wretch may don his prison dress, and march out with defiant exultation," wrote Samuel Gridley Howe, "but to a sensitive novice in crime, that dress must be the

---

[5] See particularly the statistical analysis of the first 3,000 inmates at Auburn and other figures given in DA, 60th Session (1837), Vol. I, No. 31, on and facing p. 20. According to Gustave de Beaumont and Alexis de Tocqueville (*On the Penitentiary System in the United States,* trans. Francis Lieber [Philadelphia, 1833], p. 244), less than three inmates out of 100 had been convicted for moral offenses in New York during the period from 1800 to 1830. An analysis of convictions in New York courts of record from 1830 to 1842 shows less than 400 delinquencies of a moral nature in a total list of almost 15,000 (DA, 66th Session [1843], Vol. V, No. 110, pp. 90–95). On federal prisoners see *Northern Christian Advocate,* May 31, 1848, and July 12, 1854.

[6] Levi S. Burr, *A Voice from Sing Sing* (Albany, 1833), p. 19.

[7] *Northern Christian Advocate,* Feb. 11, 1846.

poisoned shirt of Nessus, which he can never strip off until his pride and all his self-respect have been torn away by it." [8]

The clothing which the prisoner had worn upon arrival, along with any money or valuables which he might have brought with him, were taken for "safekeeping" by penitentiary officials. This was possibly the last time he would ever see them, for inmate belongings had a way of "disappearing" while their owners were confined. "Not only is his clothing treated as a forfeiture to the State as well as his liberty," a group of penal reformers once wrote of the convict, "but even mementoes of affection . . . are sometimes cast aside or destroyed with a want of feeling not particularly commendable in the administration of justice." [9]

Clad in his striped uniform, the criminal was next led before the clerk, who took down a description of his appearance and age, made notes on any other data deemed pertinent, and entered his name upon the prison register. The convict then went before the warden, who had been questioning the sheriff about the personal characteristics of the new inmate and may have received a lurid and boastful description of how hard this dangerous outlaw had been to subdue.[10] There followed a stern lecture in which the prisoner was given a preview of his future life and exhorted to strict obedience. If Gershom Powers happened to be warden at the time, the speech went approximately as follows:

You exhibit a sad picture of human degradation. From "bad example, idleness, or the indulgence of evil passions," you have been led to the commission of crime, by which you have violated the laws of your country, forfeited your liberty, and offended your God. The consequence is, that instead of now enjoying the inestimable privileges of a free American citizen, of social intercourse, and the endearments of home and friends, you appear in culprit robes, doomed to the gloomy

[8] Samuel Gridley Howe, *An Essay on Separate and Congregate Systems of Prison Discipline* (Boston, 1846), p. 43.

[9] New York Prison Association, *Seventh Report* (1852), p. 34.

[10] Gershom Powers, *A Letter . . . in Answer to a Letter of the Hon. Edward Livingston* (Albany, 1829), pp. 12–13; John Luckey, *Life in Sing Sing State Prison, as Seen in a Twelve Years' Chaplaincy* (New York, 1860), pp. 154, 197.

solitude of a prison, where the smiles of kindred and friends can never cheer your gloomy abode.

Weep not for yourself only; but remember the sighs of a father, the tears of a mother, the anguish of a wife and children, suffering and disgraced by your crimes.

Cherish no malevolent feelings against society, or the government, for arresting you in your career of criminality, but rather be thankful for the mildness of our laws; that instead of forfeiting your life on an ignominious gallows, as would have been the case under most other governments, you are only restrained for a time, for the safety of society, and your own good; that the most favorable means are afforded for repentance and reformation, by forming regular, temperate and industrious habits, learning a useful trade, yielding obedience to laws, subduing evil passions, and by receiving moral and religious instruction. If you will but faithfully improve the opportunities with which you will be thus favored, your case is far from being hopeless; your sufferings during confinement will be greatly mitigated; you will return to your friends and to society with correct views and good resolutions, and then friends and society will receive you again with open arms, and, like the compassionate father to his prodigal son, will say of you, "he was dead, and is alive again; and was lost, and is found."

It is true, that while confined here you can have no intelligence concerning relatives or friends; but they will always be informed, on request, of your behavior, health, and situation. They will be even allowed to visit the prison, and pass into avenues, from whence unseen by you at your labor, they can view your dejected visage—to a feeling heart, the exercise of a trying act of friendship. You are to be literally buried from the world; but when you return to it, the fault will be entirely your own, if you do not acquire for yourself a new reputation, become a blessing to your friends and to society, and exemplify the power of deep repentance and thorough reform.[11]

"An address of this character," declared Powers, "rarely, if ever, fails to melt a convict into the deepest tenderness." [12]

[11] Powers, *Letter*, pp. 13–14.
[12] *Ibid.*, p. 14.

Following this induction routine, the inmate was led into his new home, where he ordinarily stayed for a few days in complete solitude until assigned to a workshop. To his left as he entered the hall of the prison from the administrative offices was the old south wing. Patterned upon the layout at Newgate, it was largely abandoned for over a decade after the building of the north wing, except that its attic contained quarters for female offenders. It was converted into an island-type cellblock in 1832 by removing one of its walls, knocking out old partitions, and building five tiers of new cells. After this renovation, a wing projecting backward from its southernmost end contained a dining hall on the first floor and a chapel above. To the rear of these were more solitary cells.[13]

If the prisoner arrived before 1832, he was automatically taken to the north wing, with its island of cells banked five tiers high, and assigned to one of the cubicles. In time the wing became L-shaped when an addition was extended backward from the north end, with new cells built on the same order as the old. The walls separating the individual compartments were a foot thick and extended outward two feet beyond the cell doorways, thus greatly diminishing the chances that prisoners could communicate with one another either by word of mouth or by signals. These outward projections also created recesses in which chaplains could stand when counseling inmates without much likelihood of being heard or disturbed by convicts in the neighboring cubicles. The open space surrounding the cell island formed an effective sounding gallery. According to a report of the Prison Discipline Society, "a sentinel, in the open area, on the ground, can hear a whisper from a distant cell, in the upper story." The outer walls of the wing were pierced by a number of windows which were glazed and barred. Heat was produced by an assortment of stoves and lamps placed in the open areas in front of the cells, and some ventilation was afforded by pipes three inches in diameter which extended from the rear wall of

[13] Beaumont and Tocqueville, *On the Penitentiary System*, p. 31; DS, 70th Session (1847), Vol. I, No. 5, p. 7. Under Powers, however, the incoming convict was assigned immediately to a shop (Powers, *Letter*, pp. 14–15).

each cell to the prison roof. The whole arrangement was designed to be one of efficiency, silence, and gloom.[14]

The main administration building and the L-shaped north and south wings formed three sides of a square containing a small grass plot with gravel walks. Behind this area was a large rectangular yard covered with gravel and almost completely enclosed by workshops, most of which were built with their backs against the high wall surrounding the prison.[15] This arrangement facilitated inspection of the yard, which could be swept with a quick glance, but it proved defective in other ways. Jammed together under the shadow of the walls, the shops were dark and damp; air would not circulate properly through them; and, as their timbers rotted and industrial waste piled up in them, they became unhealthful and fetid, especially in the summertime. In addition, they increased the chances for escape, for a convict who scaled a shop roof was not very far from the top of the wall. By 1841, the shops were dilapidated, leaky, and virtually untenantable, but by this time the state had purchased a new tract of land to the rear of the prison which was enclosed by a wall and used as a site for new industrial buildings.[16]

One reason for placing the original workshops along the prison's outer wall stemmed from the desire of administrators to watch inmates surreptitiously. Running through the rear of each shop was an enclosed passageway which extended for two thousand feet around the base of the wall. From this alleyway, which was only three feet wide, visitors and prison officials could peer through narrow slits at the laboring convicts.[17] Such leaders as Gershom Powers enthusiastically endorsed this primitively Orwellian layout,

[14] Prison Discipline Society, *First Report* (1826), pp. 9–10. See also Fig. 4, facing p. 49.

[15] See Fig. 4, facing p. 49, as well as the ground plan in Powers, *Brief Account*, p. 73.

[16] Blouet, *Rapport*, p. 10; DA, 60th Session (1837), Vol. I, No. 31, p. 12; 61st Session (1838), Vol. II, No. 86, p. 15; 64th Session (1841), Vol. II, No. 28, p. 12; and 65th Session (1842), Vol. II, No. 31, pp. 2–3. The old rear wall of the prison was never torn down, and the modern institution is divided into two distinct areas by it.

[17] Prison Discipline Society, *First Report* (1826), p. 7.

arguing that it acted as a powerful check upon negligence or misconduct either by guards or by inmates, that it permitted visitors to view the shops without disturbing the occupants, and that it provided a means of convincing suspicious citizens that the penitentiary had nothing to hide.[18] Critics of the Auburn system, however, believed that this method of surveillance embodied the essence of tyranny and denounced it in unmeasured terms. "The spy system is abominable, in whatever light it is viewed," declared Harriet Martineau after visiting the prison. "It is the deepest of insults. . . . The great point to be gained with the criminal is to regenerate self-respect. A virtuous man may preserve his self-respect under the eyes of a spy . . . but a morally infirm man can never thus acquire it." [19] Complaining of the "innumerable peep holes" scattered throughout the penitentiary, another English visitor asserted that "suspicion with its hateful blast taints every Avenue of the Auburn establishment." [20]

Within an atmosphere of repression, humiliation, and gloomy silence, the Auburn convict performed an incessantly monotonous round of activity. He arose at 5:15 in the summer, or at sunrise in other seasons when the days were shorter. As soon as his cell was unlocked, he marched out carrying three pieces of equipment: a night tub used for calls of nature, a can for drinking water, and a wooden food container called a "kid." Holding this paraphernalia with his left hand, he laid his right one upon the shoulder of the felon who occupied the next cell and marched in lockstep to a washroom where the kids and cans were deposited for cleansing. He then proceeded across the yard, emptied his tub in a sewerage vault, and rinsed it at the prison pump. After this he marched to his workshop, placing the tub against the wall of the building as he entered.[21]

[18] Powers, *Letter,* p. 15; JA, 51st Session (1828), Appendix A, p. 53; JS, 51st Session, 2nd Meeting (1828), p. 100; DA, 56th Session (1833), Vol. III, No. 199, pp. 24–26, and 58th Session (1835), Vol. II, No. 135, Part 1, p. 10.

[19] Harriet Martineau, *Society in America* (New York, 1837), II, 286.

[20] Joshua T. Smith, *Journal in America, 1837–1838* (Metuchen, N.J., 1925), pp. 12–13.

[21] Powers, *Brief Account,* p. 5.

The shops were laid out so as to separate the convicts as much as possible, but it soon became evident that there was not enough space for the number of workers to be accommodated. This impeded effective supervision, and Gershom Powers at one point recommended a plan, obviously inspired by Bentham's Panopticon, for circular shops with individual stalls built around the circumference.[22] This, however, seems never to have been adopted; instead, keepers surveyed the crowded working areas from elevated stools, watching for any sign of inmate communication and giving commands when necessary. If at all possible, they used hand signals; if not, terse oral directions. An untrained person might be placed next to an experienced worker for a short time in order to learn how to do his tasks, but the convicts were normally arranged so as not to face one another. Inmate waiters passed silently among the men, distributing raw materials, removing waste, and handing out drinking water. In a corner of each shop was a privy; if a prisoner desired to use it he took with him a stick which hung from a cord in the center of the workroom. Upon returning he put the stick back in place, a silent signal that the facility was once more ready for use. Every detail possible was subjected to routine to lessen the need for verbal communication. Hours sometimes passed without so much as a word being uttered.[23]

After working until seven or eight o'clock in the morning, the prisoners marched in lockstep to the dining hall, where breakfast was served. Here they were placed at long tables, seating themselves on one side only so that there would be no opportunity for conversation or signals. If an inmate wanted more food, he raised his left hand; if he did not want all that he had, he put up his right. Convict waiters watched for such signals and provided hearty eaters with extra food taken from those who were less hungry. The prison steward looked over the men as they ate and rang a bell when he decided they had been given enough time. When this

[22] Frédéric-Auguste DeMetz, *Rapport sur les Pénitenciers des États-Unis* (Paris, 1837), p. 12; Powers, *Brief Account*, p. 75.

[23] Powers, *Brief Account*, pp. 14–15; DeMetz, *Rapport sur les Pénitenciers des États-Unis*, p. 12.

occurred the inmates stood up immediately and got into line to go back to the shops. The whole process took from twenty minutes to half an hour.[24]

If a prisoner was sick upon arising in the morning, he reported his ailment to a turnkey, who left word of it in the keeper's room for the physician when the latter arrived at about nine o'clock. The inmate himself was normally expected to go to work and remain there until summoned. Convicts who needed new clothing reported at midmorning to a room where garments were distributed. Otherwise there was only silent and unremitting labor. Dinner was served at noon, after which the men returned to the shops to work until six o'clock or sundown. When closing time finally came, they washed up in buckets provided for this purpose, marched out, scooped up their night tubs, and continued on to the prison, where they received kids and cans filled with food and water. Without breaking step they picked these up and proceeded to their respective cells, leaving their doors slightly ajar as they entered. After the turnkeys saw that the inmates were in their apartments they walked along the ranges and placed their keys in the locks. As each convict heard a key enter his lock he immediately slammed his door shut so that the keeper would know without looking that he was in his proper place.[25] To a later student the whole routine resembled the operations of a vast "human filing system, allowing the men to be removed for work in the shops during the day and then filed away at night." [26]

After eating his evening meal in solitude, the convict waited for a signal to take off his clothes and go to bed on his mat or hammock. Until this occurred he was positively forbidden to lie down. If light permitted, he could read his Bible or wait for the chaplain to come along and talk to him about educational or religious matters. Following "lights out" the prison became, in Powers' words,

[24] Powers, *Brief Account*, p. 5.

[25] *Ibid.*, p. 6.

[26] Ralph S. Herre, "A History of Auburn Prison from the Beginning to about 1867" (unpublished D.Ed. dissertation, Pennsylvania State University, 1950), p. 102.

"almost as still as the house of death." Officers prowled stealthily throughout the ranges all night in accordance with a system designed to see that they were attentive to their duties. The guard stationed in the administration building placed a little ball in the doorway leading to the south wing, where another keeper picked it up and carried it to a window at the far end of the corridor. Here it was taken by another officer who carried it through the shops and yards to the other side of the institution, where a watchman patrolling the north wing received it and took it back to the starting point. Regulations specified that the ball must make a complete revolution once every twenty minutes; if it did not, a ten-minute grace period was allowed, after which the officer who should normally have received the ball reported to the principal keeper or his deputy. The delinquent watchman was immediately sought out and summarily dismissed if he had no valid excuse for his laxity.[27] The entire procedure epitomized the way in which the administration of the prison was worked out to the tiniest detail.

The dawn of a new day merely meant that the undeviating routine began all over again, remorseless in its monotony. "It had the beauty of a finely functioning machine," stated one later penologist. "It had reduced the human beings within the prison to automata."[28] The only day that provided some respite and variety was Sunday, for then some of the least educated convicts were taken to a room for religious and educational exercises. Later in the morning the entire inmate body was marched to the chapel for divine worship. Students from Auburn Theological Seminary donated their services for the educational activities, and the chaplain or a local minister occupied the pulpit in the church service, though occasionally a guest speaker was imported, such as the noted temperance advocate John B. Gough or "the reformed gambler," J. H. Green. Singing was frowned upon in the early years,

[27] Powers, *Brief Account*, p. 7; Prison Discipline Society, *First Report* (1826), p. 37; DA, 56th Session (1833), Vol. III, No. 199, p. 33.

[28] Orlando F. Lewis, *The Development of American Prisons and Prison Customs, 1776–1845* (n.p., 1922), p. 78.

but by the 1840's it was a regular feature of the Sunday service, and a score of inmates formed a prison choir. The services and the type of preaching which predominated in them provided a badly needed emotional outlet for the convicts, who like many ordinary churchgoers "wept freely" during the sermons.[29]

The keepers, for whom Sunday offered some respite from ordinary duties, wanted the worship service to be terminated quickly; the convicts, on the other hand, had every reason to desire its prolongation, for the ensuing afternoon and evening constituted one of the most dreaded periods of the week. After being given a kid full of food and a can of water, each inmate was confined to his cell until daybreak on Monday. The "scholars" who had attended school in the morning were again taken out for instruction in the afternoon, but the rest of the convicts faced long hours of unbroken solitude in their cubicles, aggravated by the fact that they were not allowed to lie down until the night bell was sounded. The chaplain went from cell to cell and temporarily broke the monotony for the men he visited; Bible reading also offered relief from tedium as well as spiritual insight. Otherwise the prisoners could only pace back and forth like caged beasts or grasp eagerly at opportunities to volunteer for work details if various small jobs needed to be done about the penitentiary.[30] A convict who endured a succession of such Sabbaths once said that they were characterized by "short food, short sermon, short liberty; no man cares for us; long, bad, hard, painful thoughts, with a dreary day and no hope ahead."[31]

A regime imposed with such undeviating regularity inevitably

[29] *Northern Christian Advocate*, April 23, 1845, Oct. 22, 1845, and April 4, 1849; DeMetz, *Rapport sur les Pénitenciers des États-Unis*, p. 13; Powers, *Brief Account*, p. 9; JA, 51st Session (1828), Appendix A, p. 16; DA, 65th Session (1842), Vol. II, No. 31, p. 108.

[30] Fred A. Packard, *Memorandum of a Late Visit to the Auburn Penitentiary* (Philadelphia, 1842), p. 7; Powers, *Brief Account*, pp. 9–10; DA, 56th Session (1833), Vol. III, No. 199, p. 35, and 75th Session (1852), Vol. I, No. 20, pp. 137–138.

[31] New York Prison Association, *Tenth Report* (1855), p. 143.

eroded the inmate's very sense of identity and individuality. Uniformity became a fetish among defenders of the Auburn system. "A convict," stated Louis Dwight in 1827, "should have the same cell at night, the same place in the shops, and the same relative position in the column, while marching to and from the shops." [32] The same rules applied to all; the same type of striped garment was worn by everybody; each convict's cell, furniture, kid, can, and night tub were like those of his fellows. In time it seemed to some of Auburn's visitors that there was a gloomy sameness in the expressions on the faces of the convicts. "I walked through all the shops in which the prisoners were at labour," wrote an English traveler, "and I must say that so miserable, jaded, desponding a row of faces I never beheld—such sunken, lack-lustre eyes I never encountered." [33] When Richard Cobden visited the penitentiary in 1835 he was "struck with the similarity of expression in all the countenances of the prisoners," and asked himself, "does this arise from the identity of their condition, as we see a peculiar resemblance of feature or expression in the faces of almost all *deaf* men?" [34]

Aside from the stupefying effect of the discipline itself, Auburn life was filled with a variety of hardships capable of breaking the spirit of all but the most obdurate prisoners. According to Gershom Powers, the greatest of these was isolation, depriving the convict of contact with inmates, friends, or loved ones and cutting him off from all information regarding the outside world. Another privation for many prisoners was the lack of tobacco, which had been doled out to felons at Newgate but was for many years denied to convicts under the Auburn system. "Being deprived of tobacco," declared Powers, "occasions much more suffering to those who have been in the habit of using it, than the loss of ardent spirits to the drunkard. There are many who have been confined for

[32] Prison Discipline Society, *Second Report* (1827), p. 36.

[33] Murray, *Travels in North America*, I, 78.

[34] Elizabeth H. Cawley, ed., *The American Diaries of Richard Cobden* (Princeton, 1952), p. 109. Italics are as given.

years, that would cheerfully exchange half their rations of food, for a moderate allowance of tobacco." [35]

Another burden on the convict's spirit was the galling knowledge that he was in all his humiliation subject to the frequent gaze of visitors, some of whom might be former friends or neighbors. From six to eight thousand people came through the prison yearly, and the revenue from the admission fees of twenty-five cents per head sometimes determined whether or not the institution showed an annual surplus or deficit. Powers catered to this trade by writing a guidebook which was sold to the visitors for an additional twenty-five cents, and this brought in additional money.[36] There was doubtless a certain mitigating anonymity about visitation from a convict's point of view as long as the secret passageways were used, but these seem to have been discontinued with the abandonment or demolition of the old workshops in the 1840's. It must have been difficult enough for an inmate to maintain his composure and obey the regulations which strictly forbade him so much as to look at a visitor being shown through the shops, but occasionally circumstances became almost unendurable, as a prison physician once pointed out in complaining against the practice of allowing females to tour these areas. Such visitors, he stated, strongly stimulated the passions of the convicts and increased the prevalence of masturbation. Indeed, one inmate had been so overcome by the presence of a young lady in his shop that he could not restrain himself from throwing his arms about her and kissing her repeatedly until forced to desist.[37] One can only speculate about the punishment which followed so serious a breach of discipline.

The psychological pains of convict life were supplemented and exacerbated by various physical discomforts. In the first place, the cellblocks at Auburn were poorly designed with regard to heating and ventilation. Even with the addition of extra stoves it was hard to secure an even distribution of heat throughout the tiers, and

[35] Powers, *Brief Account*, pp. 16, 77.
[36] Herre, "History of Auburn Prison," pp. 203, 208–209.
[37] DA, 75th Session (1852), Vol. I, No. 20, p. 86.

conditions were not helped by the fact that the blankets provided for the inmates were made of coarse, hard-twisted thread and designed more for durability than for warmth. After examining conditions a new warden concluded in 1841 "that there has been, at times, an almost intolerable degree of suffering from cold," and called previous heating provisions "palpably wrong in principle, as well as inhumane in effect."[38]

Old and infirm convicts who had special difficulty in keeping warm were usually placed in the top range of cells, which were normally six to eight degrees more tolerable than the rest. This had a compensating disadvantage, however, for the ventilation in the upper cubicles was even worse than it was in the other tiers. Conditions were not particularly bad during the daytime, when the inmates were at work, but several hours after they had come in for the night the cellblocks were heavy with a nauseating smell of body odors and reeking night tubs. Air circulated badly even in the open areas and hung absolutely motionless in the tiny compartments. Officials tried to combat the situation by using pulverized gypsum and chloride of lime, but these were not really satisfactory even as disinfectants.[39] A long-standing practice of hanging wet clothing up to dry on the galleries only increased the dampness, as did an unsuccessful experiment with steam heating in 1839 and 1840.[40] Bedbugs and fleas, or "German ducks," as the inmates called them, added to the general discomfort.[41]

Such conditions were obviously not conducive to good health. In addition, the fact that the workshops were normally much

---

[38] JA, 51st Session (1828), Appendix A, p. 61; Dorothea L. Dix, *Remarks on Prisons and Prison Discipline in the United States* (Boston, 1845), p. 37; DA, 64th Session (1841), Vol. II, No. 28, p. 11.

[39] JA, 45th Session (1822), p. 218; Dix, *Remarks on Prisons*, pp. 36–37, 42; Blouet, *Rapport*, p. 10; DS, 67th Session (1844), Vol. I, No. 18, pp. 83–84.

[40] DA, 64th Session (1841), Vol. II, No. 28, p. 17, and 72nd Session (1849), Vol. VI, No. 243, p. 216.

[41] JA, 51st Session (1828), Appendix A, p. 20; DS, 57th Session (1834), Vol. II, No. 92, p. 32; DA, 72nd Session (1849), Vol. VI, No. 243, p. 216; Horace Lane, *Five Years in State's Prison* (New York, 1835), p. 19.

warmer than the cells meant that the inmates were often over-heated when they came in at night and were then subjected to a sudden change in temperature. On rainy days they were soaked to the skin parading across the yard and were not always able to put on other clothes or to dry the ones they were wearing. Respiratory ailments understandably became prevalent; according to the testi-mony of a prison physician in 1844, nearly half of all deaths at Auburn from 1817 to 1843 had been caused by lung diseases. This practitioner, however, asserted that the main effect of the bad con-ditions in the institution was not so much to cause sicknesses as to hinder satisfactory convalescence from them.[42]

The discomforts caused by lack of heat and poor ventilation were aggravated by an insufficiency of light in the cellblocks. The period between being locked up for the night and the signal that it was permissible to go to bed was one of tedium and ennui which con-victs tried to combat by reading, but often there was not enough illumination for this. In the summer there were usually about two hours of light remaining after the inmates came in from work, but in the winter it was dark by the time they were secured, and there was considerable fretfulness until they were allowed to lie down.[43] At Newgate there had been lamps in the convict apartments, but the cells at Auburn had no such conveniences.

One of the greatest potential sources of dissatisfaction in any penal institution is the food supply. The Auburn dining system had been designed partly to ensure that convicts with hearty appe-tites would get enough to eat, and provisions were ample at least part of the time.[44] Even so, the parsimony which was characteristic of prison management sometimes had unfortunate results. In the interest of economy, the state awarded food contracts to private suppliers who provided convict rations at the lowest possible prices.

[42] DS, 67th Session (1844), Vol. I, No. 18, pp. 81–83. Of 349 deaths among Auburn prisoners from 1818 to 1850, 121 were caused by consumption. *Ibid.*, 74th Session (1851), Vol. I, No. 13, p. 112.

[43] See Prison Discipline Society, *Eighth Report* (1833), p. 10; *Northern Christian Advocate*, May, 5, 1848.

[44] See for example Packard, *Memorandum*, p. 3; DA, 70th Session (1847), Vol. VIII, No. 255, Part 2, p. 94.

Because of business fluctuations the contractors sometimes found that they had underestimated the cost of the foodstuffs they had agreed to furnish, and tried to palm off inferior goods to the penitentiary. In 1846, for example, meat listed as "prime beef" contained swine heads, and was so full of bones and tendons that some inmates could hardly eat it. One prison agent was indicted for having knowingly fed his charges spoiled codfish, and an indignant inspector attributed an epidemic which swept the institution to bad provisions.[45] Even when the food measured up to standard it was anything but a gourmet's delight. Under Gershom Powers, for instance, the normal daily ration consisted of ten ounces of pork or sixteen ounces of beef, ten ounces of Indian meal, and a half gill of molasses. Two quarts of rye, four quarts of salt, four quarts of vinegar, one and one-half ounces of pepper, and two and one-half bushels of potatoes were also divided among every one hundred portions. This fare was washed down with rye coffee or plain water.[46]

Some convicts were mentally unbalanced upon admission to Auburn, but others became so under the rigid routine and the hardships which prevailed there. Powers admitted that it was "no uncommon occurrence" for inmates to crack under the strain, and visitors were sometimes impressed by the number of prisoners who were obviously demented.[47] Interminable brooding over past crimes may have contributed to this; when the Scots phrenologist George Combe visited Auburn in 1839, he saw a convict who had recently chopped off his left hand. This member had "offended against God and man," the felon explained, "and it was borne in upon me, that if I cut it off, as commanded by the Scripture, God would forgive me, and man also."[48] For years prison officials lacked authority to send even violent cases to insane asylums, though they

[45] DS, 70th Session (1847), Vol. I, No. 12, pp. 3–10, and 71st Session (1848), Vol. I, No. 30, p. 4; DA, 72nd Session (1849), Vol. VI, No. 243, p. 219.
[46] JA, 51st Session (1828), Appendix A, p. 20.
[47] Powers, Brief Account, p. 38; DA, 70th Session (1847), Vol. VIII, No. 255, Part 2, pp. 94, 106, and 75th Session (1852), Vol. I, No. 20, p. 40.
[48] George Combe, Notes on the United States of North America during a Phrenological Visit in 1838-9-40 (Philadelphia, 1841), II, 72.

did manage occasionally to get such inmates admitted at Blooming-dale in New York City. Convicts who were mentally unbalanced but relatively quiet remained unsegregated and were employed alongside sane prisoners in the shops.[49]

The problems created by such unfortunates vexed administrators even after their sentences had expired, for some of them were obviously too insane to make any adjustment to free society. Many of these landed in the Cayuga County poorhouse or the Auburn jail for lack of a better solution. Here they became a burden upon local citizens, who complained loudly to the legislature. In 1835, a petition to Albany reported that there were three lunatics in the poorhouse who had completed terms at the penitentiary, and that Noah Burnham, a demented murderer who had been thrown into the village jail after his prison sentence had expired, had become so deranged that it was difficult to keep clothes on him.[50] By 1842, it had been made mandatory for the principal keeper at Auburn to remove any convict whom the staff physician deemed insane to Bloomingdale, but many such inmates nevertheless remained in the penitentiary to create difficulties before and after release.[51]

Prisoners who managed to serve their time without losing their minds found serious problems awaiting them upon their return to free society. For many years it was customary to give a departing convict $3 in cash and what was supposed to be a decent suit of clothes. Such administrators as Gershom Powers readily admitted that the money was often utterly inadequate to enable the recipient to reach his friends without embarrassment. In addition, there was no systematic effort to find jobs for ex-inmates.[52] The clothes in which such persons were outfitted upon discharge were frequently bought by the agent from itinerant secondhand garment dealers

[49] Dix, *Remarks on Prisons*, p. 39.

[50] DA, 58th Session (1835), Vol. III, No. 209, pp. 1–3.

[51] *Ibid.*, 65th Session (1842), Vol. IV, No. 65, p. 103; 70th Session (1847), Vol. VIII, No. 255, Part 2, pp. 94, 106; and 75th Session (1852), Vol. I, No. 20, p. 40.

[52] Powers, *Brief Account*, p. 17, and *Letter*, pp. 18–19; JA, 58th Session (1828), Appendix A, p. 24; DS, 55th Session (1832), Vol. II, No. 74, pp. 5–6; Prison Discipline Society, *Eighth Report* (1833), p. 31.

or had been worn into the prison by other criminals. In many cases they did not fit and made their wearers look "shabby and ridiculous." It was grossly unfair, a group of prison reformers once insisted, to turn a man "adrift with the mark of a *jail bird* on his very clothing," especially taking into consideration that an ex-convict may have earned the state large sums of money through his labor.[53] One result of the meager provisions made for discharged inmates was that many of them were forced to settle in Auburn itself; in 1846, about 150 were residing in the town. "They herd here because they have no means of going anywhere else," a local newspaper stated. "And under the present circumstances of neglect, in which they are placed, they cannot but infect the character of the community." [54]

Some efforts were made from time to time to rectify these conditions. As a preliminary step, it was provided that payments to released inmates might average $3 rather than consist of an automatic grant to that amount; in this way a deserving convict could be given more and a badly regarded one less. Some men thus received the princely sum of $5 when they were returned to society.[55] In 1846, the legislature authorized an additional payment of three cents per mile of distance between the prison and the place where a discharged inmate had been originally convicted. This, however, was interpreted by Auburn administrators as a substitute for the former grant, and conditions in certain cases became worse than they had been before. In one instance, a convict from Ohio who happened to have been convicted in the town of Auburn was given three cents with which to rejoin his family in the Middle West.[56]

The inmate who found himself unable to bear the strain of con-

[53] DA, 75th Session (1852), Vol. I, No. 20, pp. 32–33; New York Prison Association, *Seventh Report* (1852), p. 33. Italics are as given.

[54] *Northern Christian Advocate*, Nov. 25, 1846. Some of these ex-convicts had probably settled in Auburn, however, because they had been offered jobs there by contractors who had liked their work in the prison shops. See JA, 50th Session (1827), p. 71.

[55] DA, 60th Session (1837), Vol. I, No. 31, pp. 84, 89, and 65th Session (1842), Vol. IV, No. 65, p. 105.

[56] *Ibid.*, 70th Session (1847), Vol. VIII, No. 255, Part 1, p. 67.

finement and did not want to wait for his going-away allowance could try to escape, but this was very difficult. One of the beauties of the Auburn system to those who administered it was the fact that the isolation of the prisoners kept escape plots at a minimum. It was not particularly hard to get out while the institution was under construction—twenty-three men broke away in the first five years of its existence—but after this escapes were rare. One seems to have occurred in 1824, another in 1837, and two more in 1842.[57] There was at least a temporary break in 1841, for a local newspaper unfriendly to the prison administration reported with great glee that a cow had been mistaken for an escaped convict and shot.[58]

If the great majority of inmates had little or no hope of escape, they could at least scheme against the administration, break prison rules when they thought they could do so unobserved, and gain possession of contraband articles whenever this was possible. As at Newgate, contractors sometimes tried to get extra work out of convicts by slipping them such bribes as tobacco, fresh fruit, or other items when guards were not watching. An especially coveted object was intoxicating drink, which could occasionally be smuggled into the institution or secured from other sources. An investigation in 1847 disclosed evidence that an inmate nurse in the prison hospital had distributed alcoholic beverages from the penitentiary's medical supply to his friends. Other drinks were stolen from the kitchen; in 1844, two convicts were flogged for getting drunk, one on vinegar and the other on "baker's beer."[59]

The urge to carry weapons was strong among imprisoned felons, and knives and other sharp objects were prominent articles of contraband. Convicts were employed at the penitentiary shops in making such items as axes, adzes, drawing knives, and chisels; inmate

[57] DeMetz, *Rapport sur les Pénitenciers des États-Unis*, p. 53; Packard, *Memorandum of a Late Visit*, p. 6.
[58] Auburn *Cayuga Tocsin*, Feb. 10 and 17, 1841.
[59] DA, 58th Session (1835), Vol. II, No. 135, Part 1, p. 22; 69th Session (1846), Vol. IV, No. 137, pp. 49, 57; 72nd Session (1849), Vol. VI, No. 243, p. 216; and 75th Session (1852), Vol. I, No. 20, p. 81.

tailors perforce worked with shears.[60] Unless friskings were frequent and thorough, some of these articles could be hidden away. "Knives, in some form," a local newspaper once stated, "are common with convicts, and edged tools in almost every shop are in their hands." [61] Stabbings occurred periodically, as in 1845 when an inmate murdered one of his fellows by plunging a scissors blade into his abdomen. The next year a burglar named Wyatt killed another convict with the same type of weapon. Wyatt also possessed a small knife blade about half an inch long which he kept hidden in a piece of plug tobacco for over a year. He attempted to commit suicide with this while awaiting punishment for the murder.[62]

Because they were deprived of all normal sexual contacts, it was only to be expected that inmates at Auburn would try to secure some form of satisfaction from various forbidden practices. The enforced isolation and constant surveillance of convicts made homosexual affairs virtually impossible, but nothing could prevent the prisoners from indulging in masturbation, which worried administrators intensely because of its supposed tendency to produce hallucinations and other forms of mental illness. "This is the besetting sin of all prisons," stated a group of investigators in 1847. "Its existence is very marked at Auburn, and is doubtless one exciting cause of much of the insanity which has prevailed there." [63]

Undoubtedly the most frequent breach of discipline at the penitentiary was talking. Inmates made every effort to communicate with one another whenever they thought they could do so without being caught. Numerous opportunities existed for furtive conversation despite the most pronounced exertions on the part of prison

---

[60] See Powers, *Brief Account*, pp. 27–28.

[61] Auburn *Weekly American*, Dec. 15, 1858.

[62] DS, 69th Session (1846), Vol. II, No. 46, p. 89; *Northern Christian Advocate*, Feb. 18 and Aug. 19, 1846. By this time, convicts at Auburn were being supplied with rations of chewing tobacco (cf. p. 242).

[63] DA, 70th Session (1847), Vol. VIII, No. 255, Part 2, p. 93. See also *ibid.*, 63rd Session (1841), Vol. I, No. 18, p. 17, and 64th Session (1841), Vol. II, No. 28, p. 16.

officials, and especially when the latter were shorthanded. The weekly scrubbing of the cells necessitated particular vigilance; twenty to thirty convicts were continually passing in and out of the cellblocks with buckets of water on such occasions, and all sorts of noise was caused by splashing, sweeping, and the scraping of crevices and corners with iron implements. On cold winter nights, guards frequently had to leave their posts to tend the heating units, and the sounds made by the opening and closing of stove doors and the moving of fuel supplies made it extremely difficult to prevent conversation. Some cells had ventilating pipes which inmates learned to use as speaking tubes.[64] Overcrowding sometimes forced administrators to put two convicts in one cell, which made communication impossible to stop.[65] Certain sections of the prison were not always well supervised by keepers; the hospital, for example, was on occasion left to the care of inmate nurses.[66] In the shops, felons could try to exchange information by means of sign language or facial expressions; some convicts who came from Newgate to Auburn in the 1820's brought with them a complete alphabet of finger motions.[67] It is conceivable that some inmates learned to make intelligible sounds without moving their lips; certainly the fact that a professional ventriloquist was at one time imprisoned at Auburn must have had interesting consequences.[68]

The extent to which communication actually took place under the "silent" system was warmly debated among reformers. Opponents of such a regime typically maximized their estimates; Fred Packard, a supporter of the methods used in the Eastern State Penitentiary at Philadelphia, visited Auburn in 1842 and claimed

[64] See especially Powers, *Brief Account*, pp. 11, 31; William Crawford, *Report . . . on the Penitentiaries of the United States* (n.p., 1834), Appendix, p. 3.

[65] At the beginning of 1832, for example, only 550 out of 622 prisoners had solitary accommodations. (DA, 55th Session [1832], Vol. I, No. 2, p. 14.)

[66] DA, 72nd Session (1849), Vol. VI, No. 243, p. 216.

[67] Powers, *Brief Account*, pp. 70–71, footnote.

[68] Beaumont and Tocqueville, *On the Penitentiary System*, p. 291; DA, 70th Session (1847), Vol. VIII, No. 255, Part 2, p. 12.

to have been assured by a trustworthy source that the inmates he saw there "very generally knew each other's names, residences, crimes, sentences, and even the courts by which they were sentenced." [69] Occasionally even persons who championed the Auburn system or at least found much to admire in it were forced to admit the possibility that some communication did take place despite all the vigilance of the keepers.[70] Some idea of the contact that did occur can be gained from prison statistics relating to the incidence of flogging for violations of the no-talking rule. Over an eleven-month period in 1845, for example, there were administered at Auburn 173 whippings for offenses consisting of or including conversation. Considering that the urge to communicate was pervasive and that some situations were favorable for undetected breaches of silence, it is quite probable that these punishments represented only a fraction of the actual violations that took place.[71]

Strict regulations and inmate determination to evade them resulted in a relatively frequent use of the lash at Auburn, with occasional instances of obvious injustice. One yearly tabulation shows that a prisoner who was found to possess a pencil in his cell and who denied knowledge of it received exactly the same number of stripes as an inmate who attempted to throw a man from the roof of a building—six. Another convict received four lashes for merely "grinning darkey fashion." Sometimes the inflictions were very severe, as in the case of a felon who received two consecutive whippings of fifty blows each for stabbing another inmate. One prisoner was given ninety-eight stripes for "feigning great weakness and swooning, and immediately thereafter violently resisting the order of the keeper to sit down," although officials stated that the strokes were not applied with much force.[72] The flogging of insane convicts to induce them to work or conform to institutional

[69] Packard, *Memorandum of a Late Visit*, p. 6.

[70] See Mathew Carey, *Thoughts on Penitentiaries and Prison Discipline* (Philadelphia, 1831), p. 35; Beaumont and Tocqueville, *On the Penitentiary System,* pp. 25–26.

[71] DA, 69th Session (1846), Vol. IV, No. 137, pp. 7–24.

[72] *Ibid.,* pp. 17, 22, 43, 53, 59.

routine constituted an especially prevalent type of abuse. In one case an inmate who had been beaten severely for supposedly feigning mental illness was shortly thereafter sent to an asylum, where he died. The incumbent prison chaplain, himself an advocate of the whip, believed that the flagellation "made the man more furious, and may have hastened his death." [73]

Despite such occurrences, one should not overestimate the amount of brutality which appeared in the normal course of operations at Auburn. It is noteworthy that two of the most lurid and highly publicized cases of alleged cruelty, involving the deaths of convicts John Winterscale and Louis von Eck, took place in 1839 during the short but sensational second administration of Elam Lynds, an atypically severe agent.[74] Probably much more representative as a warden was Gershom Powers; a variety of sources make it clear that the use of the "cat" was not excessive under him.[75] Beaumont and Tocqueville noted the relative fewness of lashings at Auburn compared to the number that took place at Sing Sing, as did the itinerant Englishman Edward S. Abdy.[76] The same contrast was pointed out by inmates who had served time at both penitentiaries.[77]

Life at Auburn was harsh, monotonous, and degrading. On the other hand, many of its features undoubtedly look much worse from the vantage point of the twentieth century than they seemed in their own age. The Cayuga County prison existed in a society in which working hours were long and exhausting even for the free laborer; in which the diet of many an artisan family was no

[73] DA, 58th Session (1835), Vol. II, No. 135, Part 2, p. 31.

[74] These events are described in Chapter IX.

[75] Report of Charles Shaler, Edward King, and T. J. Wharton, quoted in Prison Discipline Society, *Third Report* (1828), p. 21; Lane, *Five Years in State's Prison*, p. 11; Statement of [Jared Curtis?] quoted in Stephen Allen, *Observations on Penitentiary Discipline, Addressed to William Roscoe, Esq. of Liverpool, England* (New York, 1827), p. 22.

[76] Beaumont and Tocqueville, *On the Penitentiary System*, p. 41; E[dward] S. Abdy, *Journal of a Residence and Tour in the United States of North America* (London, 1835), I, 269–270.

[77] DA, 56th Session (1833), Vol. III, No. 199, p. 10.

better than that of the convict; in which many immigrants and other persons lived in squalid and overcrowded cellars or pestilential tenements that were in many respects worse than penitentiary accommodations. The discipline of the Auburn shops was severe, but even in some factories there were attempts to enforce silence among free workers and physical punishments for the recalcitrant.[78] The prison cell was not the only sleeping room that was freezingly cold in the morning, and the abstemious regime which the inmate endured through compulsion was probably not much more stringent than the self-discipline followed voluntarily by some members of a free society which regarded sobriety with something akin to worship.

"Voluntarily," of course, is an important word. Many convicts would doubtless have been glad to exchange their conditions for even less desirable ones leavened by the precious element of freedom. Nevertheless, the inmate's life was not the only one that was hard. Furthermore, if the regime at Auburn was stringent, New York possessed an institution in which matters were much worse. To appreciate this, one has only to turn to the development of a penitentiary which eventually became known as "Sing Sing," after being dubbed in its early years with the exceedingly inappropriate and ironic name of "Mount Pleasant."

[78] See for example Norman Ware, *The Industrial Worker, 1840–1860* (reprinted ed.; Gloucester, Mass., 1959), pp. 10–17, 109; William A. Sullivan, *The Industrial Worker in Pennsylvania, 1800–1840* (Harrisburg, Penn., 1955), p. 38.

# Chapter VI

# The House of Fear

IN the spring of 1825 one hundred hand-picked convicts from Auburn prison, under the command of Elam Lynds, journeyed by canal boat and freight steamer across DeWitt Clinton's "big ditch" and down the Hudson to a site known as the "Silver Mine Farm," located on the east bank of the river about thirty-three miles north of New York City. Here, on a tract containing large deposits of "marble rock easily available for quarrying," they were to implement the act of March 7, 1825, by which the legislature had provided for a new penitentiary to replace old, discredited, and ridiculed Newgate. Using marble excavated and shaped by themselves, they were to build their own prison under Lynds's harsh and ruthless supervision.[1] Although the new institution was at first given the idyllic title of "Mount Pleasant," it was soon to become world-famous as "Sing Sing," the name of a village adjoining the prison grounds. Here the doctrine of extreme coercion, with its corollary of skepticism about the possibility of rehabilitation, was to reach its apogee.

[1] JA, 49th Session (1826), pp. 304–305; Prison Discipline Society, *Second Report* (1827), p. 66; Lewis E. Lawes, *Life and Death in Sing Sing* (New York, 1937), pp. 191–192. Lynds had made a tour of eastern state penitentiaries at the behest of Hopkins, Tibbits, and Allen as a preliminary step in planning the new institution, and had been particularly impressed by the New Hampshire prison, where convicts were profitably engaged in quarrying stone. He subsequently recommended this to the New York legislature as a suitable penal industry. (JA, 48th Session [1825], pp. 112–113, 132.)

When the inmate construction workers reached their destination, they did not find so much as a temporary stockade waiting to confine them. By nightfall, however, they had thrown up a makeshift barracks one hundred feet long by thirty feet wide, and were soon engaged in quarrying and shaping rock, grading the steep slope along the river, and erecting a large cellblock. By the time seven months had elapsed, enough of the structure had been completed to permit the confinement of its builders, two to a cubicle. Meanwhile the felons lived in the barracks, held in by flimsy and hastily built walls which they could have kicked out with ease. To the amazement of contemporary observers, only two escape attempts were made, and in a period of more than two years after the founding only one convict broke away successfully.[2]

Two pioneers of the old penal system, Thomas Eddy and John Griscom, visited the project prior to the winter of 1825 and found prisoners busily cutting marble, burning lime, laying masonry, and making iron doors for their own cells. The only civilians employed were a master carpenter, a mason, a blacksmith, and Lynds himself; the state was not taking the risk of hiring free laborers who might sympathize with the felons, as had happened at Auburn. Despite his reservations about Lynds's fondness for the lash, Eddy was full of admiration for the enterprise and for the relentless

---

[2] Lawes, *Life and Death at Sing Sing*, pp. 193–195; Stephen Allen, *Observations on Penitentiary Discipline, Addressed to William Roscoe, Esq. of Liverpool, England* (New York, 1827), p. 51; Una Pope-Hennessy, ed., *The Aristocratic Journey: Being the Outspoken Letters of Mrs. Basil Hall* (New York, 1931), p. 32. The fact that many felons can safely be kept in relatively insecure quarters is well known among present-day penologists, and is reflected in such federal prisons as the one at Seagoville, Texas (see John B. Martin, *Break Down the Walls: American Prisons, Present, Past, and Future* [New York, 1954], p. 149). The example provided at Sing Sing, however, astounded such men as Allen. A comparable instance occurred at Auburn in 1828 when the entire inmate body was let out of the cells in the middle of the night to fight a fire. Although the gates were wide open and confusion prevalent, no attempt was made to escape. Such witnesses as Gershom Powers marveled at this. (Prison Discipline Society, *Fourth Report* [1829], p. 23; Gershom Powers, *A Letter . . . in Answer to a Letter of the Hon. Edward Livingston* [Albany, 1829], pp. 318–319.)

leader who was directing it. The plan of the prison, the Quaker wrote to his English correspondent William Roscoe, was "in my opinion, the best in the world." [3] The following summer, Eddy paid another visit to Sing Sing, accompanied by the famous jurist James Kent. As the two companions conversed with Lynds, they watched the inmates toiling "out under a meridian sun, pouring its fierce blaze upon the white marble blocks around them, with an ardour almost sufficient to blind the eyes." [4] Guards armed with loaded muskets patrolled the uplands surrounding the area, and keepers with full authority to use the lash at their own discretion enforced unslacking attention to the work.[5]

Despite such unremitting efforts, the main cellblock took three years to build. A veritable mausoleum of marble and iron, it was 476 feet long by 44 feet wide and contained four tiers of cells arranged like those in the north wing at Auburn. The initial capacity of eight hundred convicts, though large for the time, soon proved inadequate, and in 1830 the legislature authorized the addition of a new tier of cubicles providing space for two hundred more. Even this was not quite sufficient for the number of inmates who had been committed to the institution by the end of the next year.[6] New York had created a monster prison, setting an example for states which in future years built excessively large penitentiaries in the hope of cutting down the unit costs of confinement.[7] Expanded still more and remodeled from time to time

[3] Eddy to Roscoe, Dec. 15, 1825, in Samuel L. Knapp, *The Life of Thomas Eddy* (New York, 1834), pp. 318–319.

[4] James Kent to David Hosack, May 11, 1833, in *ibid.*, p. 14.

[5] See Pope-Hennessy, ed., *The Aristocratic Journey*, p. 32; Lawes, *Life and Death in Sing Sing*, p. 192; Knapp, *Life of Thomas Eddy*, p. 319; and John Luckey, *Life in Sing Sing State Prison, as Seen in a Twelve Years' Chaplaincy* (New York, 1860), pp. 110–111.

[6] New York State Department of Correction, *Sing Sing Prison, Ossining, N.Y.: Its History, Purpose, Makeup and Program* (n.p., 1958), p. 3; DS, 55th Session (1832), Vol. I, No. 14, pp. 1–3.

[7] Because of the great administrative problems which this practice creates, its wisdom was, and is, dubious. See Gustave de Beaumont and Alexis de Tocqueville, *On the Penitentiary System in the United States*, trans. Francis Lieber (Philadelphia, 1833), p. 102; Martin, *Break Down the Walls*, pp. 17–18.

to meet changing conditions, Lynds's marble bastille was to house over one hundred thousand inmates in its cramped and dank recesses until its final abandonment as a cellblock more than a century later.[8]

The main prison building faced the Hudson and formed one side of a hollow square containing the penitentiary yard. Extending from the southern end of the cellblock toward the river was a wing containing the kitchen, hospital, chapel, a workshop, and a storehouse. As time went on, additional workshops were constructed to form another wing running from the northern end of the main structure to the Hudson. In the center of the yard close to the water's edge was a large building used as a stone shop where blocks of marble from the quarries could be trimmed and worked into shape. As at Auburn, the shops contained partitions with peepholes through which one could peer at the convicts without being seen. Other prison structures included a wharf, built in 1830, and the residence of the agent, which adjoined the southeast corner of the cellblock. Close by were the quarries, from which inmate crews excavated marble.[9]

Despite the general resemblance between the interior of the Sing Sing cellblock and the layout of the north wing at Auburn, several differences were noticeable. One of these reflected advancing technology; the cell doors at Auburn had to be closed separately, but most of those at Sing Sing could be secured fifty at a time by means of a new invention called the "compound lever lock."[10] The most important change, however, lay in the fact that the cell doors at Sing Sing, unlike those at Auburn, were not recessed. This created more space in each cubicle, but made it much easier for convicts to talk to one another. Inmates at the

[8] J. Leland Casscles, "Sing Sing Prison Then and Now," *Correction*, XXIII (January-February, 1958), 28–29. The building still stands, and is used primarily for storage purposes.

[9] Prison Discipline Society, *Eleventh Report* (1836), Appendix, p. 6; James R. Brice, *Secrets of the Mount-Pleasant State Prison, Revealed and Exposed* (Albany, 1839), pp. 34, 36.

[10] Prison Discipline Society, *Second Report* (1827), p. 66; Brice, *Secrets of the Mount-Pleasant State Prison*, p. 31.

Cayuga County prison could not see keepers patrolling the ranges until these officials were practically in front of their cells, but the felons at Sing Sing could see them coming at a distance and time their efforts at communication accordingly. Because there was no protruding wall to block off the sound, it was not hard to hear words spoken in a low tone of voice in an adjoining compartment. The problem was further aggravated for prison administrators because the area to be patrolled at Sing Sing was much more extensive than that to be covered at Auburn. For a keeper to pass each cell in the five tiers meant a walk of about a mile.[11]

Clandestine conversation abounded under such conditions. In the words of Lewis Lawes, "It was for years the sore spot of Sing Sing's prison discipline." [12] Stopping communication at night was especially difficult; inmates would make intelligible noises and, if caught, tell the keepers that they had been talking in their sleep. Besides, it was extremely hard to identify the precise cells from which sounds were emanating in the darkness.[13] If word-of-mouth contact was impossible, prisoners scratched notes on leather, wooden chips, or anything else that was available. Hiding away scraps of paper, pencils, or even bits of coal, they tied strings around messages written with these materials and threw them from door to door. Inmate hall-boys also carried such forbidden missives.[14]

In contrast to Auburn, where communication was probably only sporadic, it was possible to organize an effective prison grapevine at Sing Sing. The French visitor Frédéric-Auguste DeMetz was

---

[11] DA, 58th Session (1835), Vol. II, No. 135, Part 1, pp. 10–11; William Crawford, *Report . . . on the Penitentiaries of the United States* (n.p., 1834), Appendix, p. 29; Powers, *Letter*, pp. 37–42.

[12] Lewis E. Lawes, *Twenty Thousand Years in Sing Sing* (New York, 1932), pp. 73–74.

[13] DS, 63rd Session (1840), Vol. II, No. 48, p. 210.

[14] DA, 70th Session (1847), Vol. VIII, No. 225, Part 2, p. 74. By this time it had become easier to acquire writing materials because the convicts had been granted permission to correspond with friends and relatives on a limited basis.

convinced that a secret association existed among prison-wise criminals at the latter institution, and that each convict knew the names and antecedents of his keepers and fellow inmates.[15] A group of reformers concluded in 1847 that any interesting information or happening was generally known throughout the penitentiary within twenty-four hours after the event. "We have been assured by an adroit rogue in the Sing Sing Prison," stated a member of this group, "that he could at all times send a message to an acquaintance and get an answer in twelve hours; and that to an entire stranger, whom he had never seen, and who had just been committed, he could do the same thing in three days." [16]

This was but one example of the ways in which Sing Sing was different from its sister institution to the west. Although both penitentiaries theoretically functioned under the same system of discipline, a combination of circumstances produced a more generally stringent—and at times actually cruel—regime at the Hudson Valley prison. A legislative investigating commission noted this in 1833 after interrogating inmates from both institutions. Prisoners at Auburn seemed relatively penitent and testified that they were properly treated, well-fed, and flogged only when they deserved it. Convicts at Sing Sing complained bitterly of unjust beatings and starvation diets. Felons who had served time in both penitentiaries corroborated these statements and told the legislators of violent chastisements at Sing Sing which were frequently administered with wooden staves in place of the ordinary "cat." [17] Another commission reported to the state assembly in 1835 "that there is a manifest difference in the two prisons, in the effect of the discipline, intended to be similar, upon the minds and feelings of the convicts." [18] This contrast was also documented in the same year in an exposé written by an ex-inmate named Horace

[15] Frédéric-Auguste DeMetz, *Rapport sur les Pénitenciers des États-Unis* (Paris, 1837), p. 26.

[16] DA, 70th Session (1847), Vol. VIII, No. 225, Part 2, p. 74, and Part 1, p. 60.

[17] *Ibid.*, 56th Session (1833), Vol. III, No. 199, pp. 9–11.

[18] *Ibid.*, 58th Session (1835), Vol. II, No. 135, Part 1, p. 5.

Lane.[19] In time Sing Sing became known far and wide as a place of unwonted severity and repression.[20]

In part, the difference between conditions at Auburn and Sing Sing was traceable to the personal beliefs of the leaders who administered the two prisons. After Lynds left Cayuga County in 1825 his place was taken by Richard Goodell, a former assemblyman who wanted to restore a degree of mildness in his relations with convicts. Unfortunately, Goodell became seriously ill and was unable to impose effective supervision upon his subordinates, with the result that such scandals as the Rachel Welch beating occurred (cf. p. 94).[21] The Powers regime, which followed in 1826, imposed tighter control over the institution but nevertheless solidified the trend away from sheer coercion. At Sing Sing, however, Lynds held sway until late in 1830 and then handed the reins to his former subordinate, Robert Wiltse. Like his famous mentor, Wiltse rejected the idea of moral suasion and governed chiefly through the use of strong-armed tactics. "The best prison," he once commented pithily, "is that which the inmates find worst." [22]

The abnormal harshness which existed at Sing Sing, however, was also partly attributable to certain special circumstances. One of these was the absence of an enclosing wall, which provided a theoretical justification for great stringency even to such humane observers as Dorothea Dix.[23] The fact that the penitentiary yard was surrounded by buildings on three sides and by the Hudson

[19] Horace Lane, *Five Years in State's Prison* (New York, 1835).

[20] See especially Frederick Marryat, *A Diary in America, with Remarks on Its Institutions* (Philadelphia, 1839), II, 56–57, and James B. Finley, *Memorials of Prison Life* (Cincinnati, 1857), pp. 295–297. Finley was chaplain of the Ohio state penitentiary at Columbus.

[21] JA, 50th Session (1827), Appendix A, *passim;* Allen, *Observations on Penitentiary Discipline,* pp. 26–28, 72–73.

[22] DS, 54th Session (1831), Vol. I, No. 3, p. 7; Guillaume Blouet, *Rapport . . . sur les Pénitenciers des États-Unis* (Paris, 1837), p. 16.

[23] Dorothea Dix, *Remarks on Prisons and Prison Discipline in the United States* (Boston, 1845), p. 18. See also a discussion on the same point in Blouet, *Rapport,* p. 19.

River on the fourth may have convinced economy-minded legislators that an expensive wall was unnecessary, even though felons daily went outside this central nucleus to quarry rock. Whatever the reason, the result was a nagging source of worry to administrators and helped to promote repressive policies. "As there is no wall inclosing the prison," declared an investigating commission in 1839, "the keepers are compelled to put the greater reliance upon the dread of the lash to terrify the convict and prevent his escape." [24] Ironically, this very reaction may have been partially self-defeating in making inmates all the more anxious to get away.

Another circumstance which contributed to harshness and brutality was the prevalence of a belief that Sing Sing's convicts were among the vilest and most dangerous in existence. This attitude was influenced by an argrarian mystique which was common in ante-bellum America. Auburn's inmates might be depraved, but they were nevertheless drawn largely from rural areas and small towns. Sing Sing's convicts, on the other hand, came mostly from the New York City area and represented the riff-raff and offscourings of urban slum conditions which many citizens regarded with horror. These feelings were reinforced by nativist prejudices, for immigrants too destitute to work their way westward clustered in port cities and helped to swell the ranks of urban criminals.[25] The impact of such ideas was obvious in various writings pertaining to the penitentiary on the Hudson. Dorothea Dix believed that Sing Sing's inmates, "coming, as they chiefly do, from the city of New York," were "the most corrupt, the most degraded, most desperate class of prisoners in any prison north of Mason's and Dixon's line." [26] A legislative document published in 1835 mentioned the prevalent assumption "that a greater degree of severity was necessary at the prison at Mount-Pleasant than at

[24] DS, 63rd Session (1840), Vol. II, No. 37, p. 78.
[25] For ante-bellum documents illustrating this nativist attitude, see Edith Abbott, ed., *Historical Aspects of the Immigration Problem: Select Documents* (Chicago, 1926), Section IV, *passim*.
[26] Dix, *Remarks on Prisons*, pp. 16–17.

any other, in consequence of its convicts being generally of a worse character than those of other prisons, from the great number of desperate villains sent there from New-York [City]." [27] Members of a senate committee argued in 1840 that felons at Sing Sing were more difficult to manage than those at Auburn because they came chiefly from the great city and thus included many foreigners or out-of-state desperadoes who had been attracted into the vortex of urban crime.[28]

For various reasons, therefore, the atmosphere at Sing Sing was constantly poisoned by apprehension and terror. Imbued with the worst possible opinion of the men in their custody, knowing that the prison was imperfectly designed for the prevention of plotting and that it contained too many felons to be administered without difficulty, keepers had reason to fear the convicts as much as the convicts feared the keepers. Visitors sensed an air of impending catastrophe. Mrs. Basil Hall, a traveler from England, remarked after touring the institution that "it was some time before I could divest myself of a certain feeling of fear when I found myself surrounded by such a set of wretches. I felt that the physical force was on their side, and that few or none of them felt any moral obligation to desist from doing us any mischief that might be in their power." [29] When Beaumont and Tocqueville visited the penitentiary they experienced the same sensations of dread, and were particularly appalled by the fact that inmates were allowed to work outside the central compound in the absence of a wall. "It is impossible to see the prison of Sing-Sing, and the system of working established there," they stated, "without being struck with surprise and fear. Though the order is perfectly kept, it is apparent that it rests upon a fragile basis. . . . The safety of the keepers is constantly menaced. In presence of such dangers, avoided

[27] DA, 58th Session (1835), Vol. II, No. 135, Part 1, pp. 7–8.

[28] DS, 63rd Session (1840), Vol. II, No. 37, p. 78. For a discussion of ante-bellum attitudes concerning urban crime, see especially David B. Davis, *Homicide in American Fiction, 1798–1860: A Study in Social Values* (Ithaca, N.Y., 1957), pp. 119, 257–265.

[29] Pope-Hennessy, ed., *The Aristocratic Journey*, pp. 32–33.

so skilfully, but with so much difficulty, it seems to us impossible
not to apprehend some future catastrophe." [30] In conversing with
the two Frenchmen, the prison chaplain likened the warden to "a
man who had tamed a tiger that one day may devour him." [31]

Such an atmosphere intensified the determination of penal
officials to break the spirit of the felons in any way possible. Although the many brutal excesses which mar the early history of
Sing Sing are ugly to contemplate, they need not be ascribed to
sheer sadism on the part of the prison staff. Keepers who were
terrified at the prospect of what might happen if the convicts got
out of hand responded by administering severe punishments for
the tiniest infractions of discipline. This, of course, only made
the victims more fearful of the keepers and more bitterly resentful
of the treatment they endured, which in turn increased the potential danger to the officers. The cumulative effect of this re-
ciprocal apprehension gradually filled the penitentiary with greater
and greater amounts of suspicion, anxiety, and hatred.[32]

The very system of government that prevailed at Sing Sing increased the tendency for disciplinary measures to get out of hand.
The loose administrative framework which was so objectionable at

[30] Beaumont and Tocqueville, *On the Penitentiary System*, pp. 26, 156.

[31] George W. Pierson, *Tocqueville and Beaumont in America* (New York,
1938), p. 102. For a contrasting view of the general atmosphere at Sing Sing,
one which is heavily outweighed by the impressions given in a great variety of
other sources, see Basil Hall, *Travels in North America, in the Years 1827 and
1828* (Philadelphia, 1829), I, 31–45 *passim*, and Thomas Shillitoe, *Journal of
the Life, Labours and Travels of Thomas Shillitoe* (London, 1839), II, 388–389.

[32] On the feeling of Sing Sing inmates toward their overseers, see particularly
Marryat, *Diary in America*, II, 56–57, and the interesting bit of convict poetry
in New York Prison Association, *Tenth Report* (1855), p. 105:

> I heer the sound of human futsteps
> Snekeing a Long and very nere
> Hes a Keeper Lurking for me
> O my hart never fear. . . .

> That Keeper's hart is full of vengeance
> He would Like my flesh to tare
> His Looks bespeak his foul intention
> Tho my suferins is not fair.

Newgate had been to some extent rectified by increased concentration of power at Auburn, and by the time Sing Sing was built the pendulum had swung to the opposite extreme of centralized control. At Auburn, the board of inspectors appointed the agent's deputy and all assistant keepers, with every officer's salary being fixed by law. At Sing Sing, the agent was allowed to choose his own staff and was given some latitude in determining matters of compensation. At Auburn, the inspectors resided in the village and took an active part in prison administration. At Sing Sing, the inspectors usually lived at a distance from the penitentiary and allowed the agent to exercise many powers not entrusted to him by law. Visiting was eagerly welcomed at Auburn, and may have acted as a check upon potential brutality; at Sing Sing, it was usually discouraged, though occasionally allowed. Even the duties of the chaplain, an official capable of exerting some moderating influence, were performed differently at the two prisons. At Auburn he was given a room in the penitentiary and normally devoted his entire professional attention to the care of the felons; at Sing Sing he lacked an office as late as 1843 and was sometimes a local village minister who had his own flock to look after, visiting the prison only on a part-time basis. After Powers took over at Auburn, the Sabbath school became a regular feature of the routine, but at Sing Sing it was only intermittently in operation.[33]

The legislature had been warned as early as 1828 that the extreme concentration of power in the hands of the agent at Sing Sing could have dangerous consequences. Officials at Auburn, including Powers, told the state senate that an administrator possessing such authority could "practice the most barbarous oppression with impunity" if he were so minded. Even if he had no such predilections, "the public, so justly jealous of power, may believe him a tyrant, because he has ample means of being so, without

[33] See especially DA, 58th Session (1835), Vol. II, No. 135, Part 1, pp. 5–6; DS, 67th Session (1844), Vol. I, No. 20, p. 229; Brice, *Secrets of the Mount-Pleasant State Prison,* p. 11; Prison Discipline Society, *Fourth Report* (1829), p. 67.

control or exposure." The dependence of subordinate officers upon the whims of their leader for their jobs and salaries, it was pointed out, might render them "mere creatures of the agent's will."[34] Convicts who served time at Sing Sing soon learned that these warnings were prophetic. In the words of Levi Burr, an offender who wrote an account of his sufferings at the institution:

The government of the Sing-Sing prison may be emphatically called, a *Cat-ocracy* and *Cudgel-ocracy;* that is, a Government instituted by a law of a free people, and entrusted in the hands of a single individual, over whose conduct there is no control; a Government whose subjects are denied the power of complaining, and over whom the Autocrat may exercise the power of life and death, without fear of censure or reproach; a Government where the subordinate officers are of that character and class of society, that for a miserable *hire,* they become the servile tools of the Autocrat, and with the Cat and Cudgel in their hands, as the representatives of their master's power, they exercise his pleasure on the subjects of his command, where there is no eye to pity, no tongue to tell, no heart to feel, or will or power to oppose.[35]

Reports of cruelty and corruption began to emanate from Sing Sing by 1828, attaining such proportions by April of that year that Samuel M. Hopkins and George Tibbits went to the institution to conduct a firsthand investigation. Finding preliminary evidence to indicate that the charges were not without foundation, they had scarcely returned home from their tour before Lynds added fuel to the fire by summarily dismissing his chaplain, Gerrish Barrett. Hopkins and Tibbits returned to the prison in July and heard testimony from an assistant keeper named Hitchcock that Lynds had been starving the convicts, defrauding the state on stone contracts, appropriating penitentiary supplies for his own use, and making personal trips at state expense. The commissioners also found evidence that Lynds had been in collusion with a meat contractor, that he had abused Barrett, and that

[34] JS, 51st Session, 2nd Meeting (1828), p. 98.
[35] Levi S. Burr, *A Voice from Sing Sing* (Albany, 1833), pp. 16–17. Italics are Burr's.

he had forbidden inmates to complain of hunger on pain of being flogged.[36]

Hopkins, who had previously defended stringent practices, was genuinely disturbed by this turn of events. He was willing to concede that the head of a prison needed extraordinary powers in order to govern such an institution effectively. On the other hand, he maintained that he and his co-workers had "never advocated such a despotism except in connection with a most effectual plan of inspection and control; with moral discipline also; with religious teaching by a devoted and attentive chaplain; and the whole plan implies, and so our reports state, that the principal should be a man of humanity, morality, and integrity." Without such necessary safeguards, Hopkins declared, he had "never supposed that the system can be, or ought to be, endured in a free country, or in any country." [37]

Convinced that he had misplaced his trust in Lynds, Hopkins now called for the agent's dismissal, but his belated attempts to secure a degree of moderation in penal affairs were unsuccessful. Lynds brazenly fired Hitchcock, and his administration was ultimately exculpated in March, 1831, by a legislative investigating committee whose members declared that the veteran keeper had "in no way impaired his well-earned fame" by his conduct of affairs at the penitentiary. It would be difficult to prove that there had been a whitewash, but as one subsequent analyst has noted, a warden armed with the despotic powers that Lynds enjoyed "could control to an amazing extent the testimony of his subordinates in any public investigation." [38]

Even before the results of the legislative inquiry were published, the tide was running strongly against Hopkins. His fellow prison commissioners, Tibbits and Allen, disagreed with him on the

[36] Prison Discipline Society, *Fifth Report* (1830), pp. 10–17.

[37] Quoted in Orlando F. Lewis, *The Development of American Prisons and Prison Customs, 1776–1845* (n.p., 1922), p. 114.

[38] Prison Discipline Society, *Fifth Report* (1830), pp. 11, 17–18, and *Sixth Report* (1831), pp. 57–58; DS, 54th Session (1831), Vol. I, No. 60, p. 33 and *passim;* Lewis, *Development of American Prisons,* pp. 114–115.

measures that should be taken against Lynds and also believed that their duties had ceased now that the facilities at Sing Sing were nearly complete. By early 1830 they had resigned, leaving their colleague to carry on the fight alone. In a letter to the legislature, Hopkins argued that the welfare of the new institution made it desirable for him to stick to his post until the state investigation had been completed, but a select committee disagreed with him and maintained that the public interest would best be served if he, too, were to retire. By April, 1830, the penitentiary was under an entirely new board whose members were frank in their admiration of Lynds.[39]

Perhaps already knowing that his honor would be publicly vindicated by the forthcoming report of the investigating committee, the controversial warden now decided to take a rest from the responsibilities of penal administration. Much to the regret of his new superiors, who commented that he possessed their "entire confidence and esteem" and lamented his departure as a "public loss," he resigned his position on October 31, 1830. The post was immediately given to his deputy keeper, Robert Wiltse, who headed the institution for almost a decade.[40] With the failure of efforts to keep the dictatorial control of the prison within bounds and with the accession of a complaisant board of inspectors, the way was open for Wiltse to govern Sing Sing as he saw fit. Under his administration, convicts experienced little if any diminution of the harshness characteristic of the Lynds regime.

Unbridled by restrictions such as Powers had imposed upon the use of the whip at Auburn, the keepers at the Hudson Valley penitentiary were permitted to strike inmates with any objects that came to hand. A contractor's agent who had no legal authority to

[39] *Legislative Documents of the Senate and Assembly of the State of New-York,* 53rd Session (1830), Vol. III, No. 255, pp. 1–2; DS, 54th Session (1831), Vol. I, No. 3, p. 7.

[40] DS, 54th Session (1831), Vol. I, No. 3, p. 7; New York State Department of Correction, *Sing Sing Prison,* facing p. 1. According to the Sing Sing *Hudson River Chronicle,* May 21, 1839, Wiltse was actually Lynds's nephew. This may be correct, but I have not found corroboration in other sources.

punish convicts in any way told investigators in 1839 that he had been instructed to knock a prisoner down with the first weapon available if the felon so much as "spoke saucy." The keepers generally carried heavy sticks or canes which saw frequent punitive use; one officer admitted striking convicts over the head with his hickory cane if they did not keep in step when marching, and administering ten or twelve blows to an inmate for smiling or laughing. An especially effective instrument was a heavy wooden rule, usually about two feet long, two inches wide, and half an inch thick. Levi Burr stated that he had often seen one of these "broken and split in pieces" over the head and shoulders of a victim. Burr also told of an incident in which a keeper had taken a lapboard from the hands of an inmate shoemaker and broken it over the convict's head. An officer named John Lent testified that he had seen a prisoner beaten with a broom, and another struck on the head with a barrel stave until the blood ran down his face. Keepers were also known to pummel inmates with their fists or to kick them sprawling to the ground.[41]

The cat-o'-nine-tails was employed often and without mercy. One convict who had menaced a prison official with a stone ax and refused to work was flogged on as many as six different occasions, with each lashing consisting of from fifty to four hundred blows. A keeper who saw the victim's back recalled that "nearly all the skin appeared to be taken off from his neck to his heels, excepting a narrow space across the loins." Nearly every officer in the prison, it seemed, had taken a hand in administering the stripes.[42] Levi Burr charged that he had counted 133 blows given to an inmate on one occasion, "and while the afflicted subject was begging upon his knees, and crying and writhing under the laceration, that tore his skin in pieces from his back, the deputy keeper

[41] DA, 62nd Session (1839), Vol. VI, No. 335, pp. 15, 24, 26, 30–31; DS, 63rd Session (1840), Vol. II, No. 48, pp. 118, 141, 145–147; Burr, *A Voice from Sing Sing*, pp. 18–19, 23, 34; Lane, *Five Years in State's Prison*, p. 13.

[42] DA, 62nd Session (1839), Vol. VI, No. 335, pp. 31, 36, 62; DS, 63rd Session (1840), Vol. II, No. 37, pp. 70–71.

approached, and gave him a blow across the mouth with his cane, that caused the blood to flow profusely." [43] A felon accused of breaking a blacksmith's punch received over one hundred lashes, "with a threat from his keeper that as soon as his lacerated back became *partially* healed, he should receive as many more stripes, unless he would confess the offence with which he was charged." [44]

Excessive severity seems at times to have degenerated into pure sadism. One assistant keeper lashed two convicts with a six-strand "cat," each tail being wound with about three-quarters of an inch of wire. Ugly charges were also made before legislative investigators that an officer had flogged prisoners across the genitals. So pronounced was the mania for flagellation that on one or two occasions keepers were permitted to strip and flog inmates who were just entering prison, "for insults offered to such keepers, or alleged offences committed previous to conviction." [45]

Insane convicts who would not work or could not conform to the rules were subjected to numerous punishments and indignities. Chaplain Jonathan Dickerson, testifying in 1839, told of one demented prisoner who was severely beaten for audibly praying, singing, or lamenting in his cell. This offender eventually found himself unable to endure such treatment any longer, and committed suicide by jumping into the Hudson. Another insane felon had been noticed about the prison area previous to his conviction, clad in feminine apparel. After he became an inmate he was forced to work for a time and then confined to his cell as an idiot. At different times he was beaten with a rattan or cane. A pole was placed near his cubicle, and turnkeys reached through the bars and prodded him with it when he became noisy. He finally died after about a year and a half of imprisonment. One keeper confessed that he had ordered a red-hot poker to be thrust into the cell of a convict who gave definite signs of being deranged. Another

[43] Burr, *A Voice from Sing Sing*, p. 17.
[44] Luckey, *Life in Sing Sing State Prison*, pp. 55–56. Italics are as given.
[45] DA, 62nd Session (1839), Vol. VI, No. 335, pp. 7, 16, 18; DS, 63rd Session (1840), Vol. II, No. 48, pp. 123, 155–156.

officer, acting under a command from the agent, fired a pistol shot through a cell door at an inmate who was later found to be mentally ill.[46]

Critics of the policies adopted at Sing Sing objected not only to the punishments meted out to the felons but also to the manner in which the prisoners were fed. Convicts at Auburn received two meals a day in a common dining hall, but administrators at Sing Sing decided against this for a variety of reasons. Because the criminals under their custody were deemed to be so vicious, it was assumed dangerous to gather them together in a single room where they might rise in a body against their keepers. If forced to eat each meal in their individual cells, they would not be able to communicate with one another or plot against the established order.[47] Throughout most of the ante-bellum period, therefore, inmates at Sing Sing had their rations delivered to their cubicles by kitchen personnel, or marched past a revolving reel which dispensed containers of food as they went to their quarters.[48] Because this system made it difficult to apportion provisions properly among skimpy and heavy eaters, convicts with well-developed appetites were allowed to report to the kitchen for extra rations or to hang the letter "E" above their cell doors as a signal for inmate waiters to leave larger helpings.[49]

Despite such modifications, the cell-feeding system had many disadvantages. It was difficult to keep the wooden food kids clean, and they gradually acquired a sour smell which did not make eat-

[46] DA, 62nd Session (1839), Vol. VI, No. 335, pp. 7, 20, 29, 32, 48, 57; DS, 63rd Session (1840), Vol. II, No. 48, pp. 119–120, 223.

[47] See Prison Discipline Society, *Second Report* (1827), p. 38; DS, 63rd Session (1840), Vol. II, No. 37, pp. 11–12, 66–67, and No. 48, pp. 1–2; Beaumont and Tocqueville, *On the Penitentiary System*, pp. 31–32. Auburn was actually atypical in feeding its inmates in groups. Most prisons, including those in Maine, New Hampshire, Vermont, Massachusetts, and Connecticut, used the cell-feeding method.

[48] See the procedures described in Shillitoe, *Journal*, II, 389, and Burr, *A Voice from Sing Sing*, pp. 24–25.

[49] DS, 57th Session (1834), Vol. II, No. 92, p. 31; DA, 62nd Session (1839), Vol. VI, No. 335, pp. 54–55.

ing from them pleasant. Because they remained in the cells all night after the evening meal, mice and other vermin could prowl about in them. Food served in these containers could not be separated, and was thus poured together in a jumbled, unappetizing mass. A contractor's agent compared the practice to "pouring swill into a trough," and pointed out that it "disgusts . . . the prisoner with his food, and brutalizes the man." If the rations had been waiting long in the kitchen or the cells, they were cold before they could be eaten. In the winter they sometimes froze in the kids before the convicts reached their quarters.[50] A group of penal officials summed the matter up in 1848 by describing the method as "depressing to the mind, brutalizing to the moral feelings, uncleanly, unhealthy, wasteful of provisions, involving an unnecessary expenditure of time, and occasioning a serious depreciation in the value of the services of the convicts." [51] Certainly it accentuated the other dehumanizing features of the Sing Sing discipline.

The administration of the labor system at the Hudson Valley prison also contributed to the animalizing effects of the daily routine carried on there. Convicts worked hard at most penitentiaries, but at Sing Sing they were literally treated like beasts of burden. Prior to 1830, most of them worked in the marble quarries, and even after the institutional economy began to be diversified under Wiltse, the cutting and shaping of stone continued to absorb the energies of many felons.[52] One of the most onerous features of the labor involved was the moving of huge blocks of marble from the excavations to the central prison yard

[50] DS, 63rd Session (1840), Vol. II, No. 38, p. 8, and No. 48, pp. 54, 238; DA, 70th Session (1847), Vol. VIII, No. 225, Part 2, pp. 70, 73–74; Dix, *Remarks on Prisons,* p. 33. Because convicts at Auburn ate their evening meals in their cells, they also experienced some of these hardships.

[51] DS, 71st Session (1848), Vol. I, No. 22, p. 10.

[52] According to Wiltse, not more than 25 or 30 inmates out of a total body of 770 were working at trades other than stone-cutting when he took office in 1830. By the middle of the decade the marble trade had proved undependable, inducing the agent to diversify the system. See DA, 56th Session (1833), Vol. III, No. 199, pp. 20–21; DS, 56th Session (1833), Vol. I, No. 27, p. 9, and 58th Session (1835), Vol. I, No. 8, p. 9.

where the stone shop was located. In this operation the workers used heavy two-wheeled carts with tongues as much as nine feet long. With the tongue in a vertical position, a mass of marble was chained to the axle, after which the inmates used the tongue as a lever and in depressing it caused the stone to be raised off the ground, where it swung back and forth between the wheels. The felons then tried to guide the cart down an incline from the quarry, at the same time maintaining enough pressure on the tongue to keep the load clear of the ground. If the cart gained too much momentum, or hit a rock and overturned, the workers stood a good chance of being maimed. When the stone had been safely deposited in the yard, the prisoners were attached to the cart with harnesses and compelled to drag it back to the quarry. On occasion, when excessively heavy slabs of marble had to be moved, combined teams of men and oxen were employed for the task and the whips of the keepers were applied to the backs of convicts and beasts with little or no differentiation.[53]

Such unmitigated drudgery became almost impossible to bear when "starving times" occurred under a system based in part upon the idea of securing a maximum of output per man with the least possible expense. The scandals of 1828 had indicated that provisions were intermittently in short supply under Lynds, and descriptions of life at Sing Sing by ex-convicts kept the dietary issue alive during the next decade. Horace Lane, a felon who had served time at both Auburn and Sing Sing, told readers he had experienced such hunger at the Hudson Valley prison that he had eaten grass and weeds to keep himself alive. Another former inmate, James Brice, made similar charges in an account of his experiences as a convict under Wiltse, particularly after that agent became his own food contractor in 1836. Most vivid of all was the

[53] Burr, *A Voice from Sing Sing*, p. 30. That this ex-inmate did not exaggerate conditions of labor at the prison is indicated by the report of a legislative commission whose members could not withhold expressions of "deep humiliation" upon witnessing "the treatment of men equal to, if not worse, than beasts of burthen" at Sing Sing in the early 1830's. See DA, 56th Session (1833), Vol. III, No. 199, pp. 11–12.

prose of Levi Burr, who told of eating the roots of shrubs and trees and described prisoners who hid clay under their shirts so that they might carry it into the institution at night and mix it with their mush.[54]

The findings of an investigating commission which visited Sing Sing in 1839 indicated that such accounts were not necessarily far-fetched. Sworn witnesses testified that convicts had been fed "poor and buggy" peas, "old and mouldy" bread, and sour mush. Although food contracts specified that meat and potatoes were to be included in each daily allotment, it appeared that on some occasions the only provisions available had been peas and bread.[55] Even these, if later testimony was correct, may have been in short supply.[56] To be sure, the commission of 1839 was dispatched from Albany by the Whig-dominated state assembly and consisted of men who had no inclination to find anything good in a Democratic prison administration, but the overwhelming mass of evidence which it gathered was difficult to controvert. Even a follow-up investigation conducted by the Jacksonian senate indicated that there had been sporadic suffering from hunger, although it was maintained that this had stemmed from inevitable shortcomings in the cell-feeding system.[57]

From the founding of Sing Sing until the close of Wiltse's regime in 1840, therefore, convict life at the penitentiary was likely to be a phantasmagoria of wretched living conditions, poor food, incessant harshness, and brutalizing drudgery. That defects in the institution's construction, honest convictions about the abnormally depraved nature of the inmates confined there, and other special circumstances made the prevailing stringency under-

[54] Lane, *Five Years in State's Prison*, p. 12; Brice, *Secrets of the Mount-Pleasant State Prison*, p. 60; Burr, *A Voice from Sing Sing*, p. 30.

[55] DA, 62nd Session (1839), Vol. VI, No. 335, pp. 6, 15, 21–22, 25, 27–28, 30, 33, 38, 44–45.

[56] See particularly DS, 63rd Session (1840), Vol. II, No. 48, p. 191.

[57] DS, 63rd Session (1840), Vol. II, No. 37, pp. 66–68. For a detailed account of these investigations and the political circumstances surrounding them, see below, pp. 204–209.

standable did not detract from the tragedies that sometimes ensued. Instead of making a felon more fit for human society than
he had been before conviction, the rigors he experienced were apt
to break him both physically and psychologically. An extreme
example was that of a discharged felon who had entered Sing Sing
"strong, healthy, and of sound mind" at the age of twenty. Twelve
years later he had been so completely institutionalized by the
routine and so mentally debilitated by the treatment he had endured that the chaplain, John Luckey, felt it necessary to escort
him personally to his relatives in New York City. Much to the
amazement of incredulous onlookers, the ex-convict dumbly followed the chaplain through the streets of the metropolis in a
lockstep. Unable to perform even the most common functions
of life without being ordered to do so, he could not so much as eat
in the absence of a specific command from Luckey. The attorney
who had procured the release of this human derelict regretted
having done so. "I did not then know," he expostulated, "that he
had had his brains knocked out at the prison." [58]

Harsh to a degree seldom attained at Auburn, life at Sing Sing
represented the culmination in actual practice of the repressive
philosophy that had come into being in New York following the
War of 1812. In 1840, the situation was to be dramatically changed;
under the leadership of new administrators, the penitentiary that
provided the most unmitigated rigor in the 1830's became the
scene of a significant experiment with new theories of mild correctional treatment. Until then, the Lyndsian outlook prevailed.
Subjected to the tender mercies of men who held that reformation
was delusory and hoped that a policy of extreme intimidation
would terrify potential wrongdoers into abstaining from crime,
the prisoner learned that every fact of existence added up to one
net result: punishment.

[58] Luckey, *Life in Sing Sing Prison*, pp. 109–121.

# Chapter VII

# The Ordeal of
# the Unredeemables

THE pessimism with which many New Yorkers viewed the reformability of the adult felon during the heyday of the Auburn
system reached an extreme with regard to one specific type of
offender: the female criminal. Not until late in the decade of the
1830's did the state provide a type of treatment for such delinquents that did not embody gross neglect and manifest a disposition to put them out of sight and out of mind. Under such
conditions the plight of the female convict was dreadful indeed.
"If there be upon the escutcheon of our State pride and greatness a
stain of reproach deeper than all the rest," asserted a sickened
legislative investigating team that had just visited the women's
quarters at Auburn prison in 1833, "it is our too great neglect of
this class of miserable beings." [1]

Why was the convicted female regarded with a special degree of
aversion and despair? A partial answer to this question could be
found in the unwillingness of American courts to pronounce
women guilty of crime unless they were habitual offenders. Indeed,
the English visitor William Crawford noted that there was a strong
tendency in the United States not even to prosecute women, espe-

[1] DA, 56th Session (1833), Vol. III, No. 199, p. 17.

cially white ones.[2] Beaumont and Tocqueville discovered when they studied American prisons that, comparatively speaking, there were five times as many female convicts in France as in the United States.[3] In 1844, the inspectors at Sing Sing remarked upon the leniency of courts in cases involving women, and argued that for this reason the females who were actually convicted were usually the most abandoned representatives of their sex.[4] In America, therefore, prison was likely to be the end of the road for women too far lost to virtue to offer much hope for redemption.

Popular attitudes toward female prisoners were also deeply affected by a belief that the consequences of delinquency and sin were more dreadful for the woman than for the man. Man had reason; woman depended upon feeling. Man was designed by God for a bold and adventurous existence; woman was created for more quiet pursuits and domestic cares. It therefore followed that a male criminal had acted partly out of an ingrained aggressiveness that was normal for members of his sex. Furthermore, unless he was hopelessly depraved he still had his reason to lead him back to rectitude if he would permit it to do so. The female offender, however, had gone against her very nature. Having thrown aside her natural sentiments and feelings, and lacking the reason that could bring the male delinquent back to decency, she was rudderless and at sea, to be tossed about by any evil temptations that might come her way. Only a miracle could ever restore her to a proper course.[5] Placed upon a pedestal as long as she lived a virtuous life, she was the victim of an inflexible double standard if she fell.

[2] William Crawford, *Report . . . on the Penitentiaries of the United States* (n.p., 1834), pp. 26–27.

[3] Gustave de Beaumont and Alexis de Tocqueville, *On the Penitentiary System in the United States,* trans. Francis Lieber (Philadelphia, 1833), p. 70.

[4] DS, 67th Session (1844), Vol. I, No. 20, p. 29. Reluctance to arrest or convict female delinquents has persisted in the United States into the contemporary era; see especially Otto Pollak, *The Criminality of Women* (Philadelphia, 1950), pp. 3–5.

[5] See especially Beaumont and Tocqueville, *On the Penitentiary System,* Introduction, pp. xiii–xvi, containing the views of Francis Lieber.

This was particularly true if the fall happened to be sexual in nature. Such a lapse blasted all hope of redemption. Beaumont and Tocqueville learned from some American correctional officials "that the reformation of girls, who have contracted bad morals, is a chimera which it is useless to pursue." [6] Staff members at Sing Sing agreed that when a woman stooped to crime her degradation was greater than that of vicious male offenders, and especially so if she had been led into delinquency by prostitution.[7] A chaplain who refused to concede the unreformability of the unchaste female nevertheless held that vice gave her nature "a more terrible wrench" than was true in the case of a man.[8] In the words of one student of ante-bellum social values, extramarital sex brought a woman "a rotting, a decomposition of human virtue and dignity. If a girl had natural warmth and passion, even a single sexual experience made her capable of any crime." [9]

Under the influence of the double standard, and especially if she had been sexually promiscuous, the female convict was a veritable pariah. Many upright citizens believed she was outside the pale of sympathy, and reformers who tried to help her faced great difficulty in overcoming harsh public attitudes.[10] A group of New York prison officials stated the matter tersely in 1844. "The opinion seems to have been entertained," they reported, "that the female convicts were beyond the reach of reformation, and it seems to have been regarded as a sufficient performance of the object of punishment, to turn them loose within the pen of the prison and there leave them to feed upon and destroy each other." [11]

[6] *Ibid.*, p. 123.

[7] DS, 67th Session (1844), Vol. I, No. 20, p. 33.

[8] Bradford K. Peirce, *A Half Century with Juvenile Delinquents* (New York, 1869), p. 95.

[9] David B. Davis, *Homicide in American Fiction, 1798–1860: A Study in Social Values* (Ithaca, N.Y., 1957), p. 160.

[10] See especially DA, 73rd Session (1850), Vol. VIII, No. 198, pp. 233, 240, as well as the remarks of Robert Kelley, later President of the Board of the Society for the Reformation of Juvenile Delinquents, as quoted in Peirce, *A Half Century with Juvenile Delinquents*, pp. 92–94.

[11] DS, 67th Session (1844), Vol. I, No. 20, pp. 32–33.

Despite the persistence of such attitudes, deeply ingrained not only in America but also in the Old World,[12] there existed portents of change. The most significant of these was the work of the great English reformer Elizabeth Fry, who became acquainted with the wretched condition of female convicts in Great Britain when she visited Newgate prison in January, 1813. Even Mrs. Fry and her followers did not believe at first in the likelihood of reforming the miserable women among whom they worked, intending merely to alleviate foul conditions and to instruct unfortunate children who had been jailed along with their mothers. Nevertheless, within five years the reform group had founded an "Association for the Improvement of Female Prisoners in Newgate," set up a school within the prison walls for the women and their children, established a system of industry, and commenced attempts to classify the inmates and to institute "marks" and rewards for the encouragement of proper behavior. The results were surprisingly gratifying. Mrs. Fry and her friends gradually became convinced that even some of the most degraded women could be restored to useful and respectable lives.[13]

It did not take long for accounts of Elizabeth Fry's work to reach America. A notable means of dissemination was provided in 1818–1819 when John Griscom, an educator and philanthropist who belonged to Thomas Eddy's circle of friends, visited Europe. After arriving in England he got in touch with Mrs. Fry, who took him to Newgate to see what had been accomplished there. Griscom was impressed, and became convinced that kind treatment of female offenders could produce desirable results. After returning to America he told of Mrs. Fry's activities in an account of his travels.[14] More important, he joined other prominent New Yorkers in founding the Society for the Reformation of Juvenile

[12] On the widespread existence of similar beliefs in Europe, see William E. H. Lecky, *History of European Morals* (3rd ed., revised; New York, 1894), II, 283–284.

[13] [Katherine Fry and Rachel E. Cresswell, eds.], *Memoir of the Life of Elizabeth Fry* (London, 1847), I, 204–206, 261–262.

[14] John Griscom, *A Year in Europe* (New York, 1823), I, 128–130, 133.

Delinquents, under whose aegis a House of Refuge for young offenders was opened in 1825.

At the House of Refuge, originally located on a pleasant rural tract bounded by what later became 23rd and 26th Streets and 5th and Madison Avenues, a separate building was provided for young female misdemeanants, and efforts were made to reform them. Superintendence of this division was entrusted to a group of benevolent women from some of the most respected families of New York City. Led by Sophia Wyckoff, the wife of an alderman, and Sarah Hawxhurst, sister of a well-known reformer named Isaac Collins, these ladies met frequently with delinquent girls and tried to inculcate moral and religious sentiments within them. A matron was appointed, and a labor system inaugurated.[15] Although the efforts of this department were limited to juveniles, an initial assault had been made upon the idea that errant females were unredeemable. "There has existed in the community, and in the minds of judges and magistrates, doubts as to the success of this department of reform, which our experience by no means justifies," stated a future president of the Society for the Reformation of Juvenile Delinquents some years after the House of Refuge was opened. "We are free to say, that with young girls, not hardened by a long-continued public life of shame, the chances of reformation are quite as good as with boys of the same age."[16]

Even before Griscom and his associates had set up the House of Refuge, the state of Maryland had inaugurated a system of penal discipline for adult female offenders which embodied many of the methods developed in England by Elizabeth Fry. In February, 1822, a matron named Rachel Perijo took over the women's department of the Baltimore penitentiary. Within three years she had established a system of industry, a school, and a religious

[15] Prison Discipline Society, *Second Report* (1827), pp. 83, 85, and *Fourth Report* (1829), p. 83; Peirce, *A Half Century with Juvenile Delinquents*, pp. 74, 92–94.

[16] Remarks of Robert Kelley as quoted in Peirce, *A Half Century with Juvenile Delinquents*, p. 97.

program. A declining incidence of sickness indicated the existence of cleanliness and order, and a drop in recommitments suggested that the new techniques were having a reformative effect.[17] After 1827, Connecticut joined the experiment by subjecting female offenders at Wethersfield prison to the same discipline as was imposed upon male convicts. Beaumont and Tocqueville examined the program, and concluded that the trial had proved the applicability of new penal ideas to the treatment of women.[18]

New York, however, was slow to profit from these examples. At Auburn about five female criminals were committed to the prison each year. Occasionally one of these, like Rachel Welch, might be placed in solitary confinement for disciplinary or health reasons; for the most part, however, such offenders were consigned to an attic room in the south wing and left to themselves. Because the penitentiary was almost exclusively occupied by men, security provisions were strict. Only two passageways led out of the attic compartment. One of these terminated in a stairway at the rear of the prison chapel, where a wooden grating hid the women from the men at the Sunday service. The other led to the administrative hall of the prison by way of the south wing, and was protected by two doors requiring different keys, although by 1832 an additional pair of bolted barriers had been installed. In order to prevent any communication with the men, the windows of the women's quarters were kept closed in all seasons. The result was a dark, stifling, nauseating atmosphere in which as many as thirty women were crowded together without supervision or proper exercise facilities. Once a day a special detail brought necessary supplies and carried out refuse. Occasionally the chaplain or the prison physician put in an appearance, accompanied by the warden or his deputy. Otherwise the unredeemable were in a limbo all their own.[19]

[17] Prison Discipline Society, *First Report* (1826), pp. 34–35.

[18] Beaumont and Tocqueville, *On the Penitentiary System*, p. 39.

[19] Gershom Powers, *A Brief Account of . . . the New-York State Prison at Auburn* (Auburn, 1826), p. 15; JS, 51st Session, 2nd Meeting (1828), pp. 102–103; DS, 55th Session (1832), Vol. I, No. 31, pp. 4–5. The total number of

The effects of such confinement upon women whose sentences ranged up to fourteen years can be but dimly imagined. No attempt was made to separate hardened criminals from young delinquents serving their first terms; little protection was afforded the weak against the assaults of the strong; rarely was segregation imposed upon those afflicted with communicable diseases. Savage fights occurred from time to time, and intermittent shrieks, screams, curses, or gales of boisterous laughter resounded throughout areas adjacent to the south wing.[20] The situation worsened as congestion increased. In 1828, Gershom Powers protested to the legislature that "if any more shall be thrown into this receptacle of wickedness and sin, *physical* as well as *moral* death will be the inevitable consequence." [21]

The policy of calculated neglect could not last forever. Prison officials could not help but worry about the presence of twenty or thirty women living in a building which was also used by men. Rachel Welch's pregnancy provided evidence that foolproof security was hard to maintain. The shrieks and other noises which came from the attic were disturbing to staff members and potentially harmful to discipline.[22] In addition, the male population of the prison was steadily increasing, and it was only a matter of time until it would be necessary to remodel the south wing to create more cell space. Finally, as Powers indicated in 1828, there seemed to be a limit to the number of females who could be jammed into a small area without risking high mortality. By 1832, the situation had become intolerable. The board of inspectors notified Albany that the women's quarters presented "a specimen of the most disgusting and appalling features of the old system of prison

---

women admitted to Auburn from 1817 to 1836 was 101; see Frédéric-Auguste DeMetz, *Rapport sur les Pénitenciers des États-Unis* (Paris, 1837), p. 53.

[20] See especially DS, 56th Session (1833), Vol. I, No. 20, pp. 16–17, as quoted in Beaumont and Tocqueville, *On the Penitentiary System*, p. 230.

[21] JS, 51st Session, 2nd Meeting (1828), p. 103. Italics are as given.

[22] See DS, 56th Session (1833), Vol. I, No. 20, pp. 16–17. Some of the remarks in this source pertain to the situation which existed after new quarters were provided in 1832, but they are equally applicable to the old arrangement.

management, at the worst period of its history." "We know of no subject of legislation," they declared, "which, in our opinion, calls more loudly for immediate action than this." [23]

Such action was forthcoming, in part because of the need for new quarters in which to house male prisoners. In 1832, the south wing was remodeled, and the attic was eliminated in the process. Temporary accommodations were provided for the women by building four large apartments above the prison mess hall, an arrangement which permitted partial separation of the females at night. Without legislative permission, the inspectors instructed the warden to hire a matron, believing that one had become absolutely indispensable. With the appointment of Lucinda Foot, who accepted the position for $16 per month, New York had finally inaugurated some form of supervision over female convicts, even though it had taken a *fait accompli* to do it.[24] The situation was now somewhat better, but some of the old defects remained. The new quarters, like the previous ones, were poorly ventilated; sickness was still prevalent; the male inmates who manned the supply detail might yet find opportunities for unauthorized contact with the women. Chaplain B. C. Smith praised the changes that had been made, but emphasized that the new provisions should be regarded only as temporary. "To be a *male* convict in this prison," he stated, "would be quite tolerable; but to be a *female* convict, for any protracted period, would be worse than death." [25]

While Auburn coped as best it could with the problem of accommodating women, Sing Sing evaded it altogether. At the time Newgate was abandoned there were women in its inmate body who should logically have been transferred to the Hudson Valley institution along with the male convicts, but Lynds and his staff wanted none of this. An attempt was made as early as 1825 to

[23] *Ibid.,* 55th Session (1832), Vol. I, No. 31, p. 5.

[24] DS, 56th Session (1833), Vol. I, No. 20, pp. 4–7; DA, 56th Session (1833), Vol. III, No. 199, p. 17; Clifford M. Young, *Women's Prisons Past and Present and Other New York State Prison History* (Elmira, 1932), p. 4. Despite its title, Young's work contains little more than a bare chronology so far as the ante-bellum period is concerned.

[25] DS, 56th Session (1833), Vol. I, No. 20, pp. 16–17. Italics are as given.

have all women convicted of felonies in New York sent to Auburn, but this brought forth a bitter protest from the inspectors of the latter prison. "A host of such abandoned wretches, from time to time let loose upon our society, to teach lessons of immorality to our youth," they declared, "would be alarming and offensive to the moral sense of this part of the state; while they would sink unnoticed in the diversified character of the dense population of our large cities." The proposal was defeated in the legislature, but its proponents brought it up again in 1827. Once more the Auburn inspectors opposed it vigorously, stating that citizens in their section could not remain silent "while threatened with such a moral pestilence." In the end, the measure failed for the second time.[26]

Defeated in their attempts to shunt an unwanted group of inmates off to Cayuga County, Sing Sing officials managed to get the female convicts in their area farmed out to the Corporation of the City of New York, which provided quarters for them at Bellevue at the rate of $100 per year for each woman.[27] The desire of the state to be rid of these creatures was amply demonstrated in 1834 when the comptroller refused to pay the traveling expenses of some Sing Sing authorities who had been conscientious enough to go to Bellevue to see how the females were doing.[28] A report on the trip had already been made, and the picture it presented was not attractive. The women were "indiscriminately mixed together," and no effort had been made to subject them to a reformatory discipline. No improvement could be expected of them, the report emphasized, as long as they were kept in this manner; "indeed, if any virtuous sentiments linger about the new convict sent to Bellevue, they are sure to be obliterated by the infamy of the character and conduct of those which whom they are associated by their confinement."[29]

[26] JS, 51st Session, 2nd Meeting (1828), p. 102.
[27] DA, 58th Session (1835), Vol. II, No. 135, Part 1, p. 11.
[28] DS, 57th Session (1834), Vol. I, No. 13, p. 4.
[29] Ibid., 56th Session (1833), Vol. I, No. 27, p. 6. Evidence on the treatment of female offenders at Bellevue, however, is confusing. According to a report of the Prison Discipline Society which was published shortly before the criti-

By the mid-1830's the females had worn out their welcome in New York City, which had criminals of its own who needed accommodations. In addition, some of the women sent by the state had proved adept at escape; twelve of them had broken out within a two-day period in 1832 amid a panic over a cholera epidemic. According to the Sing Sing inspectors, the municipal officials considered that keeping the females was "a favor accorded to the State," and wished to be released from their contract.[30] In 1835, a group of commissioners expressed grave concern about what would happen if the city authorities refused to continue the agreement, in which case the women would be "without a *lawful home,* and have to go unpunished or be again hired out to some other person or corporation." [31]

While administrators worried about such problems, the state government was not completely inactive. Gershom Powers had impressed upon DeWitt Clinton late in the 1820's "the lamentable condition of female convicts, and the manifest and gross impropriety of their ever being confined in the same prison with male convicts." [32] The distasteful bickering between Auburn and Sing Sing over the attempt to send all woman prisoners to Cayuga County may also have convinced some leaders in Albany that the situation deserved constructive thought. On April 12, 1828, the legislature appointed commissioners to secure estimates and plans for the construction of a women's prison. These officials submitted two different proposals to the senate in 1829, both of which involved building the new institution on the penitentiary grounds

---

cism quoted above, the women had one fourth of the institution fitted out for them "in a very appropriate manner, with separate dormitories, a pleasant place of worship, a convenient yard, &c." (Prison Discipline Society, *Seventh Report* [1832], pp. 41–42.) Also preplexing is the solicitude displayed by the Sing Sing officials, whose own institution scarcely manifested a rehabilitative bias.

[30] DS, 56th Session (1833), Vol. I, No. 27, Table F, and 57th Session (1834), Vol. I, No. 13, p. 5.

[31] DA, 58th Session (1855), Vol. II, No. 135, Part 1, p. 12. Italics are as given.

[32] JS, 51st Session, 2nd Meeting (1828), p. 103.

at Sing Sing with stone from the marble quarries located there. On the other hand, the commissioners also suggested that it might be a better idea to construct an entirely separate establishment in a different part of the state, possibly near a city or a populous town. The legislature accordingly directed them to see what terms could be secured, and by 1830 several locations had been found in Troy and Utica. All but one of these had been offered gratis. In March of the same year a bill was introduced into the senate to authorize building to begin, but no action was forthcoming.[33]

In the course of the next few years three different approaches to the problem emerged. The inspectors of Auburn prison were happy to endorse a separate institution for females as a means of unburdening themselves of the women under their jurisdiction. Pointing to developments at Baltimore and Wethersfield, they professed to believe that female offenders could be "as easily governed and reclaimed as male convicts." At the same time, they indicated their real convictions in preferring not to have the new prison built at Auburn. Would it not be a gross injustice to their community, they asked, to turn large numbers of female ex-inmates upon it after their discharge from the penitentiary, "and thus flood it with the accumulated depravity of all those sinks of pollution which are common and peculiar to large cities?" Seizing an opportunity to strike back at Hudson Valley officials who had tried to foist female criminals from the metropolitan area upon Cayuga County several years before, the Auburnians suggested that Sing Sing would be a fine location for the new establishment, especially since it was so close to New York City.[34]

The senate committee on state prisons disagreed with this proposal. It would be unwise, the senators declared, to build a women's prison at either of the existing institutions for men. The industrial programs of these penitentiaries would be interrupted to construct the new facilities, and potential economies which might be gained through the use of inmate labor would be

[33] DS, 55th Session (1832), Vol. II, No. 74, pp. 9–10.
[34] Ibid., Vol. I, No. 31, pp. 4–6.

negligible in comparison to the disadvantages involved. Because the employment of female convicts would probably be connected in some way with the needs of the men's prison nearby, there would be opportunities for improper communication between the sexes. Even if such contacts could be prevented, the proximity of the institutions would inevitably have a bad disciplinary and moral effect. The women's penitentiary might also become a mere adjunct to the larger establishment for men, and fall into comparative neglect. It would be far better to build it in a separate locality, such as Albany or its environs, where it could be subjected to careful governmental scrutiny. "In short," the senators declared, "a prison for this class of convicts should be differently organized; the convicts will require a different discipline, different superintendence, different employment, even different food; and the best hopes of successful treatment, seem to depend upon a separate place of confinement, unconnected with either of the other State Prisons." These views, which time would in large measure validate, were informed by a skeptical attitude about the idea of female nonreformability. "Let us not suppose that a woman, however debased or degraded, ever becomes thoroughly hardened," the committee contended in 1833. "Such a being must be as rare as a monster in the physical world." [35]

The inspectors of Sing Sing advocated a third plan. They were reluctant to have all of New York's female criminals placed in their custody, and did not respond favorably to the suggestions of the Auburn officials. "It would undoubtedly be an unpleasant appendage to either of the State Prisons," they observed, "to have one for female convicts connected in any way with the present establishments." This aversion for delinquent women might have prompted the Sing Sing authorities to join forces with the senate prison committee in calling for a separate penitentiary for inmates of this sex except for an even stronger feeling about the necessity for a self-supporting penal system. The senatorial plan,

[35] *Ibid.*, Vol. II, No. 74, pp. 10–11; 56th Session (1833), Vol. I, No. 32, pp. 2–5; and 57th Session (1834), Vol. I, No. 14, pp. 2–3.

the inspectors concluded, would be too expensive. Strange as it may seem, the appointed supervisors of a penitentiary proved to be more solicitous of the taxpayers' interests than a committee consisting of elected lawmakers. Torn between their disinclination to be given the custody of female offenders and their desire to economize, the inspectors showed how firmly exponents of the Auburn system believed in pay-as-you-go penology. They did not want all of the women, but they offered to take some of them.

If there were two regional prisons for women, the inspectors argued, it would cost less to transport inmates to them because of the shorter distances involved. By placing the institutions at Auburn and Sing Sing, the state would escape the necessity of hiring a whole new guard force. The procurement of supplies could also be integrated with the requisitioning of such goods for the men's prisons, with resulting financial savings. It went without saying, of course, that the labor of male convicts could be used in erecting the new facilities if the inspectors' approach were accepted. The possibility of attracting "pious and benevolent ladies" to visit and exhort the erring females (apparently on a voluntary basis and without pay) would be increased if there were two prisons for women rather than one. Keeping the inmates divided into two parts might also make matters easier for the matrons who would have to supervise them. Also, under the inspectors' plan no single city or village would be forced to bear the entire brunt of the moral iniquity which the discharged women would bring back into society after they were released. Obviously, the inspectors did not have much confidence that reformation would take place among the females.[36]

The state thus had three alternatives. It could establish a completely new institution, possibly in the Albany–Troy or Utica area; it could build separate quarters for females at each of the existing state prisons; or it could build a penitentiary for all convicted women at either Auburn or Sing Sing, probably the latter. Each of these suggestions had strong support. In 1832, Governor

[36] *Ibid.*, 57th Session (1834), Vol. I, No. 13, pp. 6–7.

Enos Throop, himself an Auburnian, declared that he favored sending all female convicts to Sing Sing.[37] The senate prison committee stressed the advantages of a site near Troy that provided a state-owned dam for industrial purposes. The legislators also announced that a pair of landowners had offered to donate two acres on the Hudson between Albany and Troy for a penitentiary site.[38] In 1834, a group of businessmen who called themselves the Port Schuyler Company offered to contract for the services of all able-bodied female convicts for ten years. The state would receive one dollar per week for each inmate. The Company would donate the land for the prison, and volunteered to construct the physical plant for a consideration of $23,000.[39]

For various reasons, however, the proposal of the Sing Sing inspectors received more support than the others. It had, of course, an obvious financial appeal. Furthermore, by the end of 1834 it had received the support of Levi Lewis, the agent at Auburn prison. Lewis's arguments, like those of the Sing Sing officials, were based mainly on monetary considerations. It would be possible, he declared, to put up a women's penitentiary on the grounds adjacent to his institution at a great saving to the state, using inmate rather than free labor. The new prison could be supervised by the same officers who headed the penitentiary for men, and the only additional staff members necessary would be a turnkey and two guards. Lewis stressed that if a separate institution were erected elsewhere it would need the services of male custodians to prepare fuel, make repairs, and do other jobs that females could not perform. This added expense could be eliminated at Auburn, and the women could actually provide a service for the men's prison by making, mending, and washing inmate clothing.[40]

The decisive factor that tipped the scales in favor of the Sing Sing proposal was a sudden and apparently inexplicable drop in

[37] DA, 55th Session (1832), Vol. I, No. 2, p. 12.
[38] DS, 55th Session (1832), Vol. II, No. 74, pp. 13–14.
[39] Ibid., 57th Session (1834), Vol. II, No. 84, p. 1.
[40] Ibid., 58th Session (1835), Vol. I, No. 13, pp. 14–15.

the number of female convicts. In 1832, there were eighty; a year later, only sixty-one. By January, 1834, the roster listed only fifty-five, and during the next twelve months there was a further dip to forty-six. At this point the senate prison committee capitulated. "From this unlooked for and very considerable diminution in the number of this class of convicts," the legislators conceded, "it may be doubted whether it would be expedient at this time to hazard the expense, as well as success of a separate prison. So evident the repugance to the proposition has heretofore been manifested by the Senate, from the apprehension of expensiveness without a corresponding benefit, that it will not again be recommended." [41] Obviously, the Sing Sing inspectors and Levi Lewis had not been alone in their desire to settle the female problem as cheaply as possible. Opposition to the Sing Sing plan melted away, and the legislature enacted a law "for the erection of two Prisons for female convicts, one in each of the Prison districts, in the immediate vicinity of the State Prisons." [42]

Sing Sing's victory, however, was more apparent than real. Instead of receiving only female criminals from in and around New York City, and these only because it was considered too costly to set them up in a separate institution, the Hudson Valley prison came to be saddled with the state's entire body of felons of this sex. For this outcome, paradoxically, it had its own prosperity to blame.

Although the new facilities to be erected at Auburn and Sing Sing promised to be more economical in the long run than a separate establishment, their construction involved considerable initial expense, which was to be met as much as possible from the industrial profits of the existing prisons. During the early 1830's, Auburn's inmate workshops had earned moderate surpluses, in contrast to large deficits at Sing Sing. In 1834, however, the picture had changed; Auburn's profits for that year dipped to barely a fourth of those earned by the Hudson Valley prison. Throughout

[41] *Ibid.*, Vol. II, No. 68, pp. 2–3.
[42] Prison Discipline Society, *Tenth Report* (1835), p. 20.

the next two years Sing Sing maintained its lead, and in 1837–1838 it amassed a total surplus of almost $36,000 while its sister institution showed a net deficit of almost $20,000.[43] Under these circumstances it was impossible for officials at Auburn to begin work on a building for female offenders. Even as early as 1836, when the Cayuga County prison was still earning a small profit, its inspectors announced that they could not start construction on account of insufficient funds.[44]

Sing Sing, with its handsome cash balances, was able to start work on its women's prison quickly, inaugurating the project on September 30, 1835. Several months later the foundation had been laid. The inspectors hoped that female convicts could be transferred from Bellevue during the course of the following year, and confidently expected that the work could be completed without aid from the state treasury.[45] The building operations, however, took longer than had been anticipated, for the new prison was not ready to receive its first inmates until June 1, 1839. Meanwhile, officials in New York City had manifested so clearly their unwillingness to keep state felons at Bellevue that these women were removed to Sing Sing in August, 1837, and placed in temporary quarters that had been partitioned off in the main cellblock.[46] As Auburn's financial condition deteriorated, it became clear that the Hudson Valley prison would have to shoulder alone the burden of the new program for women. In 1839, ten female convicts were moved from Cayuga County to Sing Sing. By the end of the year

[43] For comparative earnings in 1830 and 1831 see the Tables in Beaumont and Tocqueville, *On the Penitentiary System*, pp. 280, 282. Figures for 1832–1838 are given in DS, 56th Session (1833), Vol. I, No. 20, pp. 2–3, and No. 27, pp. 1–2; 57th Session (1834), Vol. I, No. 1, p. 6, and No. 13, p. 1; 58th Session (1835), Vol. I, No. 8, p. 1, and No. 13, p. 1; 59th Session (1836), Vol. I, No. 23, p. 1; 60th Session (1837), Vol. I, No. 5, p. 1; 61st Session (1838), Vol. I, No. 7, p. 1; 62nd Session (1839), Vol. I, No. 1, pp. 8–9; DA, 59th Session (1836), Vol. III, No. 133, p. 1; 60th Session (1837), Vol. I, No. 31, p. 1; and 61st Session (1838), Vol. III, No. 186, p. 1.

[44] DA, 59th Session (1836), Vol. III, No. 133, p. 10.

[45] DS, 59th Session (1836), Vol. I, No. 23, pp. 6–7.

[46] *Ibid.*, 61st Session (1838), Vol. I, No. 7, p. 5, and 63rd Session (1840), Vol. I, No. 17, p. 4.

one lone woman remained confined at Auburn, where the warden recommended that henceforth all felons of this sex should be sent to the new facilities.[47]

New York thus—quite by accident—came to have one distinct prison for women. An "imposing marble structure, after the model of a Greek temple, with massive columns," it stood "in a conspicuous place behind, but above all the other prison buildings" at Sing Sing.[48] The new institution, however, occupied a subordinate status. It was under the supervision of the same board of inspectors that managed the penitentiary for men, and its economic affairs were administered jointly with those of the latter establishment. On the other hand, it did have its own internal police.[49] By 1842, its staff consisted of a matron and two female assistants.[50] Within its walls women were to be submitted to a regular discipline, enforced if necessary with the aid of mild corporal punishments.[51]

Such, at least, was the intention. Despite its stately appearance, however, the new institution soon proved defective in many respects. Its very location made for difficulty. "It is near the male prison and between that and the quarry," the inspectors explained in 1844, "so that the male convicts are continually passing around and near it. It is impossible to prevent all intercourse, and convicts of both sexes, are from this cause, frequently tempted to be disorderly and disobedient."[52] The new building had not been provided with any equipment for cooking food, and male waiters had

---

[47] DA, 63rd Session (1840), Vol. I, No. 18, pp. 11, 20.

[48] George J. Fisher, "Ossining," in J. Thomas Scharf, *History of Westchester County, New York* (Philadelphia, 1886), II, 349. For a picture of the institution, see Young, *Women's Prisons*, p. 7.

[49] DA, 70th Session (1847), Vol. VIII, No. 255, Part 2, p. 48.

[50] *Ibid.*, 65th Session (1842), Vol. IV, No. 65, p. 22.

[51] In 1840, matron Isabella Bard admitted allowing female convicts to be struck with "a small rattan over all their clothes." Blows were subsequently forbidden, and such punishments as hair-cropping, the use of mouth-gags, and solitary confinement on stinted rations were employed. See DS, 63rd Session (1840), Vol. II, No. 48, p. 300; 66th Session (1843), Vol. II, No. 10, p. 18; and 69th Session (1846), Vol. I, No. 16, p. 92; Dorothea L. Dix, *Remarks on Prisons and Prison Discipline in the United States* (Boston, 1845), pp. 14–15.

[52] DS, 67th Session (1844), Vol. I, No. 20, p. 30.

to carry provisions to it from the men's prison. This not only increased the chances for communication but was also disadvantageous from a dietary point of view because the food was liable to become cold before the women received it. In addition, male felons were allowed into the new prison to work on industrial equipment, sometimes several days in succession.[53] The women frequently had friends or relatives among the men quartered nearby, and held strong feelings of sympathy for them.[54]

Although the female convicts were to be placed under the silent system at the new institution, it was found that the building was poorly designed to prevent communication between them. In 1844, the inspectors reported that "a continual hum of conversation" was present. Another serious defect was the lack of adequate hospital and nursery facilities for inmates who were pregnant when admitted. The room used for deliveries was badly ventilated, and the mortality rate among babies born there was exceedingly high. During one summer, eight women and five infants were confined day and night in a room eighteen feet square. Scandalized inspectors told the legislature that they "were placed in the shocking alternative of seeing these innocent children perish gradually but certainly, or of procuring the release of their guilty parents before the term of the punishment had half expired." They chose the latter option and secured the pardon of two mothers, but one infant was already dead by the time clemency was extended.[55]

Overcrowding, which must have surprised state officials in view of the previous downward trend of female convictions, was another evil that developed in the new prison. Responsible administrators, however, did not know how to enlarge the existing facilities. The manner in which the building had been constructed made it impossible to add more tiers of cells, and an addition in the rear would put the new quarters so close to the marble quarry

---

[53] *Ibid.*, p. 201.

[54] *Ibid.*, 69th Session (1846), Vol. I, No. 16, pp. 93–94.

[55] DA, 65th Session (1842), Vol. IV, No. 65, p. 44; DS, 67th Session (1844), Vol. I, No. 20, pp. 29, 37–38; Anonymous, "The Rationale of Crime," *United States Magazine and Democratic Review*, XX (January, 1847), 54.

as to endanger lives, besides giving the women a chance to communicate with inmate stoneworkers.[56] Congestion was therefore allowed to mount.

Under such conditions, disciplinary problems became so acute that mild punishments were sometimes abjured in the effort to quell misbehavior. Women were allegedly tied up by the wrists, sometimes for over an hour, in such a manner that their toes barely touched the floor. Handcuffs, stocks, and chains were also used. Despite the use of such devices, it appears that under one matron the convicts actually gained the upper hand. In May, 1843, a riot erupted after an attempt to punish a disobedient inmate. "Ten or twelve other women joined in," stated one account of the episode; "they swore and cursed, and broke benches, spoons, beds, everything they could lay their hands on. The guard was called in, but the women would not obey, and seized things to strike the guard. The whole guard was called in, or as many as could be spared from other duties." A doorkeeper testified that after the convicts had finally been forced into their cells, "they made such a noise as might have been heard in the State House." [57]

Clearly, this was not what the state had bargained for. Instead of behaving well under the new arrangements, female inmates carried knives, fought with one another, and made the air ring with ribald songs and lusty yells.[58] In 1843, less than five years after the penitentiary had been built, the inspectors recommended the construction of an entirely new establishment. Nor was this all; in the very state which had brought the Auburn system into being, these officials advocated that the women be subjected to the arch-rival Pennsylvania plan of complete solitude. They had visited the Eastern State Penitentiary in Philadelphia and, though somewhat fearful that the methods practiced there might produce "the hazard

[56] DS, 67th Session (1844), Vol. I, No. 20, pp. 37–38. See also DA, 71st Session (1848), Vol. I, No. 10, p. 81.

[57] DA, 70th Session (1847), Vol. VIII, No. 255, Part 2, pp. 58–61.

[58] See especially John W. Edmonds, *A Letter, from John W. Edmonds, One of the Inspectors of the State Prison at Sing Sing, to General Aaron Ward* (New York, c. 1844), pp. 25–26.

of stultifying the mind," they regarded this as preferable to "the certainty in our prison, of corrupting the heart and destroying the moral sense." [59] Several years later the matron of the New York institution also called for the construction of a new women's penitentiary. The ventilation of the existing structure, she contended, was poor; the hospital, kitchen, and laundry were badly designed; and it was dangerous to have a women's prison so close to one for men.[60]

By the late 1830's, therefore, New York had been forced to abandon its previous policy of virtually complete neglect with regard to female criminals. This, however, did not come about because of any great concern for the needs of the women themselves. It is abundantly clear that neither Auburn, Sing Sing, nor Bellevue wanted to accommodate a class of felons who were supposedly beyond all hope of redemption. The attempt to consign them to limbo at Auburn had simply created practical problems too great to be permanently ignored, and the need to create more space for male inmates finally dictated a change. Sing Sing's policy of sending female convicts to Bellevue was abrogated only because New York City officials were reluctant to continue this arrangement.

When the need for a new approach thus became too pressing to evade, the problem of what to do next was resolved primarily on the basis of financial considerations. Only the senate prison committee, whose members did not share the prevalent idea of female irreclaimability, showed an awareness that other criteria were relevant. The decision to build new facilities for women at each of the existing prisons for men was finally made because this solution appeared cheaper in the long run than the alternative of constructing an entirely separate penitentiary. The fact that Sing Sing ultimately became the location of the only women's prison in the state was accidental, but again attributable to financial circumstances. It soon became apparent, however, that New York had sacrificed

[59] DS, 67th Session (1844), Vol. I, No. 20, p. 34.
[60] DA, 71st Session (1848), Vol. I, No. 10, pp. 81–82.

much because of its preoccupation with economy. Less than five years after the new prison had been built, its inadequacies and faulty location had prompted its own board of inspectors to ask that it be abandoned in favor of another establishment to be constructed on radically different lines. Anything seemed better than the riot-torn institution at Sing Sing. Poorly designed and difficult to alter, the Greek temple overlooking the Hudson was an example of penny-wisdom and pound-foolishness.

Nevertheless, some gains had been made. Bad as the new women's quarters were, they were still better than the ones the state had provided before. Matrons had been appointed; there was a measure of discipline, however faulty, that had been lacking in the days of the south-wing attic at Auburn; productive employment was now possible; above all, women had been recognized as fit subjects for separate penal care. The new situation, however defective, offered an administrator with talent, vision, and courage a chance to attempt badly needed reforms. In 1844, the state was to find such a leader in a woman named Eliza W. Farnham, and a brief but significant experiment in penology was to result.

# Chapter VIII

# Prisons, Profits, and Protests

AN intense preoccupation with financial considerations, so obvious in the determination of policies involving New York's female convicts, was also very apparent in the development of the state's prison industries under the Auburn system. One of the basic differences between this mode of discipline and the rival method used in Pennsylvania lay in the emphasis which supporters of the congregate plan placed upon output and revenue.[1] As we have seen, the rapid adoption of the Auburn system in many states was due in no small measure to the desire of economy-minded legislatures to exploit convict labor. So pervasive was this attitude in many parts of the Union that the English visitor William Crawford believed it outweighed any other penological considerations in the public mind.[2]

Prison officials in the Empire State were under constant pressure to make their institutions pay. Louis Dwight, the leading champion of their system, believed that something was radically wrong if a penitentiary did not at least break even financially.[3] In 1833,

[1] On the Pennsylvania attitude see especially Harry Elmer Barnes, "The Economics of American Penology as Illustrated by the Experience of the State of Pennsylvania," *Journal of Political Economy*, XXIX (October, 1921), 618, 628–629, 638–641.

[2] William Crawford, *Report . . . on the Penitentiaries of the United States* (n.p., 1834), p. 24.

[3] Prison Discipline Society, *Second Report* (1827), p. 33.

a legislative committee took Auburn and Sing Sing to task for failing to earn profits as large as those garnered by prisons in Massachusetts and Connecticut, contending that the New York establishments could produce an annual revenue of $70,000 if proper efforts were made.[4] In the words of a document published in the following year by the state assembly, "no probable means should be left untried" to make the prisons self-supporting.[5] The eminent jurist Ambrose Spencer warned a short time later that "a permanently heavy charge upon the virtuous and industrious citizens" for the maintenance of penitentiaries "might beget such a disgust as to work a change in our ameliorated code, and might reintroduce a code much more sanguinary." [6]

Although Auburn gained some revenue from its flourishing tourist trade and Sing Sing earned a dollar here and there by carefully saving and selling old bones, swill, and empty barrels, both prisons made most of their money from the income of their workshops. These, by and large, were run on the contract system under the terms of the law which had abolished the state-account method in 1817. Private entrepreneurs were to bring raw materials to the prison, pay fixed charges for the use of inmate workers, and market the finished goods at their own risk (cf. p. 44).[7]

One of the main tasks confronting penal administrators under this system was that of finding businessmen who were willing to put their raw materials in the hands of convicts. This was not always easy. At Auburn the problem was not especially acute from 1816 to 1823, for most of the inmates were kept busy constructing the physical plant. During these years the prison did turn out small

---

[4] DA, 56th Session (1833), Vol. III, No. 199, pp. 15–16.

[5] *Ibid.*, 57th Session (1834), Vol. IV, No. 352, p. 16.

[6] *Ibid.*, 58th Session (1835), Vol. II, No. 135, pp. 63–64.

[7] Under this system the state was basically collecting wages for the services of its convicts, and it is thus only figuratively that one can speak of its earnings as profits. Because the voluminous records of the payments which the prisons received have no actual relation to the worth of the goods produced, it is difficult and in most cases impossible to determine the quantity or value of the wares which were turned out.

quantities of goods for individual villagers, but in so doing it became involved in a multitude of petty accounts and secured little
in the way of dependable income. When a concerted effort was
finally made to interest local entrepreneurs in large-scale contracts,
progress was slow. Cayuga County merchants were fearful of what
might happen to their raw materials, wary of public prejudice
against the finished products, and skeptical about the chances for
profit.[8] Their pessimism was undoubtedly increased by the attitude
of Elam Lynds, who believed that contact between businessmen
and convicts would impair discipline and therefore wanted to keep
contractors from actually supervising the manufacturing processes.[9]

Prison officials finally had to make two concessions in order to
attract bids from the entrepreneurs. First, they offered low labor
rates, hoping to raise the terms if and when the merchants found
prison industry profitable. Second, they reluctantly admitted contractors into the shops, stipulating that they were never to speak
to the convicts but to transmit all instructions through the keepers.
After the administrators had yielded on these points, the industrial program finally got off the ground. By 1826, almost a dozen
contracts had been consummated at Auburn, involving such crafts
as coopering, tailoring, shoemaking, weaving, toolmaking, and
rifle-manufacturing.[10]

It was already obvious that the contract system would create
problems in relations between officials who wanted to keep outsiders away from convicts and businessmen who naturally wanted
to oversee production. The situation was also complicated by the
fact that the prison administrators imposed labor on the inmates

[8] DA, 57th Session (1834), Vol. IV, No. 341, pp. 2–3; Gershom Powers,
*A Brief Account of . . . the New-York State Prison at Auburn* (Auburn, 1826),
p. 25.

[9] See Gustave de Beaumont and Alexis de Tocqueville, *On the Penitentiary
System in the United States,* trans. Francis Lieber (Philadelphia, 1833), p. 36.
Thomas Eddy shared this view, and told George Tibbits, Stephen Allen, and
Samuel M. Hopkins that "no contractor should be allowed to enter the prison,
or to have any intercourse whatever with the convicts." (Samuel L. Knapp,
*The Life of Thomas Eddy* [New York, 1834], pp. 88–89.)

[10] Powers, *Brief Account,* pp. 25–29, 81–82.

for a variety of reasons which could not always be reconciled in practice. The overriding concern, of course, was to defray institutional expenses or to achieve actual financial surpluses. Some officials, however, also looked upon the industrial program as a potential force for rehabilitation, through which prisoners could acquire skills and steady habits.[11] Finally, as opponents of the Auburn system pointed out from time to time, work could be imposed as a punishment in itself.[12]

In the final analysis, administrators found it necessary to stress certain objectives at the expense of others. Quite naturally, they generally placed emphasis at the point on which the interests of taxpayers, prison officers, and contractors converged, namely that of monetary return. When they compromised with what they believed to be the best disciplinary interests of the penitentiary by allowing contractors to enter the inmate workshops, officials at Auburn foreshadowed how they would respond to similar problems in the future. By 1828, they had discovered that some of the keepers did not know enough about the work being carried on under their supervision to transmit information effectively from contractors to convicts. In such cases, the businessmen or their assistants were allowed to communicate directly with the prisoners, although it was stipulated that this should take place only on a limited basis.[13] The moral was clear: output and profit were the primary goals, regardless of possible penological objections.

As taxpayers, administrators, and entrepreneurs pursued their respective economic objectives, the inmate became a living machine. His task was to produce or he would feel the sting of the lash. If he learned habits of industry and obedience, he secured such lessons at the cost of becoming a robot and a slave. Because financial considerations were paramount, rehabilitation was a mere

[11] See Prison Discipline Society, *Second Report* (1827), pp. 34–35; DA, 58th Session (1835), Vol. II, No. 135, p. 14, and Vol. IV, No. 330, pp. 3–4.

[12] DA, 60th Session (1837), Vol. III, No. 169, p. 2; Anonymous, "The Cost of Penitentiary Punishment," *Pennsylvania Journal of Prison Discipline and Philanthropy,* IV (July, 1849), 115.

[13] JA, 51st Session (1828), Appendix A, pp. 19, 26.

by-product if it occurred at all. Even the spatial distribution of convict workmen could become penologically harmful if it suited the purposes of a contractor to put a hardened criminal and a youthful offender side by side at the same bench.[14]

Whatever its merits or defects, the contract system became well established at Auburn. During the ante-bellum period the prison turned out such items as footwear, barrels, carpets, cotton ticking, carpenters' tools, steam engines and boilers, combs, harnesses, furniture, and clothing.[15] Some of these products were marketed locally; others were sold in various parts of the Union, in Canada, or even in Latin America. Light wares often found their way into the packs and carts of itinerant peddlers who hawked prison-made brooms, clocks, tools, barrels, buckets, and saddle-trees up and down the countryside from one farmhouse to another.[16]

Sing Sing's principal industry in the early years—indeed, its chief *raison d'être*—was stone-cutting. Out of its quarries came marble for Grace Church on Broadway, the Albany City Hall, the United States Subtreasury Building in New York City, New York University, and many fine residences. Even rubble had a market; the Camden and Amboy Railroad purchased large quantities of it for use in laying the roadbed of its line from New York City to Philadelphia.[17] In the 1830's, however, Robert Wiltse tried to lessen the prison's dependence upon the stone industry after suc-

[14] For a particularly trenchant criticism in this regard, see John Luckey, *Life in Sing Sing State Prison, as Seen in a Twelve Years' Chaplaincy* (New York, 1860), p. 198. The practice, however, was not solely a fault of the industrial situation. As we have seen, the belief that convicts should not be differentiated was a basic tenet of the Auburn system itself.

[15] The variety of Auburn's products is well illustrated in DS, 64th Session (1841) Vol. II, No. 28, p. 7, and No. 54, pp. 14–15.

[16] Powers, *Brief Account*, p. 28; DS, 64th Session (1841), Vol. II, No. 54, pp. 14–15; Ralph S. Herre, "A History of Auburn Prison from the Beginning to about 1867" (unpublished D.Ed. dissertation, Pennsylvania State University, 1950), p. 136.

[17] DA, 57th Session (1834), Vol. I, No. 13, pp. 61, 64, 66, 68, and No. 288, p. 5; George J. Fisher, "Ossining," in J. Thomas Scharf, ed., *History of Westchester County, New York* (Philadelphia, 1886), II, 323.

ceeding Lynds as warden, and other products became important. Inmates made barrels, boots and shoes, hats, locks, silk, chairs, brassware, tools, and other goods.[18] Contractors found outlets as far away as the West Indies, which furnished a market for molasses hogsheads.[19]

Prison-made goods were turned out under a variety of arrangements. State law gave agents considerable discretionary authority in negotiating with businessmen, and in some cases the agreements which were concluded were merely verbal.[20] Because Sing Sing owned the raw materials upon which the stone trade was based, this industry was carried on under the state account system.[21] In other cases, however, the contract method typically prevailed. In addition to providing the materials to be worked up, the entrepreneur usually furnished machinery, tools, and fuel. He also agreed to pay the state varying fees for the services of the convicts, depending upon the level of skills possessed by different inmates. Although most rates were calculated on a daily basis, piecework contracts were sometimes negotiated in such trades as coopering, blacksmithing, tailoring, and shoemaking.[22] When the latter type of arrangement prevailed, it was in the best financial interest of the prison to get a maximum of production from the inmates; under stated daily rates it was the contractor who stood to gain from an exploitative policy. Legislative investigators noted that businessmen who paid on a daily basis tended to drive the prisoners, offering them unauthorized inducements to better work or influencing the keepers to inflict severe punishments in the hope of increasing output.[23]

[18] For a representative list, see DS, 64th Session (1841), Vol. II, No. 42, p. 2.
[19] DA, 58th Session (1835), Vol. II, No. 135, Part 2, p. 14.
[20] Ibid., Vol. II, No. 106, p. 3, and 61st Session (1838), Vol. V, No. 276, p. 4.
[21] Ibid., 56th Session (1833), Vol. III, No. 199, pp. 12–13, and 58th Session (1835), Vol. II, No. 135, Part 1, p. 29.
[22] Ibid., 57th Session (1834), Vol. IV, No. 288, pp. 2–4, and No. 289, pp. 1–6; 58th Session (1835), Vol. II, No. 135, Part 1, pp. 36–38, 45–47, 49; and 70th Session (1847), Vol. VIII, No. 231, pp. 1–2.
[23] Ibid., 58th Session (1835), Vol. II, No. 135, Part 1, p. 22.

The contractor frequently had reason to be calculating and ruthless. He had to agree to take a certain number of inmates for a definite period of time; if general business conditions then got worse he could not lay these workers off as he would have been free to do with ordinary operatives. He had to relinquish part of each day for hospital calls and the distribution of clothes. Under strict administrators he had to give his orders and instructions in a clumsy and roundabout manner. His workers were likely to be substandard; many of them had practiced no trade before commitment, others were diseased or crippled, and all came from a criminal past.[24] There was always a chance that they might riot, spoil their materials, or set fire to the shops at the first favorable opportunity. In addition, many lines of work turned out to be unsuited to the peculiar conditions and levels of competence ordinarily found in a penitentiary. By 1834, the list of ventures which had been tried and found unsuitable in this regard included gunsmithing, the production of wagons and sleighs, the making of threshing equipment, and the manufacture of buttons.[25] In short, prison industry was a tricky business, and not everyone could succeed in it.

If a contractor were sufficiently clever, however, he could make money under the contract system. The prison workshop was actually a crude factory which sometimes employed hundreds of men. The entrepreneur paid no rent for his physical plant, and sometimes received his water power gratis. The labor force, despite all its shortcomings and dangerous propensities, was under the strictest type of industrial discipline. If a contractor owned a business on the outside, he might be able to integrate his prison activities with it, assigning to the inmates such tasks as were suited to their capacities and saving the more difficult operations for free workers. At Sing Sing, for example, some prisoners made only

[24] See especially *ibid.*, 57th Session (1834), Vol. IV, No. 341, p. 13, and 78th Session (1855), Vol. IV, No. 85, pp. 14, 299; DS, 65th Session (1842), Vol. II, No. 39, p. 21.
[25] DA, 57th Session (1834), Vol. IV, No. 341, pp. 10–11.

chair-bottoms; the other parts were turned out elsewhere. Some felons working in the shoe shops merely attached soles to uppers which had been made outside the penitentiary. At the Sing Sing hat shop, convicts stiffened and put plush on headwear produced in New York City by free artisans.[26] Thus the entrepreneur could gain whatever profits were attainable through subdivision of labor.

Because the financial data which appeared in prison documents related mainly to the labor fees which contractors paid the state and had little or no relevance to the value of goods produced, the ultimate prices at which they were sold, or the nature of the businessman's investment in raw materials, it is impossible to gain any clear idea of the profits which could be earned in penal industry. In 1842, however, one legislative document did estimate the value of the merchandise turned out in certain Auburn workshops, without specifying whether these were wholesale or retail figures, and presented data on some of the investments involved. Although profits cannot be calculated from this information, because the mere fact that goods are attributed a certain value does not indicate that they were actually sold at such prices, it would seem that some contractors carried on a lucrative business. One Josiah Barber, proprietor of the carpet shop, listed his total investment in raw materials and equipment at $35,000 and his labor payments to the state at $7,560.51. He estimated that the merchandise produced in the shop was worth $60,317.45. Information given by three other contractors also revealed that the value of the products manufactured in their shops during 1841 exceeded their total outlay for equipment, raw materials, and labor, and in one of these cases the margin was substantial.[27]

It is considerably easier to calculate the financial performance of prison labor from the state's point of view than it is to estimate

[26] *Ibid.*, 58th Session (1835), Vol. II, No. 135, Part 2, pp. 10, 19–20, 25.

[27] *Ibid.*, 65th Session (1842), Vol. II, No. 31, p. 7, and Vol. IV, No. 65, pp. 24–31. The figures given in Document No. 31 cover labor payments to the prison, and are based upon a fiscal rather than a calendar year. This may create a minor distortion, but the labor fees were stipulated in long-term contracts and thus had a tendency to be relatively stable.

the returns secured by contractors. From 1825 through 1829, Auburn's institutional expenses exceeded shop revenue by more than $36,000. Beginning in 1830, however, the picture brightened, and for seven years the penitentiary earned small annual surpluses aggregating slightly over $29.000. Deficits of about $10,000 each appeared in 1837 and 1838, but the prison then achieved three years of modest profits totaling more than $12,000. Although the record for this entire seventeen-year period showed a net deficit of about $14,500, the fact that Auburn's earnings had exceeded its expenses by over $21,000 since 1829 gave New York taxpayers cause for gratification.

Sing Sing's industrial program, like that of Auburn, failed in its early years to meet institutional costs. Indeed, from 1829 through 1832, the Hudson Valley prison's total deficit amounted to more than $93,000, making Auburn's figures look pale by comparison. Once the Sing Sing shops were well established, however, the prison made rapid financial progress. As convicts suffered periodic hunger and endured the harsh disciplinary measures of Robert Wiltse, there was a succession of annual surpluses. From 1833 through 1841, earnings exceeded expenses by more than $94,000, thus completely erasing the deficit accumulated in the earlier period. In addition, the institution had managed to undertake the building of a women's penitentiary, giving the state an additional monetary saving. Measured by the criterion of self-support, Sing Sing was at this point a distinct success.[28]

During the 1830's, therefore, the prisons of the Empire State provided an outstanding example of governmental frugality, performing an essential service at little or no cost to the public treasury. Such economy blended well with Jeffersonian and Jacksonian principles, encouraged advocates of the Auburn system, and spared the taxpayer. The type of penal industry which made it possible,

[28] For documentation on the earnings and expenses of New York prisons from 1825 through 1838 see above, p. 172, fn. 43. For figures on the years 1839–1841, see DS, 63rd Session (1840), Vol. I, No. 1, p. 3; 64th Session (1841), Vol. I, No. 1, p. 6; and 65th Session (1842), Vol. II, No. 39, p. 3; DA, 65th Session (1842), Vol. II, No. 31, pp. 7–9.

however, did not find favor among all citizens. In particular, the prison workshops were bitterly criticized by many free artisans who in time succeeded in obtaining restrictive legislation against what they regarded as unfair competition. These efforts, together with the activities of reformers who opposed prevailing penal methods for other reasons, helped to usher in a new phase in the development of the penitentiary system in New York.

The busy convict shops of Auburn and Sing Sing, however small and inefficient, were nevertheless similar to many factories springing up throughout the northeastern states and in other parts of the country. In both types of establishment a relatively numerous and well-disciplined labor force was employed at low rates of compensation under a system in which machinery, repetitive processes, and subdivision of effort were frequently used in order to minimize the necessity and importance of skill. In both cases this spelled trouble for many free craftsmen and other artisans who did business on a small scale, felt a strong vested interest in whatever skills they possessed, and doggedly resisted economic trends which were gradually converting them from petty capitalists into members of a wage-earning industrial proletariat.

Because they were both smaller and less numerous than the privately owned factories which they resembled, the convict workshops actually posed far less of a threat to free craftsmen than the factories did. Indeed, the testimony of an Auburn agent in 1834 suggests strongly that the prison shops were having a hard time competing with factories in New England which were flooding the Empire State with inexpensive goods.[29] Nevertheless, prison industry had certain attributes which made it a convenient scapegoat for the troubles of workingmen. These characteristics involved the nature of the labor force employed in penal workshops, the terms and conditions under which the prisons awarded contracts to entrepreneurs, the nature of the relationship between the businessman and the state which was involved in the contract system, and the way in which the existence of convict industry in given

[29] DA, 57th Session (1834), Vol. IV, No. 341, pp. 5–6, 8, 17–18.

trades intensified the status anxieties of craftsmen and artisans.

Because the felon had always been a social pariah, it was possible for the free workman to brand goods produced by criminals with a moral stigma which could impair their market value. Artisans in New York quickly discovered that the term "state prison" might have such an odious connotation in the mind of the consumer that he would be wary of buying merchandise coming from such a source. As early as 1801, protests by free shoemakers against the production of footwear at Newgate resulted in a law requiring all boots and shoes made there to be marked so that their origin could be identified.[30] In addition, it was possible for the small producer to cast aspersions upon any cheap goods which undersold his own wares by referring to the former as "prison-made," whether this was or was not actually true. During the 1830's, penitentiary officials in New York circulated questionnaires throughout the state, asking people to identify the prison-made goods which were injuriously affecting trade in their communities. Forty-one replies complained of articles which, according to the administrators, were not made in prison at all. Twenty-seven of these mentioned competition from prison-made chains, when in fact neither Auburn nor Sing Sing had produced chains in years.[31]

The penal labor system proved vulnerable to attack not only because of public antipathy toward criminals but also because the details of contracts and the manner in which such agreements were consummated sometimes smacked of monopoly and special privilege, thus arousing deep concern among citizens imbued with Jacksonian attitudes about the evil nature of such practices.[32] Successful prison contractors desired long-term agreements; penitentiary administrators wanted to avoid frequent changes in personnel which might have an unsettling influence among the convicts, and were

---

[30] Orlando F. Lewis, *The Development of American Prisons and Prison Customs, 1776–1845* (n.p., 1922), p. 48.

[31] DS, 58th Session (1835), Vol. I, No. 13, *passim*.

[32] See especially Walter Hugins, *Jacksonian Democracy and the Working Class* (Stanford, Calif., 1960), pp. 155–161.

especially eager to retain entrepreneurs who could be counted upon to observe prison rules faithfully.[33] Some contracts therefore became virtually self-perpetuating despite the existence of legal provisions which theoretically threw them open to periodic competition. In 1833, for example, the agent at Auburn prison admitted that he did not advertise for bids on contracts, stating that he felt it unfair to displace a satisfactory entrepreneur just because someone else offered to pay higher labor fees to the state.[34] If a businessman received special privileges regarding the use of water power, the employment of inmates on Sundays to repair machinery, or the utilization of extra shop space, this afforded all the more room for popular criticism. In short, there was some basis for the arguments of free craftsmen who complained that prison industries were monopolized by favored contractors.[35]

A system involving what amounted to a partnership between the state and various merchants also ran afoul of a rising tide of *laissez-faire* sentiment in the Jacksonian era.[36] To many free workmen the prison shops constituted an example of unwarranted governmental participation in economic life. One group of artisans revealed this conviction clearly when they claimed that "a competition is going on, in which the whole resources of the State are enlisted against the mechanic." [37]

Finally, and perhaps most important, penal industry served to exacerbate the feelings of workers who felt themselves slipping down the social scale. To the pain of becoming a mere wage-earner was added the outright humiliation of being thrust into competition with felons, traditionally the very dregs of humankind. Throughout the large assortment of petitions, reports, transcripts of hearings, and other official documents received and

[33] See for example DA, 57th Session (1834), Vol. IV, No. 341, pp. 14–15.
[34] *Ibid.*, 58th Session (1835), Vol. II, No. 135, Part 2, pp. 28–29.
[35] *Ibid.*, 57th Session (1834), Vol. IV, No. 352, pp. 31–33.
[36] With regard to the *laissez-faire* aspects of Jacksonianism see particularly Richard Hofstadter, *The American Political Tradition and the Men Who Made It* (Vintage ed.; New York, 1954), Chapter III.
[37] DA, 57th Session (1834), Vol. IV, No. 352, p. 30.

published by the New York legislature in its attempts to deal with the problem of prison industry during the Jacksonian period, a persistent theme appears again and again: that labor was degraded by being made a part of the punishment of criminals. This feeling was so widespread that a minority report written by members of an assembly committee in 1837 called it "the grand secret of the dissatisfaction abroad." [38]

The social consequences of convict labor, however, seemed to the free artisan to go beyond the mere stigmatization of honest work in an abstract sense. After inmates had served out their time in prison, they sought to pursue in everyday life the trades they had learned behind bars. Thus the ranks of free workingmen were infiltrated by ex-felons and the status of labor was even further demeaned in the eyes of society. Fearful of the humiliation involved in becoming associated with anyone who had been attainted by crime, many artisans harbored a flinty determination to bar all former inmates from their trades. In response to the questions of legislative investigators, they indicated repeatedly that they would not hire anybody with a known prison record. One witness told an assembly group that it was "a uniform practice among all the respectable mechanics of [New York City] to refuse to employ discharged convicts in their mechanical business." [39] In 1846, a group of reformers who tried to help ex-inmates find jobs described the case of a Sing Sing dischargee who had once been a resident of Lancaster County, Pennsylvania. Although he secured a letter of recommendation from James Buchanan, at this time Secretary of State, he could not find employment in New York. "If, with such recommendations, the discharged convict cannot obtain confidence," the reformers asked, "what can those expect who have no friends?" [40]

[38] DA, 60th Session (1837), Vol. III, No. 169, p. 2. See also *ibid.*, 58th Session (1835), Vol. II, No. 135, Part 2, p. 40, and Vol. IV, No. 330, pp. 14–15; 63rd Session (1840), Vol. VIII, No. 339, pp. 2–3; 64th Session (1841), Vol. V, No. 186, pp. 6–7; 65th Session (1842), Vol. IV, No. 65, pp. 60, 62–65, 67, 69, 72, 75, 78, 102; and 66th Session (1843), Vol. VI, No. 156, pp. 2–3; DS, 64th Session (1841), Vol. III, No. 91, pp. 6–8.
[39] DA, 58th Session (1835), Vol. II, No. 135, Part 2, pp. 40, 41, 44, 54, 57, 59.
[40] *Ibid.*, 70th Session (1847), Vol. VIII, No. 255, Part 1, pp. 92–93.

Animated by various fears and resentments, workingmen and their supporters not only made it exceedingly difficult for ex-inmates to make a successful transition into free society but also helped to propagate attitudes and beliefs which sustained the policies of such men as Lynds and Wiltse. In 1834, for example, some legislative defenders of the workingman declared that it would be a great mistake to welcome the former offender back into society with open arms. In the first place, it would reduce the exemplariness of his punishment; in the second, it was not to be expected that a criminal could ever change into a useful citizen. Efforts to reform the knaves at Auburn and Sing Sing were fanciful. "That there is more joy in Heaven over one sinner that repenteth, than over ninety-and-nine just men made perfect," the legislators argued, "is a sublime and beautiful idea, but of too refined a character to be adopted as a safe rule of conduct in the administration of criminal law among men. It is only adapted to those ethereal regions where a perfect knowledge of the human heart does not depend upon the result of experiment." [41]

Refusal to work with ex-convicts was but one way in which artisans vented their animosity toward the penal labor system. Two types of action were exemplified in 1830 by New York City stone-cutters who were aggravated by the use of granite pillars and stonework from Sing Sing in the construction of new buildings. After going on strike and finding this to be unavailing, they marched to a site where prison-cut stone was being used, ordered the masons to stop work, and made threats. Police intervention was necessary to restore order.[42] The most common way in which free workers fought the prison shops, however, was in exerting group pressure upon the legislature for the passage of restrictive laws. In 1833, for example, the newly formed General Trades' Union of New York City and Vicinity listed convict labor as one of its targets.[43] In 1834, various groups of artisans scattered throughout the state held

[41] *Ibid.*, 57th Session (1834), Vol. IV, No. 352, pp. 3–14.

[42] John B. McMaster, *A History of the People of the United States* (New York, 1893–1913), VI, 101.

[43] John R. Commons *et al.*, eds., *A Documentary History of American Industrial Society* (Cleveland, 1910), V, 203.

conventions and memorialized the lawmakers on the alleged evils of penal industry. By the end of the year, more petitions and signatures had been sent to the legislature on this topic than had ever been received on any other matter. One convention of workers at Utica had a hundred thousand copies of its proceedings printed for distribution.[44]

Such attacks on the prison workshops illustrate the complexity of New York politics during the Jacksonian period. In 1834, as the struggle against penal industry moved toward a climax, workingmen were also entering into an alliance with the Democratic party in the Empire State,[45] and were thus joining forces with the very organization under which the Auburn and contract labor systems had been developed. Such administrators as Lynds, Powers, and Wiltse were Jacksonians who owed their appointments to the Albany Regency and believed they were furthering party objectives by helping to reduce government spending. As one group of Democrats directed and defended the effort to make penitentiaries self-supporting, ostensible political associates seemed intent upon wrecking it.

Proposals to abolish or seriously modify the contract system inevitably aroused taxpayer resistance. A resident of Hornellsville, for instance, declared bitterly that the campaign against penal industry stemmed from "a wish to create a distinction in favor of the mechanic, or a wish to tax the farmer, the merchant, and professional men, to support the convicts in our State Prisons without labor, for the sole purpose of raising the wages of the mechanic." [46] On the other hand, the swelling chorus of artisan discontent could not be ignored. From the point of view of political expediency, the best solution would be one which restricted the penitentiary shops enough to satisfy the workers without at the same time ruling out the possibility of deriving sufficient revenue to meet institutional expenses. In a report smacking of fence-straddling, an

[44] DA, 63rd Session (1840), Vol. VII, No. 276, pp. 5–6.
[45] See Hugins, *Jacksonian Democracy and the Working Class,* p. 24.
[46] DS, 58th Session (1835), Vol. I, No. 13, pp. 71–72.

assembly committee in 1835 refused to admit the validity of most arguments against penal labor but nevertheless advocated a limitation upon the number of inmates who could be employed in a single prison trade, the restriction of production chiefly to goods which normally came from abroad, and a requirement of full and free competition for all prison contracts. In particular, the committee recommended that penitentiaries and county poorhouses alike might undertake the cultivation of mulberry trees and the making of silk.[47]

The legislature assented to most of these ideas in an act passed on May 11, 1835. It was stipulated that henceforth no inmate was to be taught any mechanical trade other than the making of an article which usually had to be imported into the country. Prison officials were required to give two months' notice before entering into a labor contract, and were forbidden to negotiate agreements of more than six months' duration without the "consent and direction of the inspectors." In addition, the act directed that the idea of raising mulberry trees and producing silk be given a trial at the penitentiaries.[48]

This law seemed to strike a heavy blow against established prison trades and to threaten the tenures enjoyed by favored contractors. Governor William Marcy announced in 1836 that he expected a "considerable reduction" in the amount of penitentiary earnings as a result of the statute. In 1837 and 1838, Auburn experienced deficits which were blamed on the act.[49] In actuality, however, it is doubtful that the legislation caused the prisons much hardship. Merely to stipulate that a two months' notice had to be given before a contract could be signed did not ensure that the lowest bidder

[47] DA, 58th Session (1835), Vol. II, No. 135, Part 1, *passim*. This report was denounced as equivocating by such labor advocates as George H. Evans and William Leggett (see Hugins, *Jacksonian Democracy and the Working Class*, pp. 159–160).

[48] *Laws of the State of New-York, Passed at the Fifty-eighth Session of the Legislature . . . 1835* (Albany, 1835), pp. 341–344.

[49] DA, 59th Session (1836), Vol. I, No. 2, p. 7, and 61st Session (1838), Vol. III, No. 66, pp. 9, 15.

would necessarily be chosen. The provision restricting the duration of agreements to six months could be abrogated at any time by the inspectors, who could be counted upon to be solicitous about the need for stable conditions in the shops. The portion of the act covering the employment of inmates in crafts competing with domestic producers stated that shop personnel would be limited to "the number of convicts who had learned a trade before coming to prison." Penitentiary officials interpreted this to mean that a felon who had learned any craft at all on the outside could be employed in any prison shop, even if the type of work carried on there happened to be totally different from anything he had previously done.[50]

If an incoming convict had learned no trade at all in civilian life, there was yet another way to circumvent the act of 1835; he could be assigned to a contractor who would teach him only one or two of the skills involved in a particular craft. Thus in the coopering shops one inmate was taught how to cut corners off boards and to remove sap; another was instructed in the art of boring holes; a third learned how to split wood, and a fourth how to handle a saw. In this way no single prisoner learned a trade in its entirety, and the law was theoretically obeyed. Penitentiary officials also construed the enactment to permit the employment of any felon, regardless of past experience, "upon a contract which was in existence on the 11th of May, 1835, and which had not expired at the time the convict was so put to work." By means of such devices and interpretations the apparent will of the legislature could be nullified whenever this was desirable.[51]

One section of the law, however, was temporarily obeyed and led to an interesting experiment in silk manufacturing. The inspectors at Auburn and Sing Sing grumblingly ordered mulberry trees to be planted in 1836, predicting that the effort would lead to no profitable result. By 1837, many of the trees had died at Sing Sing; three years later, the inspectors in Cayuga County reported

---

[50] DA, 63rd Session (1840), Vol. VIII, No. 339, pp. 6–9; DS, 63rd Session (1840), Vol. II, No. 48, p. 290.

[51] *Ibid.* See also DA, 64th Session (1841), Vol. V, No. 186, pp. 10–11.

much the same story.[52] In 1841, however, a new agent named Henry Polhemus took over at Auburn and began an earnest attempt to produce sewing silk. Starting with the services of two convicts who operated a single throwing mill by hand, he added various pieces of equipment until by 1843 the prison possessed twelve mills run by steam power. Forty inmates were engaged in the project by this time, and Polhemus envisioned a bright future for it.[53]

This experiment was a departure from the contract system. The state owned all the machinery, furnished the necessary capital, and tried to market the finished goods.[54] As a result of bounties which the legislature offered to farmers who would plant mulberry trees and raise silkworms, raw silk was brought to the prison in large quantities. Polhemus also advertised that he would pay ready cash for cocoons and reeled silk, and his optimistic views on the future of the experiment were published widely throughout the country. Soon the penitentiary was receiving raw silk from Pennsylvania, Ohio, New Jersey, Maryland, and Tennessee.[55] In the Auburn area itself citizens were for a time caught up in a speculative mania, some building cocooneries and others raising worms in barns, outhouses, attics, and parlors. As the craze increased, people "counted their eggs as full-grown worms, their buds as full-grown trees, and both, by the thousands, tens of thousands, and millions." Prices of eggs and plants skyrocketed until single mulberry twigs were bringing as much as one dollar each.[56]

Like many another speculative bubble, this one was fated to

[52] DA, 59th Session (1836), Vol. III, No. 133, pp. 7–8, and 63rd Session (1840), Vol. II, No. 37, p. 3; DS, 59th Session (1836), Vol. I, No. 23, p. 7, and 60th Session (1837), Vol. I, No. 6, p. 7.

[53] DA, 65th Session (1842), Vol. II, No. 31, pp. 3–4, and DS, 66th Session (1843), Vol. I, No. 23, pp. 3–5.

[54] DA, 65th Session (1842), Vol. IV, No. 65, p. 46. It does appear, however, that a local businessman named John Morrison provided assistance and advice in getting the prison silk industry established. See Elliot G. Storke and James H. Smith, *History of Cayuga County, New York* (Syracuse, 1879), p. 158.

[55] DA, 65th Session (1842), Vol. I, No. 1, p. 8, and Vol. II, No. 31, p. 14; DS, 67th Session (1844), Vol. I, No. 18, p. 15.

[56] Henry Hall, *The History of Auburn* (Auburn, 1869), p. 250.

burst. It had been hoped that Auburn sewing silk would sell for seven dollars a pound, but by the end of 1843 the price had sagged to between $5.00 and $5.25. By this time Polhemus had been succeeded as agent by John Beardsley, who presented a discouraging report to the legislature. The prison was being swamped with raw silk, and finished goods could not be sold at a profit. Knowing that many citizens were heavily involved in the silk mania, Beardsley hesitated to stop production, and temporarily kept on buying. Such a policy, however, could not long be maintained. In May, 1844, prison officials reluctantly suspended the silkmaking operation, aware that some local residents might well be financially ruined by the blow.[57] Meanwhile, a similar experiment on a smaller scale at Sing Sing had ended in failure. Begun in 1842, it had yielded only $24.02 on an investment of $3,000 by June of the following year. In addition, the noise of the silkmaking machinery had given inmates too many opportunities to communicate without being detected.[58]

The collapse of the silk venture came not long after New York's penal industries had suffered another heavy blow. Evasion of the law of 1835 had stirred up bitter protests among workingmen, who presented numerous petitions to the legislature. In 1842, an investigating committee declared that there had never been the slightest attempt to enforce the statute's provisions at Sing Sing.[59] Proposals were made to abolish the contract system altogether; to prohibit the teaching of any mechanical trades in the prisons; to disallow any machinery driven by animals, water power, or steam in penitentiary shops; to employ convicts in the macadamizing of

---

[57] *Ibid.*, p. 252; Storke and Smith, *History of Cayuga County*, pp. 158–159; DS, 66th Session (1843), Vol. I, No. 23, p. 4; 67th Session (1844), Vol. I, No. 18, p. 16; and 68th Session (1845), Vol. I, No. 8, pp. 13–14. The venture was never resumed, and the remaining stock and machinery were sold in 1846 (see DS, 69th Session [1846], Vol. II, No. 46, p. 16). A historical marker outside the main gate of the prison commemorates the silk episode today.

[58] DS, 65th Session (1842), Vol. II, No. 39, p. 18; 66th Session (1843), Vol. I, No. 10, p. 18; and 67th Session (1844), Vol. I, No. 20, p. 19.

[59] *Ibid.*, 64th Session (1841), Vol. II, No. 54, p. 1; DA, 65th Session (1842), Vol. IV, No. 65, p. 41.

roads; to use inmate labor in the production of supplies for the State Lunatic Asylum at Utica; to abandon the Auburn system and institute the Pennsylvania plan; and—most important in view of later events—to employ felons in the making of iron and steel.[60]

Although a legislative committee reporting on the prison-labor issue resisted the workers' arguments in 1841, pressure for a new and more stringent law mounted until it was too great to be withstood. On April 9, 1842, the lawmakers passed an act which tightened restrictions on penal industry and explicitly declared that "no convict who shall hereafter be sentenced to imprisonment in either of the state prisons of this state shall . . . be permitted to work . . . at any other mechanical trade than that which . . . such convict had learned and practiced previous to his conviction." In addition, the state attorney-general received authority to annul contracts which in his opinion had been made in violation of the law of 1835. As a result, eight contracts were pronounced null and void at Auburn and two were canceled at Sing Sing. Large numbers of inmates were thrown out of work, and Sing Sing's stonecutting business was badly hurt.[61]

By the mid-1840's, therefore, penal industry in the Empire State faced a crisis. The silk-manufacturing experiment had failed, and the legislature had passed new restrictive provisions which would be difficult if not impossible to evade. On the other hand, even critics of the prison labor system agreed that it would not do to let inmates be idle.[62] What was to be done? Despite the dishearten-

[60] DA, 63rd Session (1840), Vol. VII, No. 276, pp. 16–26; 64th Session (1841), Vol. V, No. 186, p. 14, and Vol. VII, No. 286, p. 11; and 65th Session (1842), Vol. IV, No. 65, pp. 45, 56–59, 84; New York *Tribune,* July 8, 1841. The *Tribune,* which had just begun operations, was a consistent supporter of the workers' arguments against penal labor; see especially the issues of June 26, July 7, and Sept. 9, 1841. These and all subsequent references to the *Tribune* are to the daily rather than to the weekly edition.

[61] *Laws of the State of New-York, Passed at the Sixty-fifth Session of the Legislature . . . 1842* (Albany, 1842), pp. 181–183; DS, 67th Session (1844), Vol. I, No. 18, pp. 3, 9, and 69th Session (1846), Vol. I, No. 16, pp. 5–8; DA, 66th Session (1843), Vol. II, No. 32, p. 18, and Vol. VI, No. 169, p. 6.

[62] New York *Tribune,* Sept. 9, 1841.

ing example of the venture in silk production, one of the best answers seemed to be the employment of convicts in trades which would not compete with domestic artisans, or in fields in which American manufacturers could not meet the demand for goods. Possibilities along these lines included the making of certain types of floor covering, such as Wilton and Brussels carpets, and the production of cutlery. Both of these industries became important at Auburn between 1842 and 1847.[63] Another idea, never adopted, was advanced by Palmer Cleveland, a businessman who wanted to employ prisoners in the mining of lead and zinc in Sullivan County. Cleveland offered to hire between one hundred and three hundred inmates, and recommended that Elam Lynds be put in charge of the operation.[64]

Of all the suggestions advanced to give convicts work without hurting free artisans in the process, the most popular was that of employing prisoners in iron production. A resident of Keeseville urged Governor Seward in 1841 to consider the possibility of using inmate labor in Clinton and Essex County iron mines, and by 1842 the state assembly's committee on prisons had taken up the idea, asserting that geological surveys had shown the inexhaustibility of ore deposits in the Adirondack area.[65] The penal labor law of 1842 authorized further study of the matter, and a Saratoga County inventor and jack-of-all-trades named Ransom Cook was given the task of exploring possibilities. In 1843, Cook presented an enthusiastic report, stating that he had located a tract of land seventeen miles west of Plattsburgh which was capable of being mined with comparative ease and possessed favorable access to fuel supplies for smelting.[66]

[63] DA, 67th Session (1844), Vol. III, No. 75, pp. 4–5; DS, 69th Session (1846), Vol. II, No. 46, p. 20, and 70th Session (1847), Vol. I, No. 11, p. 11.

[64] DA, 66th Session (1843), Vol. III, No. 96, pp. 1–3, and Vol. VI, No. 159, pp. 1–6.

[65] *Ibid.*, 65th Session (1842), Vol. IV, No. 65, pp. 46, 52.

[66] *Ibid.*, 66th Session (1843), Vol. II, No. 32, *passim.* For biographical data on Cook, see Nathaniel S. Sylvester, *History of Saratoga County, New York* (Philadelphia, 1878), pp. 204–205.

The ironmaking project attracted widespread support. The assembly committee on prisons endorsed Cook's proposals.[67] Labor groups added their influence, for few of the state's artisans at this time were engaged in iron production; in the words of one legislative document, the use of convicts in such activity would remove them from competition with free workers "as effectually as if they were transported to Russia or Sweden."[68] Powerful bipartisan support was brought to bear in behalf of the idea. The Plattsburgh *Republican,* representing such important Democratic leaders as Azariah Flagg, was active in pushing for the project, and various legislators from the northern part of the state fought for the plan as a potential benefit to their area.[69] Meanwhile, the venture enlisted the backing of such Whig organs as the New York *Tribune.*[70]

Despite opposition from critics who pointed out that the growing use of anthracite and coke for smelting was driving down the price of charcoal-produced iron and that the remoteness of the Plattsburgh area from major markets boded ill for the success of the project, a measure to establish an ironmaking penitentiary in Clinton County made steady headway in the legislature, aided by constant pressure from labor organizations and their supporters. When the bill passed the state assembly in March, 1844, a large rally of workers in New York City hailed the event enthusiastically and dispatched a memorial with forty-five hundred signatures to the senate urging similar action. Finally, after another month of agitation and debate, the upper house put its seal on the project

[67] DA, 66th Session (1843), Vol. III, No. 72, pp. 1–2.

[68] See *ibid.,* Vol. V, No. 156, p. 2, being the petition of a meeting of artisans and other citizens in Albany, and DA, 67th Session (1844), Vol. III, No. 41, pp. 3–4.

[69] Plattsburgh *Republican,* March 2 and May 4, 1844, and Feb. 15, 1845; Duane H. Hurd, *History of Clinton and Franklin Counties, New York* (Philadelphia, 1880), p. 48. There was opposition to the project from several areas in Clinton and Essex Counties, but this appears to have stemmed from dissatisfaction over Cook's choice of a site. See Plattsburgh *Republican,* March 30, 1844; DA, 66th Session (1843), Vol. VI, No. 156, p. 2, and No. 157, p. 2.

[70] New York *Tribune,* Dec. 29, 1843.

and the measure became law. Within a year the building of Clinton prison at Dannemora had begun.[71]

Penal industry in New York now stood at a crossroads. By 1844, both Auburn and Sing Sing were experiencing deficits under the impact of the restrictive legislation passed two years before.[72] If they proved unable to surmount their difficulties and the new ironmaking prison failed to operate at a profit, the idea of the self-supporting penitentiary would be direly jeopardized. Because part of the reason for the Auburn system's public appeal lay in its capacity for removing the financial burden of penal operations from the shoulders of the taxpayers, such a situation might well portend basic disciplinary changes. Indeed, there were already signs to indicate that such changes were under way, and that the convict would no longer be quite the same isolated "human working machine" that he had been in the past. Slowly the foundations upon which Elam Lynds and other reformers had built a new penal order were being undermined, and defenders of the established system had good reason to be apprehensive about the future.

[71] *Ibid.*, March 29, April 20, and May 1, 1844; *Laws of the State of New-York, Passed at the Sixty-seventh Session of the Legislature . . . 1844* (Albany, 1844), pp. 373–379; Hurd, *History of Clinton and Franklin Counties*, p. 49.

[72] DS, 66th Session (1843), Vol. I, No. 1, p. 41; 67th Session (1844), Vol. I, No. 1, pp. 24–25; and 68th Session (1845), Vol. I, No. 1, p. 30 and No. 9, p. 2.

# Chapter IX

# A New Outlook

DURING the decade of the 1840's the penitentiaries of the Empire State felt the influence of changing times. Imbued with some of the same humanitarianism which was manifested in other reform movements during this period of social ferment, new administrators began to break away from precedents which had been established by the pioneers of the Auburn system. To a certain degree these new leaders held a philosophy similar to that of Gershom Powers in that they wanted to use harsh physical punishment only when necessary and believed rehabilitation to be both possible and important. However, they lacked Powers' conviction that reformation could best be produced by breaking the spirit of a man, subjecting him to a hard and humiliating discipline, and literally burying him from the world. Instead, they tended to favor a more positive approach of attempting to bring out the best in an inmate through the use of kindness and the extension of privileges which helped to alleviate the isolation and severity of convict life. Although they sometimes differed strongly on matters of policy, they shared a common credo that can be epitomized in the words of an upstate newspaper which commented in 1845 upon the comparatively mild treatment of felons prevailing in the new prison at Dannemora:

Severe treatment has proved that men are not driven to the path of virtue. . . . Active employment—a strict but not severe discipline—the gratification of the smaller wants and desires of the convict, when it can be done without a laxity of discipline; and a kind, considerate and humane treatment, exciting self-respect, subduing evil propensities and awakening moral sentiments in the heart of the prisoner, will probably prove the true secret of success.[1]

Here, scattered throughout a few lines of type, were key words revealing an entirely different spirit from that which had influenced penal policy two decades before in a period of anxiety about the preservation of established institutions and traditional values. In talking of kindness, consideration, and gratification of inmate wants, the writer was using concepts completely foreign to the Lyndsian vocabulary. Instead of dwelling upon the degradation of the offender, as Powers did when he talked to incoming convicts, or upon the need to "let self-tormenting guilt harrow up the tortures of accusing conscience," as the inspectors of Auburn had advocated in 1825 (cf. pp. 69, 114), the newspaper account spoke of the need for "exciting self-respect." The reference to propensities and sentiments also indicated a changed outlook, for this was the language of phrenology, a pseudo-science which postulated a physical basis for deviant behavior and minimized the culpability of the offender.[2]

Such ideas reflected a softening public attitude toward the criminal, which in turn showed the influence of larger patterns in prevailing popular thought. One student of ante-bellum culture has used the term "sentimental years" to describe the period between the mid-1830's and the Civil War—an era in which Americans believed in the basic goodness of man and built a "tradition of being socially comfortable, practically successful, spiritually progressive, and privately warmed with self-esteem." [3] Other writers have noted the persistence of an optimistic point of view which was nourished by economic abundance, technological progress, the physical expansion of the country, and the achievements of natural

---

[1] Plattsburgh *Republican*, November 22, 1845.

[2] The subject of phrenology and its influence upon penal policy in New York during the 1840's will be discussed at length in Chapter X.

[3] E. Douglas Branch, *The Sentimental Years, 1836–1860* (New York, 1934), pp. 11–12.

science.[4] The prevalence of Arminianism, perfectionism, and millennialism among American Protestants was consonant with this hopeful outlook.[5]

In such a period, reform movements were more likely to be animated by faith in the future than by a desire to restore former ways or to preserve a threatened status quo. A perfect society beckoned if men would only do their utmost to root out existing evils, and the nearness of the goal heightened the reformer's sense of urgency as he strained to achieve it. Faith in the inevitability of progress and the imminence of victory served the twofold function of nerving him to supreme effort and sustaining him in case he met temporary reverses.[6]

Although the new directions taken by prison officials in New York during the 1840's were thus part of a larger picture in exemplifying the type of reform that results from hope rather than fear, it should not be assumed that the existence of considerable social optimism in this period was a sufficient cause for these changes. The disposition of penitentiary posts was first and foremost a political matter, and the nature of a prospective appointee's penological beliefs made little difference if he did not happen to belong to the right party or the right faction at the right time. So far as public opinion was concerned, the average voter's natural aversion to taxes made it likely that he would judge the achievements of prison administrators at least partly in light of the extent to which they made their institutions self-supporting, whatever his convictions might be regarding progress and human perfectability. In addition, the isolation of the convict under the Auburn system lessened the chances that his plight would receive as much attention as other social problems. Sealed off from the great mass of

[4] Carl Bode, *The Anatomy of American Popular Culture, 1840–1861* (Berkeley, Calif., 1959), p. xiii; Herbert R. Brown, *The Sentimental Novel in America, 1789–1860* (reprinted ed.; New York, 1959), pp. 181–182, 358–359; Merle Curti, *The Growth of American Thought* (2nd ed.; New York, 1951), p. 370.

[5] On the widespread influence of such doctrines among Protestants during this period see especially Timothy L. Smith, *Revivalism and Social Reform in Mid-Nineteenth Century America* (Nashville, 1957), *passim*.

[6] Curti, *Growth of American Thought*, p. 370.

citizens in a world of his own, he could easily be forgotten unless a glaring scandal, a riot, or a large financial deficit at one of the prisons brought him into the public gaze. Despite the interest in penal reform which was aroused by the recurring debate between exponents of the solitary and congregate plans of discipline, it is reasonable to assume with such analysts as Orlando F. Lewis that the average American probably knew little of day-to-day conditions behind penitentiary walls.[7]

The manner in which the way was opened for a more liberal administration of the prisons of New York illustrates how scandal and political partisanship helped to bring about change in this area of reform. Despite the profitable operations at Sing Sing under the administration of Robert Wiltse during the 1830's, the harshness of his disciplinary tactics and the parsimony with which he supplied inmate needs exposed the institution to steady, though largely ineffective, criticism by visitors, ex-convicts, and occasional legislative investigators (cf. pp. 149–155). So long as the warden's Jacksonian party-mates remained in control of the state government his position remained secure, particularly since his frugality was well calculated to please the taxpayer. In the event of a political shift, however, he would be vulnerable to charges of cruelty and misconduct.

Wiltse's downfall began in 1838. In the pages of the *Hudson River Chronicle,* a Whig newspaper published in Sing Sing village, editor Alexander H. Wells began attacking conditions at the penitentiary, charging that punishment had been "merged in torture" and that barbarism had taken the place of "wholesome chastisement." Economizing on inmate rations, he declared, had reached a state at which "the scum of meat kettles, which had formerly been sold to a soap-boiler in the village," had been substituted for molasses in the prison dietary.[8] Similar charges had been made before, but by 1838 something could be done about them. In the

---

[7] Orlando F. Lewis, *The Development of American Prisons and Prison Customs, 1776–1845* (n.p., 1922), p. 329.

[8] *Hudson River Chronicle,* Vols. I and II (1837–1839), *passim,* especially the issues of May 29, June 19, and Oct. 2, 1838.

state elections of that year William H. Seward defeated the Jacksonian incumbent, William Marcy, for the governorship. The party to which Wells belonged was now in the ascendancy.

Although the Democrats still controlled the state senate, the Whigs had picked up a majority in the assembly, which shortly dispatched a group of investigators to Sing Sing to check the veracity of Wells's accusations. From a succession of prison officers and shop supervisors the legislators elicited an impressive array of data relating to brutal floggings and starving times under Wiltse's regime, and drew up a report which roundly condemned the warden's tactics. Seward then asked the senate to remove Sing Sing's board of inspectors from office. "If our system of imprisonment," he asserted, "cannot be maintained without the constant infliction of such punishments as are disclosed by this report, it was established in error, and ought to be completely abandoned." [9]

Undismayed by the damning evidence which the assembly committee had collected, Wiltse and his supporters fought back. Knowing that they would receive a sympathetic hearing from the Jacksonian upper house, they memorialized the senate for a reinvestigation on the grounds that the previous one had been unfairly conducted.[10] This request was granted, and a three-man committee was appointed to conduct the new inquiry. Meanwhile, the powerful Albany *Argus,* one of the leading Jacksonian newspapers in the country, took up Wiltse's cause, declaring that the assembly committee had been politically motivated and branding Seward's demand for the removal of the Sing Sing inspectors as inquisitorial. Not to be outdone, ninety-six Whig legislators attacked the senate in a stinging manifesto issued on May 7, 1839. On his part, Wells predicted that the senate investigating team would produce a whitewash.[11]

---

[9] Quoted in Prison Discipline Society, *Fourteenth Report* (1839), pp. 40–42. For the text of the assembly report see DA, 62nd Session (1839), Vol. VI, No. 335.

[10] DS, 62nd Session (1839), Vol. III, No. 99, pp. 1–2.

[11] Albany *Daily Argus,* April 22, 26, and 27, 1839, quoting in part from Westchester *Herald; Hudson River Chronicle,* May 28 and June 18, 1839.

When the senators reached Sing Sing they were confronted with fifty-five separate charges of improper conduct on the part of Wiltse and his fellow officers. Not unexpectedly, the committee finally issued a majority report defending the warden from his attackers, but the moral force of the verdict was weak. The findings of the assembly group were in many instances impossible to controvert, and the best the senators could do was to hunt for extenuating circumstances. As a result, the ensuing report was more an excuse than an exculpation. Furthermore, one of the senators, Henry Livingston, refused to sign the document and drew up a minority statement denouncing Wiltse's regime.[12]

Although Wiltse retained his position for the better part of another year, therefore, the effort to vindicate him had been distinctly less than victorious. In addition, a significant blow to the warden and his defenders came from a person who had once found little but good to say about penal developments in New York, Louis Dwight. The leader of the Prison Discipline Society had visited Sing Sing late in 1838, and subsequently reported that he "saw enough to satisfy his mind that the punishments were odious and detestable, both in manner and degree." He was convinced that the inmates were not properly fed, and that the sick were inadequately cared for. He had watched an officer beat a convict in a way which he believed would have caused "the prosecution of a truckman, in the streets of Boston, who should beat a dumb beast in the same manner." Surely, he contended, there was a better way to deal with felons than this. Public opinion could not long tolerate officials who subjected fellow mortals to the inhumanities he had witnessed.[13]

If these developments were not sufficiently disturbing to those who looked upon prisoners merely as scoundrels to be subdued and exploited, defenders of this theory suffered another setback at Auburn, where indignant citizens ended a regime which had been

[12] DS, 63rd Session (1840), Vol. II, Nos. 37 and 38, *passim*.
[13] Prison Discipline Society, *Fourteenth Report* (1839), p. 42, and *Fifteenth Report* (1840), p. 36.

blamed for the death of two convicts. The success of this effort showed clearly how moral and political forces were being effectively marshaled against excessively stringent penal policies as the 1830's came to a close.

The crisis at Auburn began in 1838 when the board of inspectors, worried by financial deficits which had occurred under the administration of agent John Garrow, decided that the situation called for a strong leader who could somehow restore efficient and profitable operations. Their choice was none other than Elam Lynds, who returned to the Cayuga County institution for a second tour of duty in May and began a sweeping economy drive. Abolishing the previous practice of having two meals a day in the mess hall, he established the Sing Sing method of feeding inmates in their cells, and thus dispensed with the services of four keepers who had supervised the dining room. In other moves he abandoned the Sabbath school, forced contractors to submit to stringent regulations, and greatly tightened institutional discipline.[14]

Controversy quickly ensued. Evidence on the preliminary skirmishing is scanty, but it appears that a dispute broke out between Lynds and the prison physician, Leander Fisher, over the feeding of convicts. Fisher was summarily dismissed, and his place taken by Lansingh Briggs, a man whose penal philosophy was closer to that of the warden. Shortly thereafter, dissension erupted among the inspectors, leading to the resignation of one board member and the onset of a pamphlet war in which the Auburn public was treated to a series of charges and countercharges on the merits or shortcomings of the new administration.[15]

This was but a prologue to more serious matters that occurred in 1839. On March 1 of that year a convict named John Winterscale choked to death while trying hastily to swallow a piece of

[14] DS, 62nd Session (1839), Vol. I, No. 11, pp. 2–12, and 63rd Session (1840), Vol. II, No. 48, p. 84. On the deficits that occurred under Garrow, see DA, 60th Session (1837), Vol. I, No. 31, p. 1, and 61st Session (1838), Vol. III, No. 186, p. 1; DS, 62nd Session (1839), Vol. I, No. 1, pp. 8–9.

[15] See especially Ezra the Scribe [pseud. for Rev. Silas E. Shepard], *The Chronicles of Auburn* (Auburn, 1838), *passim*.

boiling beef which he had stolen from the prison kitchen. Critics of Lynds asserted that the incident would not have occurred had Winterscale not been famished because of the warden's dietary economies.[16] A matter of even greater notoriety was the death of Louis von Eck, an immigrant forger who had been sentenced to Auburn. Von Eck was a frail inmate who suffered from tuberculosis, intestinal disorders, intermittent paralysis, and apparent insanity, but Lynds and the new physician, Briggs, decided that he was a hypochondriac who deserved no consideration or mercy. On one occasion, according to later testimony, Lynds pulled the ailing felon out of a hospital bunk, kicked him, and called him a lying scoundrel. Following a series of beatings, von Eck declined further in health and went on protracted hunger strikes. He eventually died in the prison hospital on April 8, 1839.[17]

Lynds and the inspectors met after von Eck's death and decided that no coroner's inquest would be necessary. Word of the episode, however, leaked out to a public which was already inflamed by discussion of previous incidents. Within a short time an angry crowd appeared at the prison gates and demanded an inquest, after which several local physicians were admitted into the penitentiary. Their verdict merely fanned the flames higher. Von Eck, they decided, "came to his death from disease, the fatal termination of which was hastened by flogging, labor and general harsh treatment, imposed by the agent Elam Lynds, and Galen O. Weed, one of the keepers, and also by inexcusable neglect and want of proper care on the part of the physician Lansingh Briggs, who reported him from time to time well, when actually sick." [18]

As a result of popular protest, a series of hearings was held in June before the same committee which had been appointed by the

[16] DA, 63rd Session (1840), Vol. I, No. 18, p. 19; DS, 63rd Session (1840), Vol. II, No. 37, pp. 10–11. See also Elliot G. Storke and James H. Smith, *History of Cayuga County, New York* (Syracuse, 1879), p. 156.

[17] DS, 63rd Session (1840), Vol. II, No. 37, pp. 6–9, and No. 38, pp. 7–38; George Combe, *Notes on the United States of North America during a Phrenological Visit in 1838-9-40* (Philadelphia, 1841), II, 22.

[18] DS, 63rd Session (1840), Vol. II, No. 37, p. 6.

state senate to examine the situation at Sing Sing. Again the commissioners showed the same partisan bias that they had displayed in their investigation of Wiltse's regime; two of them voted to uphold Lynds, and Henry Livingston drew up a minority statement in opposition.[19] The hearings, however, were actually somewhat anticlimactic, for intense local disapproval of Lynds's policies had already made his position untenable. Public unrest was so acute, according to one Auburn newspaper, "that serious threats were made of razing the prison to its very foundation, and setting the convicts at liberty." As could be expected, local Whigs made political capital out of the embarrassments of a Democratic penal administration.[20] On April 19, 1839, Lynds bowed to his foes. Resigning his position, he called himself a victim of personal animosity and denied that his regime had been cruel.[21] His detractors had thus accomplished one of their main goals before the senate committee hearings started.

Thanks to the sensational disclosures at both Auburn and Sing Sing and the advent of a Whig administration in Albany, the way was now prepared for a new dispensation in the prisons of the Empire State. After Lynds had been succeeded at Auburn by two short-term replacements, Noyes Palmer and Robert Cook, the Whigs placed a party member named Henry Polhemus in charge of the Cayuga County institution. Polhemus quickly provided better living conditions for the convicts, and made a serious attempt to comply with the labor law of 1835 by his vigorous experiment with silk manufacturing (cf. p. 195).[22] More significant, however, was the dramatic change which occurred at Sing Sing after April 24, 1840, when the regime of Robert Wiltse came to an end. The

---

[19] *Ibid.*, Nos. 37 and 38 *passim.*

[20] Auburn *Cayuga Tocsin*, April 22, 1840, and Jan. 6, 1841, recalling events in 1839. See also *Hudson River Chronicle*, April 23, 1839, reporting on the situation in Auburn.

[21] DS, 63rd Session (1840), Vol. II, No. 37, pp. 39–40.

[22] See especially Storke and Smith, *History of Cayuga County*, pp. 155–156; DA, 64th Session (1841), Vol. II, No. 28, pp. 11–12, and 65th Session (1842), Vol. II, No. 31, pp. 3–4; DS, 66th Session (1843), Vol. I, No. 23, pp. 3–5.

Whig appointee who took his place, a Peekskill foundry operator and stove manufacturer named David L. Seymour, proceeded to inaugurate policies based upon an outlook which had never before prevailed at the bastille on the Hudson: that the chief purpose of a penitentiary was not to punish, but to rehabilitate.[23]

Cognizant of the excesses which had resulted from the unregulated use of the lash by underkeepers during the Wiltse regime, the new administration moved quickly to set up a different system under which such subordinates were required to report convict misbehavior to the principal keeper, Angus McDuffie, who then determined the extent of the punishment to be meted out.[24] By 1841, McDuffie was able to report that the number of stripes inflicted upon inmates had already been cut in half, and was looking forward to the time when the use of the lash would be "a rare occurrence." [25] In another major departure from Wiltse's policies, Seymour considerably augmented the role of religion in penitentiary life, personally taking part in worship services, delivering tracts to the convicts on Sundays, and assuming charge of the Sabbath school. His solicitude for the inmates extended into other areas of activity as well; on one occasion he spent an entire night in the prison hospital during an epidemic, helping to care for the sick and the dying.[26] Educational opportunities for the convicts were also enhanced when, with the encouragement of Governor Seward, an institutional library was established. Characteristically,

[23] New York State Department of Correction, *Sing Sing Prison, Ossining, N.Y.: Its History, Purpose, Makeup and Program* (n.p., 1958), facing p. 1; George D. Seymour, *A History of the Seymour Family* (New Haven, Conn., 1939), pp. 359–360.

[24] By this time the offices of agent and principal keeper had been separated, probably with the despotism of Wiltse's administration in mind. The agent was to concern himself chiefly with financial matters, and the principal keeper with the supervision of discipline. Nevertheless, Seymour played an active part in the everyday life of the institution. See especially DA, 64th Session (1841), Vol. II, No. 28, pp. 2–3.

[25] DA, 64th Session (1841), Vol. II, No. 42, pp. 5–6, 25–26.

[26] John Luckey, *Life in Sing Sing State Prison, as Seen in a Twelve Years' Chaplaincy* (New York, 1860), pp. 26–27.

Seymour personally charged the books out and distributed them among the inmates.[27]

Under the policies adopted by Seymour and McDuffie the isolation which the prisoner endured under the Auburn system was partially broken. Convicts were allowed a limited amount of face-to-face visiting with parents and other relatives, and were also permitted to send and receive occasional letters under the supervision of the chaplain.[28] When a lack of teachers threatened to shut down the Sabbath school, it was decided that the "better sort" of inmates could be used as instructors, much to the horror of skeptics imbued in the Lyndsian tradition.[29] Eager to assist discharged offenders in making a successful transition to free society, Seymour believed that a farm on the prison property at Sing Sing should be set aside as a sort of halfway station where ex-inmates who had no friends on the outside might obtain work at fixed wages, as well as moral training and instruction in husbandry.[30] Small wonder, then, that memories of the agent and the work he had done lingered on at Sing Sing years after he had left the institution. As a convict poet wrote in the mid-1850's:

> Giv us Christiens like David L. Semore
> And this prisen is like heven above
> He is one that used kindness
> And he has the prisners luv.[31]

In restricting the use of the lash, emphasizing the role of religion, and trying to make confinement reformative, Seymour and McDuffie had something in common with Gershom Powers, who had regulated flogging, advocated the appointment of a chaplain so that inmates would have a "benevolent and pious friend, to

[27] DA, 64th Session (1841), Vol. II, No. 26, p. 40, and No. 42, pp. 6, 13, 17–19; New York State Department of Correction, Sing Sing Prison, p. 5.

[28] DS, 65th Session (1842), Vol. II, No. 39, pp. 25–26.

[29] Ibid., 66th Session (1843), Vol. I, No. 10, p. 19; Luckey, Life in Sing Sing State Prison, p. 348.

[30] DS, 65th Session (1842), Vol. II, No. 39, p. 20.

[31] New York Prison Association, Tenth Report (1855), p. 106.

instruct and console" them, maintained faith in the reformability of felons, and tried to do for his men what "humanity and Christian charity demanded." The new administrators at Sing Sing, however, were not merely emulating the techniques and beliefs exemplified by Powers. In many ways, they were reverting to ideas advanced by Thomas Eddy, who believed in giving convicts incentives for good behavior, and by John Stanford, who had not hesitated to use inmate instructors at Newgate. Like Eddy, they were willing to allow their charges visiting privileges, something that Powers had never condoned. They were also far from sharing Powers' belief that prisoners should be "literally buried from the world." [32]

In yet another respect the Seymour administration went beyond the accomplishments of Powers, thanks to the activities of a Methodist preacher named John Luckey, who had become chaplain at Sing Sing shortly before the end of the Wiltse regime. An ardent exponent of what one historian has called "Evangelical Arminianism," Luckey had a deep concern for the outcast and destitute which was exemplified not only in his prison work but also in subsequent activities for the Ladies' Home Missionary Society at the Five Points Mission in New York City, one of the earliest institutional manifestations in America of Methodist concern for the urban poor.[33] Taking advantage of the opportunities afforded him by the policies of Seymour, he threw himself into the task of reforming the felons committed to his spiritual care.

One of Luckey's main objectives was a better understanding of the backgrounds from which his charges came, which he hoped would provide insight into the operations of the criminal mind. Powers had shown a similar interest, but had confined himself mainly to preliminary interviews before convicts began their sentences and parting conversations just prior to their release.

[32] See above, pp. 32–33, 39, 105–106, 115.
[33] Luckey, *Life in Sing Sing State Prison, passim;* Smith, *Revivalism and Social Reform, passim,* especially Chapter II, "The Churches Help the Poor"; New York *Sun,* Aug. 22, 1846; *Northern Christian Advocate,* May 2, 1855.

Luckey, on the other hand, spent much time questioning visitors and sheriffs about the personal histories of the inmates with whom he worked; studying the letters to friends and relatives which the Seymour administration permitted prisoners to write; calling upon people with whom the convicts under his care had been associated in civilian life; and having repeated conversations with the felons themselves. He took down his findings in notebooks which were carefully indexed so that he could refer to a particular case at a moment's notice; by 1846, he had filled about fourteen of these with information, and as he counseled his charges he tried to apply the understanding he had gained from his research. Like Powers before him, he maintained an interest in these men after they had been released, but in a much more personal and direct way than the Auburn warden had found possible. Since most Sing Sing inmates came from New York City and its environs and returned to that area after confinement, their homes were easily accessible to Luckey, who managed to secure free passage down the Hudson from obliging river captains. He frequently accompanied ex-convicts back to the city, helped them to find jobs, tried to protect them from the blandishments of former associates in crime, and made periodic checks on their progress in free life.[34] In a real sense he was New York's pioneer penal caseworker, using for the first time methods which were later to become staple techniques.

The Seymour administration thus broke away from the Lyndsian approach and established the most liberal prison regime that had existed in the Empire State since the days of Thomas Eddy. The Auburn system remained, with its routine of silence and hard labor enforced, if necessary, by recourse to physical punishment.[35] Nevertheless, the spirit which motivated the operation had changed. Reformation, rather than deterrence, was the primary

[34] DA, 64th Session (1841), Vol. II, No. 42, pp. 19–24; DS, 65th Session (1842), Vol. II, No. 39, pp. 25, 27–28, and 69th Session (1846), Vol. I, No. 16, p. 104; Luckey, *Life in Sing Sing State Prison*, pp. 67, 353–354, 368.

[35] My research has failed to substantiate the statement made in New York State Department of Correction, *Sing Sing Prison*, p. 5, that lashing was abandoned under the Seymour administration.

goal of the new leaders; kindness, not coercion, was the favored means of securing compliance among the inmates. The isolation of the prisoner was mitigated under rules which now permitted visiting and writing privileges; an effort was being made to understand the felon as an individual; and responsible officials were showing an awareness of the ex-convict's need for help and guidance in the difficult period of readjustment to free society.

A more humane spirit was likewise in evidence at Auburn as the Polhemus administration carried out its program of reform. By the end of 1842 it was reported that the death rate at the Cayuga County institution was the lowest in thirteen years; that the shops and cells were now properly warmed; and that inmates were provided with ample shoes, clothing, and blankets. Even the use of the whip was temporarily abandoned as officials experimented with a new disciplinary device known as the shower bath, in the hope that this would prove to be a viable substitute for the lash.[36]

The Seymour and Polhemus administrations, however, lasted only about three years. In 1842, the Democrats scored an overwhelming victory in the race for the governorship, and the prisons were soon under their control once more. At Auburn, the disciplinary experiments of the previous regime were abandoned, and the lash was restored.[37] It was at Sing Sing, however, that the most noteworthy changes occurred. Here the chairmanship of the board of inspectors was placed in the hands of John Worth Edmonds, a native of Columbia County who had distinguished himself in the course of a varied career as newspaper editor, lawyer, Jacksonian politician, and state senator.[38] Under his leadership, the repressive spirit of earlier administrations was quickly reintroduced.

[36] DS, 66th Session (1843), Vol. I, No. 9, pp. 2, 72–73. This device became especially important in the 1850's, and its development is described in Chapter XI.

[37] DS, 67th Session (1844), Vol. I, No. 16, pp. 76, 84.

[38] A short and not always reliable sketch of Edmonds' career is contained in John Livingston, *Portraits of Eminent Americans Now Living: With Biographical and Historical Memoirs of Their Lives and Actions* (New York, 1853), II, 797–803. For other details of his activities as a Jacksonian spokesman, see Arthur M. Schlesinger, Jr., *The Age of Jackson* (Boston, 1945), pp. 179, 197, 339, 341, 412.

Edmonds was convinced that disciplinary and industrial affairs had deteriorated badly at Sing Sing under Whig control, and shortly presented to the legislature a gloomy account of the financial situation confronting the institution. After an investigation had been held and witnesses questioned under oath, the new inspectors charged that accounts had been improperly kept under Seymour, and that the total deficit for the preceding three years aggregated nearly $50,000.[39] Well before this report was issued, Edmonds had come to the conclusion that drastic action was imperative if proper discipline and fiscal order were to be restored. He desired at first to return Robert Wiltse to power, but could not secure the consent of his fellow inspectors. Instead, the position of agent was given to William H. Peck, an obscure figure who, unlike Seymour, appears to have confined himself to his financial duties while in office. The disposition of the principal keepership was much more significant, and caused some angry citizens to burn Edmonds in effigy. From Utica, where he had recently been serving as one of the commissioners supervising the construction of a new state insane asylum, Elam Lynds returned to the prison on the Hudson as its chief disciplinary officer.[40]

A program of severity and retrenchment was swiftly put into effect. The prison staff was reduced in size, and salaries were cut. Despite an actual increase in the inmate population, less money was spent on food, clothing, and hospital stores. Prisoners were no longer allowed to teach in the Sabbath school, and when sufficient civilian instructors could not be found to take their place the

[39] Luckey *Life in Sing Sing State Prison*, pp. 29–30; DS, 67th Session (1844), Vol. I, No. 20, pp. 8–11, 199; John W. Edmonds, *A Letter . . . to General Aaron Ward* (New York, c. 1844), p. 4; DA, 66th Session (1843), Vol. VI, No. 176, p. 5. The spending record of the Whig administration at Albany had been a major issue in the gubernatorial campaign of 1842; this probably intensified the new inspectors' concern about prison deficits. See especially David M. Ellis *et al.*, *A Short History of New York State* (Ithaca, N.Y., 1957), pp. 217–218.

[40] Edmonds, *Letter*, pp. 5–7; DS, 69th Session (1846), Vol. IV, No. 120, p. 10; New York State Department of Correction, *Sing Sing Prison*, facing p. 1; DS, 67th Session (1844), Vol. I, No. 20, pp. 24, 209; Federal Writers' Program, *New York: A Guide to the Empire State* (New York, 1947), pp. 359–360.

entire venture was abandoned. The restrictions that had been placed upon lashing under Seymour and McDuffie were speedily rescinded. The cells were frisked, and all sorts of forbidden articles from knives and alcohol to French and Latin grammars were confiscated, after which the inmates who had possessed them were summarily flogged.[41] All reading materials except the Bible and a prayer book were now prohibited, and the convicts were forbidden either to write or to receive letters. The chaplain was ordered to tell the felons nothing about their friends and relatives except for the laconic remark, "Your friends are well." If Lynds wished, even this minor indulgence could be disallowed.[42] Visiting privileges, although not completely eliminated, were abridged. Meanwhile, the incidence of flogging climbed sharply.[43]

For Edmonds, who had wanted tighter discipline and had braved popular hostility to return Lynds to power, these developments should have been gratifying. Such, ironically, was not the case. It is highly probable that the chief inspector had known little about penal affairs prior to assuming his new post at Sing Sing; his reputation as a lawyer and legislator was based largely upon his record in matters pertaining to banking and the rights of labor. His overriding concern upon taking over the prison position had been to improve fiscal conditions, and he appears to have regarded increased stringency as a means toward that end. In addition, he came from a Quaker background which may have predisposed him to view the violence of Lynds's tactics, once he witnessed them in action, with a measure of dismay.[44] As the use of the whip became

---

[41] DS, 67th Session (1844), Vol. I, No. 20, pp. 5, 237.

[42] Luckey, *Life in Sing Sing State Prison*, pp. 31, 185. Although Edmonds was technically correct in asserting that the inspectors refused to abolish correspondence privileges, Luckey is undoubtedly accurate in stating that these were forbidden to the convicts. On July 22, 1843, the board stipulated that no inmate could write a letter, but that the principal keeper could do it for him if he deemed it proper. In view of Lynds's ideas, this was surely tantamount to a complete prohibition. See Edmonds, *Letter*, p. 7; DS, 67th Session (1844), Vol. I, No. 20, pp. 21–22.

[43] DS, 67th Session (1844), Vol. I, No. 20, pp. 21–22.

[44] See especially Livingston, *Portraits of Eminent Americans*, pp. 797, 799–800; Schlesinger, *Age of Jackson*, pp. 179, 197, 339, 341. In 1846, Edmonds

5. John Worth Edmonds, 1799–1874. Engraving from John Livingston, *Portraits of Eminent Americans Now Living, With Biographical and Historical Memoirs of Their Lives and Actions* (New York, 1853).

more and more frequent, Edmonds became less and less enthusiastic about what he saw happening. When the number of stripes inflicted by the keepers reached a reported monthly total of fifteen hundred, not counting those administered by Lynds himself, the new chairman decided that things had gone too far.[45]

Searching for new ideas, Edmonds approached John Luckey, who was still chaplain, and asked for his views on penitentiary discipline. Luckey knew that several keepers were opposed to the reintroduction of Lyndsian tactics, and that these officers had made a secret agreement to maintain the "mild system" in their shops. Informing Edmonds of this, he urged that the chairman visit these shops and see the results for himself.[46] When Edmonds and a fellow inspector investigated the situation, they found that the number of lashes inflicted on some inmate gangs averaged only six per month, while other groups received as many as four hundred. Surprisingly, the state of discipline in the latter was no better than that which prevailed in the former.[47]

Modifying his previous views, Edmonds now became an exponent of regulating the use of the whip. Late in July, 1843, he and another inspector named Isaac Birdsall recommended a number of changes to their colleagues. Henceforth, no keeper was to strike a convict with any other instrument than the ordinary "cat" except in self-defense; no assistant keeper was to inflict more than ten blows upon an inmate in any case; and no felon was to be flogged more than once for a single breach of discipline without specific orders from the board. Lynds himself was to administer no more than twenty-five lashes for any one violation, and was to render to the inspectors an account of all the punishments he inflicted. Finally, no prisoner was to be whipped in any event until

informed a correspondent that he had diligently sought knowledge about penal matters during his inspectorship by visiting other institutions and doing extensive reading on the subject. This strengthens my belief that he did not assume his post with any well-developed ideas in this field. See DS, 69th Session (1846), Vol. IV, No. 120, p. 11.

[45] DS, 69th Session (1846), Vol. IV, No. 120, p. 10; Edmonds, *Letter*, p. 6.

[46] Luckey, *Life in Sing Sing State Prison*, pp. 31–34.

[47] Edmonds, *Letter*, p. 8.

a period of twelve hours had elapsed since his infraction of the rules.

The board was not ready to authorize these changes, but it did give Edmonds permission to admonish Lynds about his mania for flogging. The principal keeper "strenuously remonstrated" at this warning, but the incidence of lashing nevertheless diminished temporarily. By September, however, the smoldering dispute between Lynds and his critics within the institution flared into the open. A charge that a released convict had been brought back into the prison and flogged was referred to the inspectors, as well as accusations that a recent escape was due in part to the principal keeper's negligence. Lynds appeared before the board accompanied by counsel and denied these allegations, but a majority of the inspectors decided that they were substantially true. A motion to dismiss the veteran official, however, was temporarily tabled.[48]

Administrative squabbling continued to build up at Sing Sing, increasing in bitterness until Lynds and his superiors were in a state of open hostility. Edmonds subsequently charged that on one occasion, while numerous convicts were within earshot, the principal keeper audibly expressed a desire to see the inspectors thrown into the Hudson. Finally, in January, 1844, a keeper named Joseph Requa confronted the board with a series of allegations that Lynds had been intoxicated while on duty, had countermanded orders given by the agent, had made abusive remarks about the inspectors, and had used state property for his personal needs. Requa later tried to withdraw these charges, but a majority of the board had by this time reached the end of their patience. On February 9, 1844, Elam Lynds's last tour of duty in the prisons of New York came to an end. He was never again to be involved in their management.[49]

[48] *Ibid.*, pp. 8–11; DS, 67th Session (1844), Vol. I, No. 20, pp. 236, 241, 243, 246–252.

[49] Edmonds, *Letter*, pp. 18–23. An appeal by Lynds to the state senate for redress failed; see DS, 67th Session (1844), Vol. II, No. 91, and Vol. IV, No. 155. Lynds lived for another eleven years, dying in South Brooklyn on Jan. 8, 1855; see Thorsten Sellin, "Lynds, Elam," DAB, XI, 527; New York *Times*, Jan. 9, 1855.

The way was now open for significant changes to take place in the administration of discipline. In April, 1844, the inspectors embarked upon an experiment in which the lash was to be used only as a last resort. Two months later they issued an explicit directive to the keepers to substitute other punishments for flogging whenever possible, using such methods as solitary confinement, deprivation of food or bedding, changing an inmate's employment from a given task to a less pleasant one, or subjecting prisoners to the shower bath. By the end of the year the new principal keeper, Harman Eldridge, estimated that the number of stripes administered to the felons had fallen off by 75 per cent, and stated that this had been accompanied by an actual decrease in the number of disciplinary violations.[50] While this change was taking place, other steps were taken to liberalize policy. Luckey and Eldridge, for example, were directed to reassemble the prison library.[51] In addition, an "out-ward" was erected on the penitentiary grounds where insane convicts could receive proper care and treatment instead of being lashed as before.[52]

Edmonds was not willing to stop at this point. Through visiting other penal institutions, corresponding with such reformers as Dorothea Dix, and reading a variety of works pertaining to prison discipline—in itself a striking departure from the activities of administrators who had trusted in "common sense"—he became interested not only in making policy changes at Sing Sing but also in trying to stimulate thought and action on a broader and more general level. With the exception of the Society for the Reformation of Juvenile Delinquents, which naturally confined its atten-

[50] DS, 68th Session (1845), Vol. I, No. 9, pp. 6, 38. The average number of lashes administered each month at Sing Sing in 1843 was 1,121. The corresponding figure for 1844 was 787, still relatively high and reflecting in part the heavy incidence of flogging early in the year. By the end of 1845, the monthly average was down to 366. See DA, 71st Session (1848), Vol. I, No. 10, p. 17.

[51] DS, 68th Session (1845), Vol. I, No. 9, p. 37; Luckey, *Life at Sing Sing State Prison*, p. 36.

[52] DS, 68th Session (1845), Vol. I, No. 9, pp. 4–5; Dorothea Dix, *Remarks on Prisons and Prison Discipline in the United States* (Boston, 1845), pp. 14–15, 39–40.

tion to young offenders, New York had no organization of its own devoted to penal reform. Louis Dwight's Boston-centered Prison Discipline Society, which had pre-empted the field many years before, was now as always mainly a mouthpiece for the thoughts of one man, and was intellectually strait-jacketed by its leader's continued control and stubborn resistance to change. In addition, it had the further disadvantage of being so blindly opposed to the Pennsylvania system and so slurring in its official pronouncements concerning the solitary method that no fruitful interchange of ideas could possibly take place between it and reform groups reflecting the Philadelphia point of view. Although he remained committed to the basic features of the congregate system, Edmonds apparently became convinced by the end of 1844 that a new society was needed if there was to be any chance of cutting through the increasingly sterile debate which had been taking place for years between exponents of the two competing approaches to penal discipline. Early in December he published a newspaper notice, co-signed by over sixty leading citizens of New York, calling for a public meeting at which a "Prison Association" could be organized.[53]

Edmonds had evidently laid the groundwork carefully, for within a week the New York Prison Association (N.Y.P.A.) had been formed at a well-attended meeting in New York City at which the inspector was one of the chief speakers. Two errors, he told his audience, prevailed on the subject of penitentiary punishments. One was the belief that all criminals were vicious and hardened; the other was the idea that the offender deserved nothing but compassion. Edmonds pleaded for a middle ground, "a common sense view of the matter, which did not regard a prison as a place of ease, nor yet as a place devoted to torment only, but as a house of repentance, where the most hardened might be taught the useful lesson that the way of the transgressor is hard, and that virtue is sure of its reward here and hereafter." The

[53] New York *Tribune*, Dec. 3, 1844; Anonymous, "Prison Discipline," *United States Magazine and Democratic Review*, XIX (August, 1846), 132.

speaker's study of earlier works on penal matters was evident as he harked back to Thomas Eddy's idea that prisoners should be divided into three groups: the innocent (those who had committed offenses only under the direst need or with dubious intent), the doubtful, and the irreclaimable. The last, Edmonds stated, should be deprived of all opportunity to injure society, although the way of repentance should always be held open to them. The others should be subjected to continued rehabilitative treatment. Vengeance should be ruled out as an object of punishment; the system should aim "not at the infliction of retributive pain upon the prisoner, but at his reformation." Finally, Edmonds adopted a conciliatory tone with regard to the Pennsylvania system and its exponents. The new prison association, he said, should wed itself to neither the congregate nor the solitary method, but rather "select from both that which is wisest and best." [54]

After listening to other speeches which emphasized the potentialities of kindness in penal policy, the ways in which environment was related to crime, and the necessity for preventing politically motivated changes of prison personnel, the assembly formally organized the new association and approved the appointment of committees to effect "the amelioration of the condition of prisoners, whether detained for trial, or finally convicted, or as witnesses; the improvement of prison discipline and the government of prisons; and the support and encouragement of reformed convicts, after their discharge, by affording them the means of obtaining an honest livelihood, and sustaining them in their efforts at reform." [55] After the new society was well launched in the New York City area, Edmonds traveled to Auburn, where on November 17, 1846, he addressed "a numerous and respectable meeting" at

[54] New York Prison Association, *First Report* (1844), pp. 23, 26–27, 29. Note the similarity of some of these ideas to those of Eddy as given in Samuel L. Knapp, *The Life of Thomas Eddy* (New York, 1834), pp. 60–61, and [Thomas Eddy], *An Account of the State Prison or Penitentiary House* (New York, 1801), pp. 50–51.

[55] New York Prison Association, *First Report* (1844), *passim;* DA, 68th Session (1845), Vol. IV, No. 96, p. 1.

the Cayuga County Court House on the need for a milder system of penal discipline, calling for an end to flogging and to political machinations in prison management. Partisanship was pushed into the background as the leading Auburn Whig, ex-Governor Seward, aided Edmonds in establishing a western branch of the Association.[56] During this same period, another division was set up in Troy.[57]

The activities of the New York Prison Association soon revealed the many ways in which its outlook differed from that which had prevailed during the previous generation among penal reformers in the Empire State. At the second-anniversary meeting of the society in December, 1846, for example, Edmonds stated that a considerable effort had been made during the past year to correspond with foreign experts on penal affairs. From the very beginning the organization had maintained close ties with Johann Ludwig Tellkampf, a German penologist who was visiting the United States on an official tour of prison inspection for the Prussian government and had delivered an address to the N.Y.P.A. at its first meeting. At the 1846 gathering, Edmonds also read a communication to the members from Nicolaus Heinrich Julius, another German correctional expert who had inspected a number of American penitentiaries in the mid-1830's.[58] New Yorkers, once proud in the belief that their state possessed the ultimate wisdom in penal matters, were finally returning to Thomas Eddy's conviction that America had much to learn in this area from the Old World.

Another departure from the past occurred in October, 1847, when Edmonds and other members of the N.Y.P.A. participated

[56] *Northern Christian Advocate*, Nov. 25, 1846; DA, 70th Session (1847), Vol. VIII, No. 255, Part I, p. 32. It is pertinent to remark in this connection that Horace Greeley was also a consistent supporter of the N.Y.P.A. See New York *Tribune*, Dec. 3, 1844; Dec. 7, 1844; and Feb. 4, 1847.

[57] New York *Tribune*, Dec. 23, 1846.

[58] *Ibid.* For Julius' own account of his American tour, see his work *Nordamerikas sittliche Zustände, Nach eigenen Anschauungen in den Jahren 1834, 1835, und 1836* (2 vols.; Leipzig, 1839).

in a "Prison Discipline Convention" in New York City in which correctional ideas were discussed with a delegation from Pennsylvania headed by such exponents of the solitary system as Richard Vaux. On a previous occasion, Edmonds had indicated that he feared the effects of prolonged solitude upon the mind and believed that the Philadelphia method was "applicable only to a short term of punishment." On the other hand, he was ready to concede that those who defended the system were animated by a just and humane spirit, and that their plan of discipline, with certain modifications, might work with tolerable success. It is not apparent that either the New Yorkers or the Pennsylvanians backed down on their ideas at the 1847 meeting, but the mere fact that they had gathered together for discussion was in itself a significant indication that the rancor of previous years was to some extent dissipating. Before adjourning, the participants actually talked over the idea of forming a National Prison Association, and scheduled another meeting to be held at Philadelphia in June, 1848.[59]

Most of the activities of the New York Prison Association, however, were confined to the Empire State itself, where its efforts also demonstrated the dimensions of the change that had come about in penal affairs since the halcyon days of the Auburn system. Securing a charter of incorporation from the New York legislature, it conducted investigations of state, county, and city penal establishments under a special grant of authority permitting N.Y.P.A. representatives to question inmates in private about the treatment they were receiving. In 1846 alone, the Association examined fifteen county prisons and all of the state penitentiaries. Facts gathered on such missions were printed in the organization's annual reports, which were distributed to members of the legisla-

[59] New York *Tribune,* Oct. 8 and 9, 1847; New York Prison Association, *First Report* (1844), pp. 23–24, 44, 47–48. The proposed National Prison Association did not come into being until 1870, when a meeting of penal reformers from all parts of the nation was held in Cincinnati. Although subsequent conventions were held at Baltimore, St. Louis, and New York City, internal dissensions and financial troubles had caused the organization to wither away by 1875. See Blake McKelvey, *American Prisons* (Chicago, 1936), pp. 69–73.

ture and among the public at large.[60] Another important aspect of the society's operations was the maintenance of an office in New York City to which released inmates might come for money, clothing, and aid in finding jobs. Managed by Isaac Hopper, a Hicksite Quaker who had previously been involved in prison reform as a resident of Pennsylvania, this division had by 1846 assisted 506 ex-convicts in one way or another and found employment for 205 of them.[61]

In 1845, a female department of the N.Y.P.A. was established under the leadership of such women as Mrs. John W. Edmonds, Mrs. William Cullen Bryant, Mrs. Freeman Hunt, and Miss Catherine M. Sedgwick. The main focus of this group's efforts was an asylum for discharged female prisoners opened on June 12 of the same year. Hopper assisted the women in this phase of the Association's activities, aided by his daughter, Abby H. Gibbons, and by Caroline M. Kirkland, an enthusiastic N.Y.P.A. worker who later aided the asylum by writing a book in its behalf. In a dilapidated three-story house at 191 Tenth Avenue in New York City, these leaders and their helpers carried on "a death grapple with sin in its strongest dominion—the heart of a disgraced and ruined woman." Female ex-convicts who sought refuge in the "Isaac T. Hopper Home," as it came to be called, entered on a voluntary basis and were free to terminate their stay whenever they wished. Strictly forbidden to smoke, drink, or curse so long as they remained in residence, and given only a frugal diet, they were employed in sewing and laundering and given instruction in

[60] See DA, 70th Session (1847), Vol. VIII, No. 222, pp. 1–2, and 72nd Session (1849), Vol. VI, No. 243, pp. 213–215. The special powers granted to the N.Y.P.A. aroused considerable opposition among conservatives, who managed as early as 1847 to push through the senate a bill to take away the society's inspection rights, particularly those allowing inmates to be questioned in private. (DA, 70th Session [1847], Vol. VIII, No. 256, pp. 1, 4.)

[61] Lydia Maria Child, *Isaac T. Hopper: A True Life* (Boston, 1853), pp. 212–214, 273–296, 410–411; DA, 70th Session (1847), Vol. VIII, No. 255, Part 1, p. 66. Hopper, who had been active in the N.Y.P.A. from its beginning, had accompanied Edmonds to Albany to lobby for its incorporation.

elementary subjects. In addition, they were required to attend worship services on Sunday, and were given frequent religious advice during the week.

From the beginning, the asylum was a shoestring operation. As the New York *Tribune* commented, "the house has in it scarcely anything; it is a true Lazarus establishment, asking for the crumbs that fall from the rich man's table." Nevertheless, the dedication of those who operated it enabled the Hopper Home to survive and render a valuable public service. When it was believed that a woman had shown evidence of reformation, a position was secured for her as an operative in a factory or a domestic helper in a private household, and she was obliged to accept the assignment or be expelled from the asylum. By 1848, the managers had found employment for 175 of the inmates, a figure which increased steadily as the years went by.[62]

In addition to exposing improper penal conditions, aiding discharged convicts, and attempting to reform fallen women, the New York Prison Association also acted as a gadfly in advocating departures from long-accepted correctional policies. Its third annual report, published in 1847, contained trenchant criticism of several time-honored ideas, including the belief that the success of a penitentiary should be judged primarily by the amount of the financial surplus it was able to produce. The Association bowed to public sentiment in conceding that self-supporting prisons were desirable, but argued that "if this cannot be effected but at the expense of reformatory action, it had better be abandoned than attempted." Only about 1 per cent of the annual expenditure for the penitentiaries, it informed the reader, was spent on bettering the mental or moral condition of the convicts.

The same report also took issue with another sacrosanct idea

[62] Caroline M. Kirkland, *The Helping Hand: Comprising an Account of* THE HOME, *for Discharged Female Convicts* (New York, 1853), *passim;* John F. Richmond, *New York and Its Institutions, 1609–1872* (New York, 1872), pp. 456–460; DA, 72nd Session (1849), Vol. VI, No. 243, p. 194; New York *Tribune,* June 19, 1845.

associated with the Auburn system, namely, the theory that inmates should not be allowed to communicate with one another. The rule of silence, the Association maintained, was "at war with one of the strongest principles of our nature, and impracticable in point of fact." Representatives of the society had become convinced through interrogating offenders and officers alike that it was impossible to maintain complete noncommunication without appointing a keeper for each individual convict. "To make laws . . . which violate the social order of our being, which are at war with the law of our nature, and are impracticable in execution," it was asserted, "is to sustain a system by a refined species of torture, suited perhaps to the walls of an inquisition, but not at all in unison with the benevolent breathings of the age." [63]

The concluding words of this statement furnished one key for understanding the great changes that had come about in the prisons since the beginning of the decade. In an era characterized by optimism, humanitarian striving, and social experiment, new penal policies could be put into practice as long as political circumstances allowed such leaders as Edmonds to remain in power. The transformation that had occurred in New York afforded only one example of this, for old correctional ideas were being attacked, reconsidered, and modified in state after state throughout the 1840's. In Vermont, revelations of the abuses which had taken place under Lynds and Wiltse at Auburn at Sing Sing had stimulated reformers to inaugurate milder methods at Windsor prison.[64] Similar tendencies were at work in New Hampshire, where convicts were now allowed to read books and to correspond with people in the outside world. "The spirit of philanthropy that now is hovering over [our] land, does not only shower down its blessings on the poor drunkard, but it has come into our prisons," wrote one inmate in a contribution to a temperance paper called the *White Mountain Torrent.* "Yes, notwithstanding our prisons are made of stone and

[63] DA, 70th Session (1847), Vol. VIII, No. 255, Part 2, pp. 33, 35–36, 45.
[64] David M. Ludlum, *Social Ferment in Vermont, 1791–1850* (Montpelier, Vt., 1948), pp. 211–212.

iron, the spirit of kindness and love has found a passport." [65] In Ohio, a new warden named Lauren Dewey inaugurated a notable series of reforms in the state penitentiary at Columbus after replacing an exponent of harsh methods. Lashing was greatly restricted, and the previous "rule with a rod of iron" was replaced by a "law of kindness." [66]

The challenge to the penal thinking of the past quarter-century was particularly well revealed in Massachusetts, stronghold of Louis Dwight's Prison Discipline Society. Under the leadership of Frederick Robinson, once described as "a man remarkable for his kind disposition and for his confidence in the power of love to reform the degraded," the lash was abandoned almost entirely in the state prison at Charlestown and one of the basic rules of the Auburn system, that which prescribed the "downcast eye," was revoked.[67] Another citizen of the Bay State, Dorothea Dix, championed not only the cause of the insane but also that of the convict. Her quest for a more humane penal system was highlighted in 1845 by the publication of her *Remarks on Prisons and Prison Discipline in the United States,* advocating mild policies and commending Edmonds for the efforts he was making in New York.[68] Finally, rebellion flared in the Prison Discipline Society itself as Samuel Gridley Howe, Horace Mann, and Charles Sumner, who favored the Pennsylvania system, launched a campaign against Louis Dwight. Howe tried unsuccessfully to block a legislative appropriation to the organization in 1843, and by the middle of the decade the hostility of the minority toward Dwight erupted in a series of bitter speeches at Society meetings, including performances by Sumner that amounted to dry-runs for his tirade on the "Crime against Kansas" delivered in the United States

[65] Quoted in New York *Tribune,* Dec. 31, 1844.

[66] See the long anonymous letter quoted in *ibid.,* supplement to the issue of March 20, 1847.

[67] *Ibid.,* Jan. 22, 1847.

[68] Albert Deutsch, *The Mentally Ill in America: A History of Their Care and Treatment from Colonial Times* (Garden City, N.Y., 1937), p. 173; Dix, *Remarks on Prisons, passim.*

Senate in 1856. In the end, Dwight retained majority support, but was unable to prevent Sumner, Howe, and Mann from printing a minority statement strongly deprecating his tactics.[69] In 1847, Sumner's younger brother George carried the fight to the Second International Penitentiary Congress at Brussels, telling the delegates not only that American public opinion on the subject of prisons had been shaken, but also that "the idea of the infallibility of the system of Auburn has been done away with." [70]

However biased the source, this was a fair estimate.[71] In a period of humanitarian ferment, the old penal order seemed to be crumbling and a new one gradually emerging to take its place. Nowhere did this appear to be more true than in the state which had pioneered the Auburn system only a generation before. Nevertheless, as the New York Prison Association indicated by the strictures contained in its 1847 report, the basic features of that system, though softened, still remained. If penal officers now tended to believe in reformative treatment, effective financial support was still lacking. If the inmate's former isolation had been partially broken, the rule of silence still prevailed. If the N.Y.P.A. itself was nonpartisan and opposed to the practice of making sweeping changes in prison personnel, the penitentiaries were far from immune to the operations of the spoils system.

[69] Samuel Gridley Howe, *An Essay on Separate and Congregate Systems of Prison Discipline* (Boston, 1846), pp. v–ix; Harold Schwartz, *Samuel Gridley Howe: Social Reformer, 1801–1876* (Cambridge, Mass., 1956), pp. 147–149; David Donald, *Charles Sumner and the Coming of the Civil War* (New York, 1960), pp. 120–128.

[70] DA, 72nd Session (1849), Vol. VI, No. 243, pp. 137–138, 140; John H. Cary, "France Looks to Pennsylvania: The Eastern Penitentiary as a Symbol of Reform," *Pennsylvania Magazine of History and Biography*, LXXXII (April, 1958), 200. See also George Sumner, *The Pennsylvania System of Prison Discipline Triumphant in France* (Philadelphia, 1847), *passim*.

[71] Sumner went on to contend, however, that the Pennsylvania system was "gaining ground every day." This was plausible with regard to Europe, where the solitary method secured acceptance in such countries as France, Belgium, Sweden, and Denmark and was endorsed by penal congresses held at Brussels and Frankfort-am-Main. In America, on the other hand, the existence of such a trend would have been difficult to prove.

In short, though much had been changed, much remained to be done. In addition, there was no real assurance that the reforms which had been brought about thus far could be indefinitely maintained. Furthermore, by 1847 it was abundantly clear that those who wanted to break away from the harsh methods of the past were by no means agreed on the modes of discipline that should prevail in the future or on the rationale which should undergird a new order. In the end, the bickering produced by this state of affairs helped to undermine the progress of a movement which was enjoying only a precarious existence to begin with. Seymour and Polhemus had learned in 1843 that it was easier to start a trend than to perpetuate it, and the lesson was to be repeated before the decade came to an end.

# Chapter X

# Radicalism and Reaction

ALTHOUGH the reform administrators who came into power in the prisons of New York during the 1840's agreed upon certain fundamental premises, they were by no means in complete accord on all matters of penal policy. They shared a common disinclination to use violent punishments, a belief that criminals could and should be rehabilitated, and a disposition to use kindness whenever this did not impair discipline. On the other hand, there remained considerable room for disagreement on the causes of crime, the nature of guilt, and the precise means that should be taken to produce amendment of the offender. Some officials were more eager than others to break away from traditional ideas involving the felon and his treatment. As a result the period between 1844 and 1848, during which the movement for a more humanitarian administration of New York's penitentiaries reached its peak, was marked by acrimony and debate. Disputes over certain ideas and techniques became so acute that a split occurred between reformers who shared a common aversion to older methods. This played into the hands of critics who had never wanted a change in the first place, and reaction set in before the decade came to an end.

Foremost among the tendencies to which penological conservatives objected during the 1840's was the way in which popular sympathy and pity were replacing the aversion and animosity with which criminals had only recently been regarded. Paradoxically, some of this sympathy and pity had unquestionably been stimulated by the excesses which had occurred under the stringent rule of such men as Lynds and Wiltse, so that the repressive school was being haunted by its own zeal. The roots of the new attitude, however, could be found in the same optimism which was reflected in the increased emphasis upon rehabilitation in the prisons. In a period of lessened concern about the safety of democratic institutions, and of faith in the inevitability of progress, hatred of the offender could not feed upon widespread fears of social upheaval and citizens could afford to be indulgent. The spread of sentimentalism, which exalted pity as a virtue, also contributed to the new image of the lawbreaker, and was especially influential in the progress of the antigallows movement.[1] In addition, the romantic emphasis upon the organic unity of mankind reinforced latent Christian attitudes about human brotherhood and the implication of the group in the sins of the individual.[2] The result, in the eyes of some critics, was a further threat to property and morality in an age of misguided reformism. "Nobody has any *rights* except scoundrels, and slaves and debtors," exclaimed James Watson Webb's New York *Courier and Enquirer* in 1847 in an attack upon current penal practices. "Laws must consult their convenience and advantage solely." [3]

One manifestation of a sympathetic outlook toward the criminal in the 1840's was the willingness of many citizens to absolve him from guilt, either wholly or in part, by shifting blame to various environmental deficiencies. The influential *Democratic Review* asked its readers in 1846 to consider the extenuating circumstances

[1] See Herbert R. Brown, *The Sentimental Novel in America, 1789–1860* (reprinted ed.; New York, 1959), p. 142; David B. Davis, "The Movement to Abolish Capital Punishment in America, 1787–1861," *American Historical Review,* LXIII (October, 1957), 29–30.

[2] See especially Merle Curti, *The Growth of American Thought* (2nd ed.; New York, 1951), pp. 372, 381.

[3] New York *Courier and Enquirer,* May 5, 1847, as quoted by New York *Tribune,* May 7, 1847. Italics are as given.

which existed with regard to certain illegal acts, and "to inquire how far even the most virtuously disposed might have fallen before them." [4] Even more outspoken was a statement by Lydia Maria Child to the effect that "Society is answerable for crime, because it is so negligent of duty," printed in the New York *Tribune* in 1844.[5] Popular novelists who had been influenced by such European works as Edward Bulwer-Lytton's deterministic *Paul Clifford* portrayed felons as victims of circumstance. In *The B'hoys of New York* and *The G'hals of New York,* for example, Ned Buntline (Edward Z. C. Judson) cast young delinquents in the role of frustrated and injured persons who had been corrupted and wronged by relatives and acquaintances.[6] The influence of environmentalism was apparent at the first meeting of the New York Prison Association in 1844 when William Henry Channing, one of the charter members of the organization, spoke of "the conviction, fast becoming general, that the community is itself, by its neglects and bad usages, *in part responsible* for the sins of its children; and that it owes to the criminal, therefore, aid to reform." [7]

Such arguments obviously ran counter to the beliefs of those who regarded the felon as a strictly accountable being. So did the contentions of reformers who asserted that criminality indicated disease or faulty cerebral endowment rather than willful depravity. Although Anglo-American jurisprudence had accepted the M'Naghten Rules of 1843, based upon John Locke's theory that a man should be adjudged legally sane if he understands the nature and quality of his actions and can distinguish right from wrong, this principle had already come under vigorous attack by such eminent alienists as Isaac Ray, whose arguments greatly concerned citizens fearing that the worst types of crimes might now be excused on the grounds of insanity. Such terms as "homicidal mania,"

[4] Anonymous, "Prison Discipline," *United States Magazine and Democratic Review,* XIX (August, 1846), 129.

[5] Lydia Maria Child, "Kindness to Criminals—The Prison Association," copied from Boston *Courier* by New York *Tribune,* Dec. 20, 1844.

[6] David B. Davis, *Homicide in American Fiction, 1798–1860: A Study in Social Values* (Ithaca, N.Y., 1957), pp. 217–221.

[7] New York Prison Association, *First Report* (1844), p. 31. Italics are as given.

"moral insanity," and "irresistible impulse" were cropping up in popular discussion and seemed slippery indeed to those who insisted that some hard and fast line of demarcation, such as Locke provided, was needed to separate the guilty from the innocent. Ray's theories received a particularly spectacular airing in New York in 1846 when William H. Seward based his famous defense of William Freeman in part upon them.[8]

The idea that criminal acts were attributable in many cases to defective endowments received considerable support from the pseudo-science of phrenology, which was particularly distasteful to defenders of traditional moral theories. Phrenology postulated that the human mind was composed of various faculties, generally grouped into "propensities" and "sentiments." Under the heading of "propensities" were subsumed such characteristics as amativeness (the desire for sexual love), combativeness, destructiveness, secretiveness, and acquisitiveness. The "sentiments" included benevolence, veneration, self-esteem, conscientiousness, and love of approbation. Each of these faculties was controlled by a given area of the brain. The "propensities" had their proper uses; they gave people courage to face difficulty, determination to resist aggression, and the desire to provide against want. Nevertheless, they could become so overdeveloped as to induce men to commit savage crimes. The "sentiments" were also potentially liable to abuse. Firmness, which could be manifested in such desirable characteristics as perseverance, could also produce intransigence and "tenacity in evil." If the various faculties were improperly developed or out of harmony with one another, criminal behavior might occur. This would be especially likely if the propensities were stronger than the sentiments that should normally have held them within bounds.[9]

[8] Davis, *Homicide in American Fiction,* Chapter III, *passim.* Freeman, part Indian and part Negro, had murdered four members of the wealthy Van Nest household near Auburn and wounded others. Seward failed to secure an acquittal, but the prisoner died in his cell before execution. See Frederic Bancroft, *The Life of William Seward* (New York, 1900), I, 174–180.

[9] See the list in George Combe, *The Constitution of Man Considered in Relation to External Objects* (Boston, 1836), pp. 50–53, and the diagram in

To the phrenologist, therefore, wrongdoing did not stem from depravity; it had a physical basis. Because the strength of each faculty was governed by the extent of a given brain area's development, one could sometimes identify a criminal merely by looking at him. He was likely to have a "ruffian head," characterized by a low forehead, a flat or depressed skull, and large amounts of brain area behind his ears. By spotting which propensities were especially well developed, one might even be able to tell the precise crimes such a man was most likely to commit. If he had pronounced areas of covetiveness and combativeness, for example, he was probably an armed robber; if he possessed marked covetiveness with cautiousness, however, he might well be a sneak-thief or a pickpocket.[10]

If these theories were true, it was wrong to hold a criminal strictly responsible for his offenses. The cerebral organization of certain people, stated a New York phrenologist in 1835, was such as to produce strong impulses to steal. To require the same behavior from such individuals as was expected of citizens with good phrenological developments was just as senseless "as it would be to require of man, constituted as he is, that he should visit the depths of the ocean with the fish, or penetrate the mid-heavens with the eagle." A person could be held responsible only for the proper exercise of faculties which he actually possessed.[11] This did not mean, however, that the criminal's mental processes were unchangeable. "The condition of the brain, like that of the muscles and organs of sense," affirmed a prominent phrenologist, "can be altered, and greatly improved by exercise." If one wished to weaken

---

John D. Davies, *Phrenology, Fad and Science: A 19th-Century American Crusade* (New Haven, Conn., 1955), p. 6.

[10] Charles Caldwell, *New Views of Penitentiary Discipline, and Moral Education and Reform* (Philadelphia, 1829), pp. 18, 25. See also the analysis in Amos Dean, *Lectures on Phrenology: Delivered before the Young Men's Association for Mutual Improvement of the City of Albany* (Albany, 1834), pp. 103–104. For a brief general treatment of the relation of phrenology to penology, see Davies, *Phrenology, Fad and Science*, pp. 98–105.

[11] Dean, *Lectures on Phrenology*, pp. 102–103, footnote.

a dangerous propensity, he should place the person who possessed it in an environment which would give such a faculty little chance for activity. At the same time, he should surround the afflicted individual with uplifting influences. These would gradually strengthen the areas of the mind that controlled the higher sentiments. The criminal could thus be changed into a better man.[12]

Rehabilitative treatment was therefore the only phrenologically intelligent policy; subjecting a culprit to violent punishment merely strengthened the very faculties that needed to be inactivated. Flogging was a great mistake, for it excited resentment and hatred, and stimulated a desire for revenge. Traditional methods of dealing with offenders were also unsound in other respects. The fact that a man committed repeated crimes, for example, served only to show that he had an especially bad cranial development and was in critical need of therapy. Because of public ignorance, however, multiple offenders were usually treated with ever greater severity. The concept of "making the punishment fit the crime" was another fallacy. Instead, the treatment should fit the cerebral development of the individual offender.[13]

Phrenology had not been unknown to early New York prison reformers. During his trip to Europe in 1818, John Griscom had attended a lecture by Franz Joseph Gall, the father of studies in this field, but had come away from it filled with skepticism.[14] In the 1820's, however, phrenology gained several notable exponents in the United States. One of these was Charles Caldwell, a professor at Transylvania University; another was John Bell, an outstanding Philadelphia physician who edited the *Eclectic Journal of Medicine*. In 1832, the visit to the United States of Gall's leading disciple, Johann Gaspar Spurzheim, also stimulated great interest

[12] Caldwell, *New Views of Penitentiary Discipline*, pp. 3, 14–15, 22–23.

[13] *Ibid.*, pp. 3–4, 41; Marmaduke B. Sampson, *Rationale of Crime, and Its Appropriate Treatment: Being a Treatise on Criminal Jurisprudence Considered in Relation to Cerebral Organization*, ed. Eliza W. Farnham (New York, 1846), p. 11, footnote.

[14] John Griscom, *A Year in Europe* (New York, 1823), I, 259, and II, 56, 259, 351–353.

in phrenology, as did the American tour of the Scots writer and lecturer George Combe later in the decade. After Combe spoke in New York City in December, 1838, a distinguished group of jurists, physicians, university professors, and philanthropists tendered him a resolution asserting that phrenology opened up "a new era in mental and physiological science, in which we believe human inquiry will be greatly facilitated, and the amount of human happiness essentially increased." The list of believers in the theories of Gall and Spurzheim included such eminent men as Nicholas Biddle, Henry Ward Beecher, Horace Mann, Samuel Gridley Howe, and Henry Schoolcraft. Amariah Brigham, who became supervisor of the New York State Lunatic Asylum at Utica and founder of the *American Journal of Insanity,* was also a disciple.[15]

The moral relativism associated with phrenology, however, appalled various citizens in New York. David Meredith Reese, a critic of many popular "isms," contemptuously attacked the ideas of Gall and his followers as devices for "easing a loaded conscience." [16] Another detractor feared that "the midnight assassin may go with Phrenology in one hand and the dagger in the other, and execute his dark design without compunction and without responsibility." [17] When phrenology began to be applied in the New York prison system, therefore, it was not surprising that it encountered strident opposition from those who believed that man was a free moral agent who should be held strictly accountable for his transgressions. Typical was the reaction of the New York *Courier and Enquirer,* which complained bitterly in 1847 about new ways of dealing with convicts according to cranial bumps and propensities. "The quacks that now vex the public ear with their

---

[15] Davies, *Phrenology, Fad and Science,* pp. 13–14, 16–20; Arthur E. Fink, *Causes of Crime: Biological Theories in the United States, 1800–1915* (Philadelphia, 1938), pp. 4, 9–10, 12; Robert E. Riegel, "The Introduction of Phrenology to the United States," *American Historical Review,* XXXIX (October, 1933), 75–76, 78; Roswell W. Haskins, *History and Progress of Phrenology* (Buffalo, N.Y., 1839), pp. 199–200.

[16] David Meredith Reese, *Humbugs of New-York: Being a Remonstrance against Popular Delusion* (New York, 1838), pp. 75–76.

[17] Quoted in Plattsburgh *Republican,* Jan. 13, 1844.

clamor, and threaten utterly to destroy the body politic with their nostrums," it confidently predicted, "will have their day, and then go to their own place and be heard of no more. Heaven speed the day!" [18]

The principal target of this criticism was Eliza W. Farnham, who was chiefly responsible for introducing phrenology into the state penal system after becoming matron of the woman's prison at Sing Sing in 1844. Reading about the work of Elizabeth Fry among criminals had stimulated in Eliza, as a young orphan growing up in western New York, "an intense curiosity to penetrate the innermost centre of the stained soul, and observe the mysterious working of that machinery by which so fatal a result was produced." [19] Years later, as the articulate and reform-conscious wife of a young lawyer, explorer, and author named Thomas Jefferson Farnham, she received her chance when John W. Edmonds, looking for someone who might be able to establish order among the female convicts, interviewed her and gave her the job. [20] A woman of independent mind who not long before had returned with her husband to New York after a few years of pioneering on the Illinois prairies, Mrs. Farnham was not hesitant about introducing new techniques at Sing Sing, and was prepared to defend her ideas in print with considerable writing ability. Firmly convinced of the rightness of her views, and tending to make harsh judgments with regard to those who opposed them, she had all the makings of a controversial figure and quickly became one. [21]

So far as the new matron was concerned, her charges could not

[18] Quoted in New York *Tribune,* May 7, 1847.

[19] Eliza W. Farnham, *Eliza Woodson, or, The Early Days of One of the World's Workers: A Story of American Life* (2nd ed.; New York, 1864), pp. 248, 350–351.

[20] Georgiana B. Kirby, *Years of Experience: An Autobiographical Narrative* (New York, 1887), p. 190.

[21] The matron's former experiences in Illinois are recounted in Eliza W. Farnham, *Life in Prairie Land* (New York, 1846), *passim.* Her occasional censoriousness was clearly revealed in her correspondence with John Bigelow, a member of the Sing Sing board of inspectors. See especially Eliza W. Farnham to John Bigelow, Dec. 28, 1845; July 20, Aug. 6, and Oct. 1, 1846; Feb. 20 and 22, 1847; and June 29, 1848, Bigelow Papers, New York Public Library.

be held fully responsible for the crimes which they had committed. "We knew that they were the products of their circumstances," stated an assistant matron and intimate friend who shared Mrs. Farnham's philosophy; "of their inherited tendencies and the conditions into which they were born. Given ignorance and weakness in the blood, and back alleys populated by the degraded and friendless, who can wonder at the outcome?"[22] The proper way to treat a felon, the matron believed, was to follow phrenological doctrines and remove those elements from his environment that stimulated his animal propensities. The substitution of proper influences would in time strengthen his better faculties while the vicious ones withered away. "Those sentiments which have lain dormant or been crushed by outrage and defiance," Mrs. Farnham declared somewhat rhapsodically, "must be gently summoned into being, and tenderly and patiently nursed by continual influences, which fall pleasantly upon and around them like dew upon the sickly seedling."[23] Such a process could never be consummated through the use of harsh and violent punishments; nor could it be furthered by harping upon an inmate's degraded past. Instead, the emphasis had to be upon positive and hopeful incentives. "We never spoke to them of their past as vicious," recalled a co-worker in later years; "it . . . pleased us to love these low-down children of circumstances less fortunate than our own. We gloried in being able to lift a few of them out of the slough into which they had fallen, or in which they had been born, and to sustain them while they were trying to take a little step upward in the direction of the light."[24]

One of the most efficacious of the "continual influences" which could be brought to bear, the matron believed, was education, previously hampered by the practice of instructing the inmates only singly in their cells. Soon she broke precedent by assembling

[22] Kirby, *Years of Experience*, p. 200.
[23] See Mrs. Farnham's editorial comments in Sampson, *Rationale of Crime*, pp. 66, 73.
[24] Kirby, *Years of Experience*, pp. 225–226.

all of her charges in the chapel every morning for schooling. On some occasions she lectured to them on American history, astronomy, geography, physiology, and personal hygiene; on others she read to them out of "some instructive or entertaining book." Women who knew how to read and maintained a good behavior record were given books to take to their cells, especially George Combe's phrenological treatise, *The Constitution of Man*. Illiterates were allowed to have picture books. Starting with a library which was limited to seventy-five copies of Richard Baxter's *Call to the Unconverted,* Mrs. Farnham was able to prevail upon friends for such works as "Sergeant's Temperance Tales, Hannah More's Domestic Tales, Miss Edgeworth's Popular Tales, Miss Sherwood's Works, and some little books of history, geography, and travels." Some volumes were obtained through the efforts of Margaret Fuller, who visited the prison in December, 1844, and delivered a lecture to the women.[25]

Books and lectures, however, were not enough. To the matron, the very environment of a penitentiary, with its despondency and gloom, was calculated to have a bad influence upon minds aspiring to better things. She therefore set out to brighten the tone of inmate life. Flowerpots were placed in the windows, maps were hung from the walls, and large lamps with reflectors were installed in the ceilings. Holidays were observed, and on one Fourth of July Mrs. Farnham and her staff chipped in to buy candy and other delicacies for the convicts. Music became a part of institutional life when Georgiana Bruce, a former participant in the Brook Farm experiment, became an assistant matron and brought her piano to the prison. The temper of one unruly inmate was calmed when she was allowed to have a rag doll and cradle, much to the indignation of a conservative critic who happened to visit the peni-

[25] DS, 69th Session (1846), Vol. I, No. 16, p. 94; DA, 70th Session (1847), Vol. VIII, No. 255, Part 2, p. 49; Sampson, *Rationale of Crime*, p. 66, footnote; Anonymous, "The Rationale of Crime," *United States Magazine and Democratic Review*, XX (January, 1847), p. 53; Kirby, *Years of Experience*, pp. 192–194; New York *Tribune*, Dec. 26, 1844.

tentiary. In addition, the women were encouraged to engage in handicrafts, and a glass case was set up where the items they produced could be displayed for purchase by outsiders who toured the institution. The proceeds went toward the acquisition of more books for the library.[26]

Mrs. Farnham believed that positive incentives should replace coercive measures whenever this was practicable, and inaugurated a system of classification soon after her administration began.[27] On July 4, 1844, she arranged to have Edmonds visit her department and award large bouquets to the inmates who were chosen by their peers as the kindest and "most amiable." Each of the other convicts received a smaller bunch of flowers on the same occasion.[28] Although the matron was encouraged by the results of such experiments, she found that strong disciplinary measures could not be eliminated completely. "There is a class of criminals who are susceptible to nothing but fear of punishment," she concluded sadly in 1847. "They are incapable of appreciating the motives which would prompt other treatment, and are quite certain to misconstrue them, and so meet it with contempt or ridicule rather than respect." [29] She was therefore constrained on occasion to use chains, mouth gags, strait jackets, and other devices, however reluctantly.[30]

In general, she believed, moral growth presupposed a certain degree of liberty, and could not be achieved by overburdening the prisoners with rules and regulations. "The nearer the condition of the convict, while in prison, approximates the natural and true condition in which he should live," she declared, "the more perfect will be its reformatory influence over his character." She therefore considered "the smallest number of rules with which our prison can be soundly governed, the most favorable for the improvement and elevation of its inmates." With such precepts in mind, she threw out the rule of silence in January, 1846, and allowed con-

---

[26] Kirby, *Years of Experience,* pp. 190–226 *passim;* New York *Sun,* Aug. 19, 1846; DA, 70th Session (1847), Vol. VIII, No. 255, Part 2, p. 49.

[27] DS, 68th Session (1845), Vol. I, No. 9, p. 7.

[28] New York *Tribune,* July 27, 1844.

[29] DA, 71st Session (1848), Vol. I, No. 10, p. 78.

[30] *Ibid.,* 69th Session (1846), Vol. IV, No. 139, pp. 113–122.

versation "at all convenient times when it would not interrupt or retard labor." This privilege was at first allowed only to certain inmates, but by the end of the year it had been extended to every woman.[31]

In pursuing her reform program, Mrs. Farnham enjoyed the support of valuable allies both within and without the institution in which she worked. One consistent defender was Horace Greeley, who had known her before her appointment and praised her efforts despite the fact that she was a Democrat who owed her position to a Jacksonian board of inspectors.[32] As chairman of that body, Edmonds gave her solid backing until he resigned early in 1845 to accept a judgeship in New York City. His successor, James Powers, was an elderly jurist from Catskill who favored mild policies, as did another new inspector, a young lawyer from Newburgh named Benjamin Mace. Two other appointees of the incoming Wright administration were conservative in their approach, but the fifth inspector swung the balance against them. This was John Bigelow, who not only worked for humanitarian methods at the men's prison but also became a strong source of assistance to the matron.

Bigelow was young, well educated, and idealistic. He had tried his hand at being a lawyer, a writer, and a journalist, and at this stage of his career was dissatisfied with his accomplishments. At first, he appears to have accepted the inspectorship primarily as "an office which without complicating my position in politics establishes me in the confidence and respect of men whose consideration it is desirable to maintain," but he soon became genuinely interested in penal problems. Ambitious, and not afraid to suggest new ideas, he was determined to "make a mark" on the development of penitentiary methods before leaving his post.[33] Throwing his

[31] *Ibid.*, 70th Session (1847), Vol. VIII, No. 255, Part 2, p. 62; DS, 70th Session (1847), Vol. I, No. 5, p. 89.

[32] See New York *Tribune*, March 18, 1844; April 11, 1844; Feb. 25, 1846; and Jan. 28, 1847.

[33] Ms. diary of John Bigelow, New York Public Library, entries of April 20 and May 11, 1845; Margaret Clapp, *Forgotten First Citizen: John Bigelow* (Boston, 1947), pp. 3–39, 41; John Bigelow, *Retrospections of an Active Life* (New York, 1909–1913), I, 67–68.

weight on the side of Powers and Mace, he helped to decrease the incidence of flogging until by the end of 1846 the prison went through an entire month in which not a single lash was administered.[34] Punishments, he held, were of two classes: those which "quicken the moral sensibilities," and those which "merely afflict them." The former helped the convict to acquire self-respect, and the latter caused him to lose it. In Bigelow's words, "all punishment which merely insults, depraves." [35]

Bigelow's receptivity to new ideas was exemplified by his reaction to an experiment being conducted at Auburn and at the new ironmaking prison in the Adirondacks, where inmates were being given rations of chewing tobacco. To the young inspector this appeared to be a good means of allowing a "gentle stimulant" to men who were deprived of normal sexual outlets, the companionship of friends, and even the right to speak. In February, 1846, he submitted a report to his fellow board members advocating such a concession, and secured its approval. "It was highly complimented," he confided to his diary, "& it will be the source of great happiness to the poor devils." [36]

Actively sympathizing with the changes Eliza Farnham was putting into effect in the woman's prison, Bigelow was soon able to help the matron in a way highly displeasing to some Sing Sing staff members who favored humane methods but were strongly opposed to what they regarded as radical ideas, especially phrenological ones. Most prominent among these moderates was the prison chaplain, John Luckey. By the middle of 1846, internal bickering at the penitentiary had produced a crisis which foreshadowed the eventual collapse of the reform administration less than two years later.

[34] See DA, 69th Session (1846), Vol. IV, No. 139, p. 105, and 70th Session (1847), Vol. VI, No. 160, p. 1, Table 3, and p. 5. It should be stressed that the trend was steadily, but not precipitously, downward. The general decline of lashing from 1843 through 1848 is shown by the statistics given in DA, 71st Session (1848), Vol. I, No. 10, p. 17.

[35] Bigelow diary, entry of March 15, 1846.

[36] DS, 70th Session (1847), Vol. I, No. 5, pp. 10–11, 16–22; Bigelow diary, entries of Feb. 6 and 10, 1846.

It is not surprising that Mrs. Farnham and Luckey failed to get along with one another, for the matron's background was not calculated to promote friendship with clergymen. She had been brought up by a stepmother who was a self-professed atheist, and her childhood reading included a number of books by freethinkers. Later, as a student at a Quaker boarding school, she had been unenthusiastic about meetings she had attended, recalling in later years the "musty moralities," "religious saws," and "ancient truisms" which were "alternately aired, in dolorous sing-song tones." After being reunited with other members of her family who had been reared in religiously orthodox surroundings, she had shocked them with her lack of faith.[37] She appears to have become more moderate in her views over the years; as matron, for instance, she had a group of religious singers perform at the prison and wrote approvingly to a friend about the effects produced by such songs as "My Mother's Bible," sung in "half-tremulous tones." [38] On the other hand, she objected to "forcing theology on the prisoners," and opposed the efforts of an assistant who was bent upon converting Catholic convicts to Protestantism.[39] Her espousal of phrenological doctrines which seemed at variance with biblical concepts of free will and moral responsibility, as well as her encouragement of novel-reading among the inmates under her charge, were not popular with the Methodist chaplain and his wife, Dinah. It is clear from Mrs. Farnham's correspondence with Bigelow that by December, 1845, if not sooner, she and the Luckey family were on bad terms.[40]

Bigelow became involved in the Luckey–Farnham dispute by helping the matron to publish an American edition of some writings on criminal behavior by Marmaduke B. Sampson, an English phrenologist. Among other things, he gave her permission to have

[37] Farnham, *Eliza Woodson*, pp. 74, 236–246, 311–314, 349–350; see also the matron's *Life in Prairie Land*, pp. 233–235.

[38] New York *Tribune*, April 22, 1845.

[39] Kirby, *Years of Experience*, p. 199.

[40] Farnham to Bigelow, Dec. 28, 1845, Bigelow Papers.

an artist visit Sing Sing to make outline drawings of convict head-formations for inclusion in the volume. Much to Luckey's disgust, the chaplain's office was selected to be the studio for this effort.[41] When the book was finally published under the title *Rationale of Crime,* neither the deterministic outlook of Sampson nor the editorial comments by Mrs. Farnham could be approved by the Methodist parson. Although the matron hedged a bit on the problem of moral responsibility, asserting that "the possession of a faculty in any degree implies some capacity to use it," she made it clear that she had a relativistic conception of guilt.[42] Not surprisingly, the work met a storm of denunciation by such newspapers as Webb's *Courier and Enquirer* and the New York *Observer.* "They say it destroys accountability," wrote Bigelow contemptuously. "Let them slide." [43]

In addition to broadcasting her skepticism about free will, Mrs. Farnham also encroached upon the prison library, which had previously been Luckey's preserve. Nobody had defended the inmate's right to read more vigorously than the chaplain, but this advocacy did not extend to the novels of Dickens, Combe's *Constitution of Man,* and such works as Orson Fowler's *Amativeness: or, Evils and Remedies of Excessive and Perverted Sexuality.* Deeming these books potentially harmful to the minds of the convicts, he tried to prevent them from being kept in the library, against the matron's stalwart opposition.[44] By July, 1846, the situation had become so bad that either Mrs. Farnham or the chaplain had to go. In a showdown before the board of inspectors the position of the former prevailed, and Luckey was relieved of his job.[45]

Neither Luckey nor his supporters accepted this outcome without a fight. The New York *Sun* took up the chaplain's defense,

[41] Clapp, *Forgotten First Citizen,* p. 42; Farnham to Bigelow, Aug. 6, 1846, Bigelow Papers; New York *Sun,* Sept. 23, 1846.
[42] Sampson, *Rationale of Crime,* p. 15, and *passim.*
[43] Bigelow diary, entry of Nov. 17, 1845.
[44] See especially New York *Sun,* Sept. 23, 1846.
[45] See Farnham to Bigelow, July 20, 1846, and to Rev. C. H. Halsey, Aug. 1, 1846, Bigelow Papers.

praising him as "a much esteemed Methodist Clergyman" and charging that he "was dismissed from his position simply because he exercised his judgment in excluding immoral and irreligious books from the cells of the prisoners." Mrs. Farnham's phrenological doctrines, it was alleged, were designed to keep the inmates subdued "by gratifying the very tastes which brought them under her charge." [46] Bigelow's support of the matron brought down upon him bitter letters from defenders of Luckey, one of them reminding him that his "constitutional power as Inquisitor" did not extend beyond the limits of Sing Sing.[47] Luckey himself took his case to the public through the press, telling of "innumerable petty annoyances and embarrassments" to which he had been subjected and maintaining the unjustifiability of his dismissal through the "connivance of a majority of the Board of Inspectors." [48] When Matthew Gordon, a young graduate of Union Theological Seminary in New York City, was appointed to take the chaplaincy, it was charged that he disbelieved in the divinity of Christ.[49]

When the New York Prison Association sent an inspection team to Sing Sing later in the year, the whole affair became the subject of a special hearing. Dinah Luckey accused Mrs. Farnham of inculcating "a love for novel reading averse to labor," and asserted that the Scriptures had not been sufficiently emphasized under the matron's regime. She very sternly disapproved of discussions which she had heard among the inmates on the subject of women's clothing fashions. The Luckey group also protested the reading of *Nicholas Nickleby* and *A Christmas Carol* to the convicts, even though defenders of Mrs. Farnham gravely assured the investigators that these stories had been bowdlerized before the prisoners had heard them. It was also charged that the matron had made personal use of state property, that she had unlawfully employed inmates to

[46] New York *Sun,* Aug. 19 and 22, 1846.

[47] T. W. Niven to Bigelow, Aug. 8, 1846; B. W. Morse to Bigelow, Aug. 10, 1846; and Rev. C. H. Halsey to Bigelow, Aug. 18, 1846, Bigelow Papers.

[48] New York *Sun,* Sept. 23, 1846.

[49] Niven to Bigelow, Aug. 8, 1846, Bigelow Papers.

work for herself and her family, and that she was capricious and unjust in her administration of discipline.[50]

The Prison Association took no action on these complaints. In following this course it incurred the animosity of Luckey's supporters and became identified with the views of the matron and Bigelow. The ex-chaplain made public his loss of confidence in the organization and said that he would hereafter go directly to Albany with his complaints. The N.Y.P.A. was also castigated by Alexander Wells, who was once more happy to censure a Democratic prison administration, even one espousing policies diametrically opposed to those practiced by the regime he had condemned before. The Prison Association, he charged, was but the complaisant tool of Mrs. Farnham and John W. Edmonds.[51] Meanwhile, the matron's edition of Sampson's writings continued to come under public attack despite the pleas of such men as Horace Greeley that it be given a fair hearing. If its doctrines were invalid, the New York *Tribune* urged, they should be rejected "dispassionately and under the influence of reason, not in a tempest of obloquy and passion." [52]

Soon trouble was brewing again at Sing Sing. The new chaplain, Gordon, quickly aligned himself with the Farnham–Bigelow group, and before long he was having differences with Harman Eldridge, who had replaced Lynds as principal keeper in 1844. Like Luckey, Eldridge was a moderate. Although he had been attacked in the press on one occasion for alleged cruelty, he had been exonerated by Edmonds, and even Mrs. Farnham had called him a man of "humanity and good judgment." [53] His association with the Auburn system, however, stretched back as far as 1826, when Ger-

---

[50] DA, 70th Session (1847), Vol. VIII, No. 255, Part 2, pp. 50, 52, 57.

[51] *Ibid.*, pp. 64–65; DS, 70th Session (1847), Vol. I, No. 5, pp. 90–91.

[52] New York *Tribune*, Nov. 11, 1846.

[53] *Ibid.*, May 18 and 28, 1844; Sampson, *Rationale of Crime*, pp. xx–xxi. See also DA, 69th Session (1846), Vol. IV, No. 139, pp. 106–107; 70th Session (1847), Vol. VIII, No. 255, Part 2, pp. 74, 78–79; and New York *Tribune*, Feb. 21, 1845, characterizing Eldridge as "mild and kind," but "by no means deficient in firmness."

shom Powers had singled him out as an especially valuable keeper at the Cayuga County institution, and his long habituation to old ways hardly fitted him to sympathize with ideas as advanced as those held by the Farnham group.[54] The precise grounds of his difficulty with Gordon are not clear, but it is possible that he was disgruntled over the firing of Luckey and critical of the new chaplain's youth and inexperience. His position forced him to work closely with whoever occupied the chaplaincy, which had been placed under his general supervision by a law passed several years before.[55]

Whatever the causes, the dispute between the chaplain and the principal keeper was clearly in evidence by early 1847, and Mrs. Farnham was just as clearly embroiled in it. In February, she carried the matter to Bigelow, informing him that a conspiracy was under way between Eldridge and an assistant matron whom Mrs. Farnham described as a "most unscrupulous and . . . accomplished *liar*." [56] A short period of administrative infighting was followed by the principal keeper's resignation, although there was dissension among the inspectors and a countermove to fire Gordon. Bigelow, of course, threw his weight in favor of the chaplain, who with but nine months' experience was soon elevated to the position Eldridge had vacated.[57]

The triumph of the Farnham–Bigelow group now seemed assured, but such was not the case. The victories over Luckey and

[54] Gershom Powers, *A Brief Account of . . . the New-York State Prison at Auburn* (Auburn, 1826), p. 76. On the conservatism which tempered Eldridge's views, see especially Edmonds' comments in DS, 69th Session (1846), Vol. IV, No. 120, p. 17.

[55] DA, 65th Session (1842), Vol. IV, No. 65, p. 106.

[56] Farnham to Bigelow, Feb. 20, 1847, Bigelow Papers. Italics are Mrs. Farnham's.

[57] Bigelow diary, entry of March 7, 1847; DS, 70th Session (1847), Vol. IV, No. 153, p. 4; DA, 71st Session (1848), Vol. I, No. 10, p. 15. The assembly document dates Gordon's accession to the principal keepership as May 14, which may be an error in view of the fact that Eldridge's resignation came in early March. Eldridge remained in penal work, becoming superintendent of the New York City Workhouse (see DA, 73rd Session [1850], Vol. VIII, No. 198, pp. 50–53).

Eldridge had been won only at the cost of alienating reformers whose humanitarianism was tempered with a distaste for phrenology and moral relativism. The extent of this alienation was clearly revealed in 1847 when the senate prison committee was authorized to conduct an investigation of the situation at Sing Sing.

This committee, composed of Frederick Backus, Saxton Smith, and Abraham Gridley, was far from subscribing to the views of Elam Lynds and Robert Wiltse. Only a year before, Backus and Gridley had helped to prepare a bill to restrict the amount of corporal punishment that could be administered to a convict. Backus himself wanted the flogging power completely removed.[58] The three men, however, issued a caustic report on the state of affairs at the Hudson Valley prison. The institution, they maintained, was "under a feeble state of discipline," and there was "nothing *masculine* in its composition." The rule of silence was almost completely disregarded when the inmates mingled, and was generally unobserved in the shops. The convicts were saucy and worked only reluctantly; as a result, the value of their labor was diminishing. The time was coming when the contractors might fail to renew their agreements with the prison and legislative appropriations would be required to keep it in operation. Indeed, it was over $29,000 in debt already. The committee believed that a mild philosophy could be implemented without impairing discipline, and cited recent happenings at the Charlestown penitentiary in Massachusetts to substantiate this claim. On the other hand, the senators declared in sarcastic words obviously aimed at Bigelow and Gordon, such an administration could not be maintained without "the aid of full grown *men* to superintend its introduction, and carry it into full operation."

The committee then assailed phrenology and its disciple, Eliza Farnham. Referring sarcastically to the matron's activities in examining convict head-formations, the members asserted "that the State cannot afford to sustain so large an institution for a course of experiments on so baseless a theory," and called for a return to common sense and "old fashioned wisdom." The next object of

[58] DS, 69th Session (1846), Vol. IV, Nos. 120 and 121, *passim*.

attack was the New York Prison Association, which the legislators believed had been a pernicious influence at Sing Sing. Members of the reform organization, animated by an undue sympathy for felons, spied upon and annoyed keepers who were trying to maintain a "mild but healthy discipline," and thus made the convicts impudent and hard to control.[59]

The fact that such a document could be written by penological moderates shows clearly the lacerated feelings that had been produced by the squabbles of the preceding two years. The reform front had been split wide open. This could not help but encourage conservatives who did not subscribe to the views of either the moderates or the Farnham–Bigelow group and who wanted to see a return to severe methods. Late in 1847, Amzi L. Dean and John Fisher, who as inspectors at Sing Sing had been outvoted by the Powers–Mace–Bigelow coalition, refused to sign the annual report of the board and sent the legislature a minority statement denying that reformation was the chief end of penal treatment and subjecting Farnham and Gordon to merciless criticism. In places their declaration was reminiscent of the harsh philosophy expressed in 1825 by Hopkins, Tibbits, and Allen when those men attacked the alleged softness of Thomas Eddy's generation (cf. pp. 102–103). In the words of Dean and Fisher:

Let prisons cease to be a terror to the depraved, and a warning to others who may be disposed to wander from the highway where travels [sic] the good and virtuous—let a phrensied sympathy excite the passions and swell the bosom of community in soothing the imaginary wrongs of criminals, and misguided philanthropy seek to mitigate the ills of mankind in converting our penitentiaries into schools for the instruction alone of its inmates—let the principle that punishment is no part of our prison system, and moral suasion and reformation obtain the ascendancy over the calm judicious observance of an "enlightened policy"—a policy that would be a terror to the depraved and evil doers, and terrify the youthful rogue, and prevent a continual drain upon the treasury for the support of those who [sic] the taxpayers are under no obligation and should not be compelled to support, and then the

[59] *Ibid.,* 70th Session (1847), Vol. IV, No. 153, pp. 4–6. Italics are as given.

period will arrive when insurrection, incendiarism, robbery, and all the evils most fatal to society and detrimental to law and order, will reign supreme.[60]

Under severe attack from within the prison and without, the experiments of such leaders as Mrs. Farnham and Bigelow soon came to an end. The reform tempo slowed in November, 1847, when the matron restored the silent rule at the women's prison. Three new inmates had escaped, and she felt it advisable to re-affirm the old regulation. In addition, she reluctantly suspended other personal freedoms and confined the convicts to closed rooms when they were not working. An added retrogression was the discontinuance of the morning lectures which had previously been given to the women, a step necessitated by the consummation of a contract to employ the inmates in button-making.[61]

The heaviest blow of all, however, was undoubtedly Bigelow's failure to secure another term on the board of inspectors. A new state constitution drawn up in 1846 had made such posts elective rather than appointive. Legislation passed in 1847 stipulated that the voters were to choose three men to supervise the entire New York penal system and that the terms of office were to be staggered so that a vacancy would occur each year. When Bigelow tried to secure a Democratic nomination to become a member of the new group, he was defeated, possibly because of his Free-Soil leanings.[62] Already facing serious discouragements, Mrs. Farnham clearly had little future at Sing Sing with her chief supporter on the way out, and left the penitentiary early in 1848. Soon she was in Boston, helping Samuel Gridley Howe care for such handicapped patients as the celebrated Laura Bridgman at the Perkins Institution and Asylum for the Blind.[63] The great reform period at Sing Sing was coming to an end.

[60] DS, 71st Session (1848), Vol. I, No. 17, pp. 2–5.

[61] Ibid., Vol. I, No. 10, pp. 74–75, 80–81.

[62] Laws of the State of New-York, Passed at the Seventieth Session of the Legislature . . . 1847 (Albany, 1847), p. 396; Clapp, Forgotten First Citizen, p. 44.

[63] See Eliza Robbins to Samuel Gridley Howe, Feb. 20, 1848, Letters in

Despite disagreements and setbacks, however, moderates and radicals alike could find grounds for satisfaction in one final achievement capping the humanitarian trend that had been in existence since the scandals of 1839. Late in 1847, at the very end of the reform cycle, the state legislature abolished flogging in the prisons of New York. Although public sentiment had been growing against this form of punishment throughout the decade, its final abandonment came about in large measure because of a highly controversial whipping that occurred at Auburn in January, 1846, followed by the death of the inmate who suffered it, a felon named Charles Plumb.

Plumb had earned his flogging by behaving in an undeniably bad manner. He had emptied his night tub down the stairs of a cellblock, smashed two windows, and littered a workshop with containers of ink, turpentine, paint, oil, and varnish, besides threatening to "split the brains out" of a keeper who attempted to pacify him. After being punished for this conduct, he tore up his Bible, a library book, and his bed clothing. It was not clear that his death shortly thereafter was directly attributable to the lashing he received, and the official cause was stated to be "bilious intermitting fever." Nevertheless, local citizens became deeply aroused because of the incident, and by March the principal keeper, Hiram Rathbun, had been forced out of his job. An attempt by reformers to end flogging once and for all by legislative proscription, however, failed of adoption, much to the gratification of the Auburn inspectors. Corporal punishment, they stubbornly insisted, was necessary if a proper state of discipline was to be maintained.[64]

But the fight against the whip continued. "There is no degrada-

---

Blindiana Library, 1848–1849, No. 18, Perkins School for the Blind, Watertown, Mass.; Farnham to Bigelow, June 29, 1848, Bigelow Papers; New York *Tribune*, Dec. 16, 1864; Maud H. Elliott and Florence H. Hall, *Laura Bridgman: Dr. Howe's Famous Pupil and What He Taught Her* (Boston, 1903), pp. 232–233.

[64] DA, 69th Session (1846), Vol. III, No. 83, *passim,* and 75th Session (1852), Vol. I, No. 20, pp. 7, 74; DS, 70th Session (1847), Vol. I, No. 11, pp. 2–3.

tion like the lash," asserted an article in the *Democratic Review*. "We confess that if we believed it to be indispensable, we should be prepared to abandon the whole system. . . . The other improvements in our prison discipline are overshadowed, and sink into comparative insignificance, before this towering atrocity." [65] Two special reports were submitted to the state senate on the matter of corporal punishment, one favoring legal restrictions on flogging and the other advocating outright prohibition.[66] The New York *Tribune*, which had called for the abolition of whipping at the time of the Plumb scandal, reiterated its feelings on this score early in 1847 in the course of an article praising the virtual abandonment of flogging at Sing Sing.[67] Later in the year the assembly committee on prisons rejected the entire theory of deterrence, criticized the use of the lash, and envisioned a time when penitentiaries would become "great MORAL HOSPITALS, where the State, like a good Samaritan, binds up the wounds and heals the maladies which *sin* and *ignorance* have engendered." [68] Meanwhile, dissension among the inspectors at Auburn over the merits of whipping had been revealed when Luman Sherwood, a member of the board, came out against the "cat." [69]

As the 1847 session of the legislature neared its close, the lawmakers responded to such pressures by enacting a lengthy and detailed statute which abolished flogging and formally sanctioned some of the innovations that had been taking place in the state prisons. Thenceforth, blows could be inflicted upon inmates only "in self-defence or to suppress a revolt or insurrection." Unusual punishment, when deemed necessary, should consist of solitary confinement on stinted rations. The act directed Sing Sing, Auburn, and Clinton prisons to erect special cells for such contin-

[65] Anonymous, "Prison Discipline," *United States Magazine and Democratic Review*, XIX (August, 1846), 138.

[66] DS, 69th Session (1846), Vol. IV, Nos. 120 and 121, *passim*.

[67] New York *Tribune*, Feb. 4, 1846, and Feb. 25, 1847.

[68] DA, 75th Session (1847), Vol. VIII, No. 241, *passim*. Italics and capital letters are as given.

[69] DS, 70th Session (1847), Vol. I, No. 12, p. 11.

gencies, and also stipulated that convicts suffering from insanity were to be removed to the state asylum at Utica. Penitentiary administrators were ordered to respect inmate property by taking care to return upon discharge all money and other articles which had been received from a convict at the beginning of his sentence. In addition, the going-away allotment was to be increased by three cents for each mile between the penitentiary and the home or place of conviction of a released offender. In another move the legislators directed the prisons to hire part-time instructors for the education of inmates and authorized annual grants of $100 to each institution for the purchase of library books, maps, and writing supplies.[70]

This act would have been a milestone in the history of correctional policy in New York had it done nothing more than abolish the whip. In addition, it consolidated some of the gains that reformers had made in the prisons since the beginning of the decade. On the other hand, its significance should not be overestimated. In the first place, it reflected the recent past more than it foreshadowed the immediate future. Most of the officials who took over the penitentiaries in the remainder of the ante-bellum period were men whose outlook differed materially from that of Seymour, Edmonds, Farnham, and Bigelow, and who could find ways to circumvent the law when it suited their purposes to do so. The act of 1847 was also of limited usefulness as far as rehabilitation was concerned, even though it represented an improvement over the previous situation. The addition of five part-time teachers under its provisions was an inadequate answer to the educational needs of inmates in three (or if the women's penitentiary is counted separately, four) different institutions. The sum of $100 per year allotted to each prison for educational supplies was also manifestly small; in the case of Sing Sing, with approximately one thousand inmates, it amounted to about ten cents per convict.

In short, the statute passed in 1847 was the last noteworthy accomplishment of a reform era that was about to end. Although

[70] *Laws*, 70th Session (1847), pp. 600–608.

short in duration, this period was vital and significant. For the greater part of a decade, the former emphasis upon deterrence and repression had given way to faith in the reformability of the offender and concern for his essential dignity as a human being. In the attempt to bring out the best in prisoners, resort had been made to kindness rather than to intimidation. The use of the lash had been curtailed and finally abolished. The convict's isolation from society had been partially alleviated by allowing him to read books, to write and receive letters, and to have occasional visitors from the outside world. An energetic reform group, the New York Prison Association, had been founded to spread new ideas, to investigate improper penal conditions, and to assist ex-convicts who needed jobs, lodgings, clothing, and advice.

Eventually, matters progressed too far and too rapidly to suit reformers whose humanitarianism was tempered by a fear of becoming too lenient with offenders and a distaste for moral relativism. New theories stressing the physical and environmental basis for crime seemed at variance with traditional concepts of guilt and personal accountability. When such persons as Eliza Farnham attained positions of leadership, a struggle ensued, ending in bitterness and recrimination among reformers who shared a common desire to rehabilitate but who disagreed irrevocably about what this goal meant and how it could best be achieved. By 1848, this factionalism had produced wounds that would be slow to heal.

Had the reform movement of the 1840's continued on into the decades that followed, the Auburn system might have come to an end in the mid-nineteenth century. As it was, the system had been modified by 1847, but its essential features remained. With the exception of the unsuccessful attempt to introduce communication under Mrs. Farnham at the women's prison, nothing had been done to alter the rule of silence. The labor law of 1842 had shaken the industrial program, but the old ideal of the self-sustaining penal system had not yet been discarded. The lockstep, the stripes, the cramped and lonely cells, the monotonous and dehumanizing routine were all present, and remained as part of the ordeal to be faced by the ordinary adult offender while the state progressed in its treatment of misdemeanants, first-term convicts, and juvenile delinquents. The lash was gone, but equally painful instruments of coercion could be, and were, substituted in its place. If a new order was to be achieved, much remained to be accomplished. That this was not to be done in the near future, however, can be observed by taking a brief glance at the penological backwater of the 1850's.

# Chapter XI

# Ebb Tide

LATE in February, 1848, one of Mrs. Farnham's admirers wrote to Samuel Gridley Howe in an effort to help the former matron secure a position at the Perkins Institution in Massachusetts. Pointing out that there had been a "recent overturn in the prison government" at Sing Sing, Eliza Robbins stoutly defended the regime that had just collapsed and asserted that the persons who now controlled the penitentiary were animated by narrow and selfish motives which doomed their administration to failure from the start. The progress of penal reform in New York, she believed, was now "completely suspended" and "indefinitely retarded." [1] Time substantially validated this estimate, for the state prisons now entered a period of comparative stagnation under the leadership of officials who lacked either the power, the money, the inclination, or the public support to overcome the ever mounting problems that faced them.

The difficulties that befell the prisons during this period were attributable to a number of adverse circumstances. It is clear at the outset that the public became less and less interested in penal reform. In 1854, for example, the New York Prison Association lamented growing apathy on the subject; the organization's complaints were borne out by its own experience, for it was plagued

---

[1] Eliza Robbins to Samuel Gridley Howe, Feb. 20, 1848, Letters in Blindiana Library, 1848–1849, No. 18, Perkins School for the Blind, Watertown, Mass.

by a lack of financial support. When Louis Dwight died in the same year and his once powerful Prison Discipline Society quickly collapsed, a scarcity of funds prevented the N.Y.P.A. from stepping into the position of leadership which the Boston group had held. Three years later, the Association blamed inadequate financial backing in large part for its inability to maintain an energetic program of prison inspection.[2] In 1859, a reform-minded Albany pastor could only decry "the wicked indifference of the masses of our people to the whole subject of crime." "A vast majority of those who choose judges, legislators, inspectors, and appoint virtually all the officials of justice," declared the Rev. Amory D. Mayo, "neither know what our criminal system is, nor concern themselves for its operation."[3]

Why such apathy in what was still an age of considerable humanitarian striving? It is possible that some citizens channeled their reform energies so completely into the burning cause of the day, antislavery, that they had little time for any other benevolent activities. Others were probably discouraged by the fate of the Farnham–Bigelow regime at Sing Sing. The demise of the Prison Discipline Society may have contributed to the growing indifference, for its annual reports on penal questions were now no longer circulated. Perhaps the most important cause, as the New York Prison Association suggested in 1854, was that the public was simply tired of the protracted struggle which supporters of the Auburn and Pennsylvania systems had waged since the 1820's. By this time every conceivable argument that could be enlisted in defense of either plan had been thoroughly aired, and it seemed that "the States which have adopted either system, appear to rest contented with it, or at least to endure it, with apparently no disposition to change or improve."[4]

---

[2] New York Prison Association, *Ninth Report* (1854), p. 61, and *Eleventh-Twelfth Report* (1857), pp. 24–25; Blake McKelvey, *American Prisons* (Chicago, 1936), pp. 21, 48.

[3] Amory D. Mayo, *Symbols of the Capital: or, Civilization in New York* (New York, 1859), p. 61.

[4] New York Prison Association, *Ninth Report* (1854), p. 61.

New administrative regulations also contributed to the backwardness of penal policy. The three-man board of popularly elected prison inspectors provided for by the constitution of 1846 represented a public desire to extend democratic procedures, as well as a feeling that the consolidation of power in one group of officials would be more efficient than the previous system of individual boards at each penitentiary. Unfortunately, matters did not work out as well as had been hoped. Under the terms of legislation enacted in 1847, each member of the new board was to take one of the three state prisons as his special responsibility for a quarter of a year and then rotate to another institution. As it turned out, inspectors frequently evaded this requirement, and it was possible for a prison to become the private satrapy of a single official armed with sweeping powers of appointment and dismissal. In addition, the election of one new inspector each year under a system of staggered terms intensified political pressures in the penitentiaries. The kettle of intrigue simmered constantly, and no staff member felt secure in his tenure.[5]

The great power which could be wielded by an inspector who entrenched himself at a prison could obviously be used for improper ends. Political morality was at a low ebb in the Empire State during the 1850's, and it is not surprising that the penal institutions experienced some of the same types of skulduggery that were going on in the legislature at Albany and in New York City's municipal government.[6] In the middle of the decade, a scandal of major proportions broke at Sing Sing after an inspector named Henry Storms had managed to entrench himself there. The prison had never recovered from the effects of the convict labor law of 1842, and was continually in debt to creditors who were put off

[5] *Laws of the State of New-York, Passed at the Seventieth Session of the Legislature, Second Meeting . . . 1847* (Albany, 1847), pp. 396, 600, 602; DA, 78th Session (1855), Vol. III, No. 60, pp. 507–509, 554–556; DS, 75th Session (1852), Vol. I, No. 35, p. 10, and 81st Session (1858), Vol. I, No. 4, pp. 20–21; Auburn *Weekly American*, April 1, 1857.

[6] See David M. Ellis, *et al.*, *A Short History of New York State* (Ithaca, N.Y., 1957), p. 238, and Glyndon G. Van Deusen, *Thurlow Weed: Wizard of the Lobby* (Boston, 1947), p. 229.

with promises to pay until periodic special appropriations were received from the state treasury. Taking advantage of this situation, Storms and the agent he appointed, Munson J. Lockwood, set up an office in New York City at which they trafficked in Sing Sing notes and payroll funds. In addition, they systematically used bogus grocery and supply receipts to squeeze illicit gains out of the public coffers. Drunkenness, bribery, and other evils flourished at the prison until Thomas Kirkpatrick, the inspector in charge at Auburn, managed to secure a legislative investigation. The malodorous details which were elicited from a parade of witnesses revealed clearly the insufficiency of safeguards against venality and incompetency within the prison system.[7]

Penal reform was also retarded after 1848 by bitter feelings hanging over from the administrative disputes of recent years. Because the conduct of the New York Prison Association in the Luckey–Farnham struggle had caused it to be identified with the more radical faction, some officials who now came into power refused to cooperate with the organization and were especially adamant against allowing it to exercise its statutory rights to inspect the penitentiaries. This not only removed a potential check upon brutality and maladministration but also impeded the N.Y.P.A. in its efforts to promote rehabilitation and assist released offenders. One warden, for example, actively discouraged inmates from seeking the organization's help.[8]

One of the most disturbing aspects of penal operations during the closing years of the ante-bellum era, depressing in its effects upon the morale of administrators and staff members alike, was the increasing inability of the prisons to achieve self-support under

[7] DA, 78th Session (1855), Vol. III, No. 60, *passim*.
[8] Voluminous material exists on the running feud between the N.Y.P.A and hostile administrators during this period, particularly with reference to inspection rights. See DA, 72nd Session (1849), Vol. VI, No. 243, p. 31; 73rd Session (1850), Vol. VIII, No. 198, pp. 9, 13–19, 21, 24, 38–39; and 74th Session (1851), Vol. IV, No. 120, pp. 17–39; DS, 72nd Session (1849), Vol. I, No. 50, pp. 233–234, and 76th Session (1853), Vol. I, No. 20, p. 24; New York Prison Association, *Ninth Report* (1854), pp. 21, 132, 166; *Eleventh-Twelfth Report* (1857), pp. 24–25; and *Thirteenth-Fourteenth Report* (1859), pp. 12, 14.

the restrictive labor legislation enacted in 1842. Despite great efforts to make industrial operations financially profitable, the penitentiaries became more and more dependent upon legislative relief and emergency appropriations. The crowning disappointment in this regard was the dismal record of the new ironmaking institution established in Clinton County in an effort to produce a commodity which would not injure the interests of free workers.

The early years of the Clinton prison had been marked by considerable hopefulness. Influenced by a report drawn up by Ransom Cook, the Saratoga County inventor who had scouted the Adirondacks for iron deposits after the passage of the convict labor law of 1842, a special committee headed by Silas Wright selected a site seventeen miles west of Plattsburgh for the new institution late in 1844. Cook became the first warden of the prison the following year and pursued an energetic program of construction and iron mining while admirers predicted that the project would "create an era in the history of penitentiary reform." [9] In anticipation of the institution's success, citizens named the agglomeration of dwelling houses and log shanties which came to be scattered throughout the woods near the prison "Dannemora" after the well-known Swedish iron center.[10]

Cook proved to be a skillful administrator. Sharing many of the ideas which motivated the contemporaneous efforts of Mrs. Farnham and John Bigelow at Sing Sing, he believed the power of kindness to be "the strongest known to human nature," used the lash sparingly, took pains to establish a prison library, lectured to the convicts on scientific subjects, and allowed the inmates such indulgences as chewing tobacco.[11] A group from the New York

---

[9] See especially Anonymous, "The Clinton State Prison, Clinton County, New York," *United States Magazine and Democratic Review*, XVII (November, 1845), 345–352; Duane H. Hurd, *History of Clinton and Franklin Counties, New York* (Philadelphia, 1880), p. 49.

[10] Plattsburgh *Republican*, Aug. 16, 1845.

[11] On Cook's administration of prison affairs, see especially DS, 69th Session (1846), Vol. I, No. 14, pp. 3–4, 12–15, 21–23, 30; 70th Session (1847), Vol. I, No. 5, pp. 17–18, and No. 10, pp. 9–17; Plattsburgh *Republican*, Nov. 22, 1845.

Prison Association visited Dannemora in 1846 and praised the methods which prevailed there, asserting that "cruelty is unknown, and disobedience infrequent." [12] Cook also seemed to have been a wise choice for the wardenship because of the mechanical aptitudes which he brought to a novel industrial experiment. Two pieces of machinery to be used at the new institution, a steam-powered forge and an electro-magnetic ore separator, were of his own design.[13]

Despite a promising beginning, however, the penitentiary never fulfilled the hopes of those who had fought to establish it. Cook could not bring the complex plant and machinery required for mining, smelting, and forging into being rapidly enough to suit critics of the venture, and also irked religious elements by requiring the convicts to work on occasional Sundays. In addition, he aroused charges of nepotism by purchasing supplies from a firm to which his son belonged. When the Whigs gained control of the new board of prison inspectors elected in 1847 his removal became certain, and early the following year he shared the fate of the Farnham–Bigelow group at Sing Sing.[14]

A change of wardens, however, did nothing to improve matters. Remote from the state's major centers of population and connected with the outside world only by the poorest of roads, the institution could not market its products effectively and was expensive to provision with food and other supplies.[15] The Adirondack iron indus-

[12] DA, 70th Session (1847), Vol. VIII, No. 255, Part 2, p. 117.

[13] On Cook's mechanical abilities and achievements, see particularly DS, 68th Session (1845), Vol. I, No. 16, pp. 1–5, and 70th Session (1847), Vol. IV, No. 122, pp. 5–6; Nathaniel B. Sylvester, *History of Saratoga County, New York* (Philadelphia, 1878), pp. 204–205; Plattsburgh *Republican,* Oct. 12, 1844, and Feb. 19, 1848.

[14] DA, 70th Session (1847), Vol. VIII, No. 236, pp. 2–5; DS, 70th Session (1847), Vol. I, No. 10, pp. 3–5, and Vol. IV, No. 122, pp. 3–4; Plattsburgh *Republican,* Feb. 19, 1848.

[15] DA, 69th Session (1846), Vol. II, No. 55, pp. 7–8, 10, and 72nd Session (1849), Vol. II, No. 94, p. 3; DS, 69th Session (1846), Vol. I, No. 14, p. 7, and 82nd Session (1859), Vol. I, No. 20, p. 155; Plattsburgh *Republican,* Aug. 16, 1845.

try was in a generally depressed condition during the late 1840's and early 1850's, and the prison shared in the difficulties of the times.[16] In addition, initial estimates of the ore contained in the penitentiary tract proved overly sanguine. By 1852, the supply had virtually given out and the state was forced to pay heavy rents to private interests for the privilege of working adjacent lands.[17] As deficits mounted, critics demanded that the entire project be given up, and a number of convicts were actually transferred to Auburn and Sing Sing in anticipation of the prison's abandonment.[18]

In the end, this step was not taken. The other state penitentiaries were already too overcrowded to absorb all of Dannemora's inmates, labor groups were fiercely opposed to the termination of the iron venture, and various legislators were unwilling to write off the extensive investment which had been made in physical plant and equipment at the Adirondack site. Still, it was obvious that the whole experiment had turned out badly. In 1860, Governor Morgan told the legislature that the "disproportionate cost of maintaining the prison at Dannemora . . . shows that its original design and location there was an error." [19] The Albany *Daily Knickerbocker* agreed, reflecting the thinking of many citizens when it stated that the institution was "too inaccessible—too much surrounded by intense cold and snow storms—to ever be other than a losing concern—an extravagant folly, tolerated for the sole purpose of proving that there are men in the world sufficiently empty-headed to spend twelve shillings every time they make a dollar." [20]

The prison at Dannemora, however, was only the most conspicu-

[16] Hurd, *History of Clinton and Franklin Counties*, p. 49; Plattsburgh *Republican*, March 22 and Dec. 27, 1851.

[17] DA, 75th Session (1852), Vol. I, No. 1, pp. 12–13.

[18] See especially Plattsburgh *Republican*, Feb. 24 and March 24, 1849; Anonymous, *Prison Labor . . . in the Prisons of the State of New York, and of the United States* (Albany, 1885), p. 41; DS, 73rd Session (1850), Vol. I, No. 16, pp. 3–4.

[19] DA, 83rd Session (1860), Vol. I, No. 12, pp. 11–12.

[20] Quoted from Plattsburgh *Republican*, Feb. 4, 1860.

ous example of the failure of Empire State penitentiaries to make a satisfactory adjustment to restrictive labor legislation. Under the law of 1842 it was still possible to use inmates who had learned trades prior to conviction in similar work under the contract system, and this was of some help to administrators. The chief stumbling block was the problem of what to do with the unskilled offender, or the felon who knew only a trade which was not used in the prison shops.

One available gambit, sanctioned by the law, was the use of such inmates in producing supplies for publicly owned institutions. Under the name of the "state-use system," this eventually became a mainstay of American penal industry. In 1847, the legislature encouraged this type of work by providing that all clothing for the convicts at Dannemora was to be made at Auburn and Sing Sing.[21] Prison officials also found ways to secure income by using inmates in unskilled manual labor. Much of Sing Sing's support in 1849, for example, came from the employment of felons in building a portion of the Hudson River Railroad that ran directly through the penitentiary grounds.[22] Administrators pinned their greatest hopes, however, upon the provisions in the law of 1842 which encouraged the prisons to make goods that would compete mainly with foreign manufacturers. After the collapse of the silk venture at Auburn, the first major test of this idea, the Cayuga County institution turned to the production of rugs and cutlery, which soon supplied most of its revenue. Sing Sing resorted to the making of Brussels carpets, file manufacturing, and fur cutting.[23]

The attempt to secure steady and adequate income from the production of nondomestic items continued at the prisons throughout the rest of the ante-bellum period, but the risks were great and the results unimpressive. The hard fact was that some industries had failed to thrive in the United States because they were not well

[21] *Laws*, 70th Session, 2nd Meeting (1847), p. 625.
[22] DS, 73rd Session (1850), Vol. I, No. 16, p. 162.
[23] *Ibid.*, 67th Session (1844), Vol. I, No. 18, p. 5, and No. 20, p. 16; 70th Session (1847), Vol. I, No. 11, p. 11.

suited to American conditions; it was unrealistic to expect the prisons to make flourishing enterprises out of manufactures that nobody else had been able to establish on a profitable basis. On the other hand, if a foreign product could be successfully made in America, there was nothing to prevent native artisans from entering the field. In time such a product would become domesticated and thus illegal to be made in prison shops. This nearly happened to saw-making, which was introduced at Sing Sing as an industry that would not compete with American manufacturers. In 1855, a senate committee which had received a protest from free saw-makers reported that this line of business, "although a comparatively new department of industry in the United States, has within the past ten years increased . . . to one of imposing magnitude, and is without doubt at the present time entitled to exemption from prison competition to the extent contemplated by existing statutes." [24] The legislature apparently failed to follow this recommendation, but the threat to penal industry was clear. How could administrators plan intelligently if they did not know how long the nondomestic ventures they established would remain lawful?

The greatest danger inherent in the production of imported goods, however, was that a prison might stake its industrial program too heavily upon one or two relatively exotic lines and court disaster if one of these failed. For reasons which are not clear, the Auburn cutlery contract was not continued after 1848. As a result, the institution depended increasingly upon its carpet shop, which was run by a local entrepreneur named Josiah Barber. This proved dangerous. Within a few years Barber suffered some business setbacks, and was allowed extensions of time on his labor payments by the administration, which "secured" his debts to the institution by obtaining a claim upon his prison stock and equipment, supposedly worth $60,000. When Barber informed penitentiary officials in 1851 that he could not meet his obligations, the agent decided to terminate his contract and sell the assets he had pledged as security. It was soon discovered, however, that the American rug

[24] *Ibid.,* 78th Session (1855), Vol. III, No. 71, p. 1.

business was in such a depressed state that no fair price could be realized on this property, and no sale was made.

By now the prison was in a grave situation. Approximately three hundred and fifty convicts faced idleness if the carpet shop closed down. In addition, the prison's main source of financial support was gone. The outcome clearly revealed the inability of the institution to defend its position if an important contractor fell into arrears. Despite Barber's indebtedness, the inspectors intervened in his favor. He was awarded a new contract requiring him to pay less for his inmate labor than before, containing nothing on the subject of security for his old obligations, and awarding him the free use of inexperienced convicts for three months.[25]

The altered situation created by the labor law of 1842 also posed problems for contractors. Entrepreneurs who ran shops turning out nondomestic goods shared the prevailing uncertainty about whether or not these would remain indefinitely legal. Businessmen who produced domestic wares could not count upon a steady flow of workers, being limited to the employment of inmates who had learned to make such products on the outside. Because the contractor could not plan ahead, he was tempted to cut corners and maximize short-run gains while the opportunity allowed. The system of inspectorships under which such men as Henry Storms could entrench themselves heightened the possibility of collusion.

It is not surprising, therefore, that numerous methods were used to defraud the state of income during the 1850's. Contracts were drawn up, for example, with loopholes and ambiguities affording grounds for dispute about the proper definition of such terms as "able bodied men" and "full day's labor." Squabbles involving such matters actually led to the resignation of one Auburn agent early in the decade.[26] The Storms–Lockwood regime at Sing Sing provided tremendous opportunities for the unscrupulous. Particu-

[25] *Ibid.*, 72nd Session (1849), Vol. I, No. 30, p. 26, and 74th Session (1851), Vol. I, No. 13, p. 43; DA, 78th Session (1855), Vol. III, No. 60, pp. 224, 932.
[26] DA, 78th Session (1855), Vol. III, No. 60, pp. 918–920, and Vol. V, No. 85, pp. 386–387; 75th Session (1852), Vol. I, No. 20, p. 157.

larly nefarious were a number of agreements concluded with a contractor named Alfred Walker, who gained virtually free use of the prison marble quarries, bought state-owned equipment at knock-down prices, and actually received state money for dumping into the Hudson, as "fill," quantities of dirt and rubbish which he excavated in his quarrying operations. Walker also managed to hire a staff member to visit courts of justice and pay bribes in an effort to have convicted men falsely certified to be hatmakers.[27]

One popular means used by a number of contractors to defraud the state was the contrived damage suit. It was possible for goods to be spoiled by inmate workers, or for fires to be set by convict incendiaries, and in such cases damages might fairly be claimed by businessmen who suffered them.[28] Some entrepreneurs, however, gained unconscionable advantages. Conspicuous was a firm which entered into a five-year contract for contract labor at a total charge of $33,485.70. In addition to inmate workers it received thirteen thousand square feet of floor space heated at state expense, janitorial help, and the assistance of three keepers to maintain order. Through the use of various devices it managed to cut the charges to $26,717.51, after which it recovered $25,017.74 through a damage suit for losses allegedly suffered in a fire. It had thus secured five years of convict labor and other concessions for only $1,699.77.[29] In 1857, the prison inspectors complained that it was a standard practice for contractors to claim damages if they were behind in their remittances for inmate labor and did not wish to pay the fees.[30] At this time the state was involved in a large and controversial damage suit with a Dannemora contractor named Jacob Kingsland which ultimately resulted in an award so exorbitant that Governor Morgan refused to pay it.[31]

[27] *Ibid.*, 78th Session (1855), Vol. III, No. 60, pp. 140, 147–150, 406–407.

[28] See DS, 66th Session (1843), Vol. III, No. 83, p. 5; *Northern Christian Advocate,* Dec. 12, 1855; Auburn *Weekly American,* March 17, 1858.

[29] DS, 78th Session (1855), Vol. I, No. 22, pp. 7–9.

[30] *Ibid.*, 80th Session (1857), Vol. III, No. 110, p. 25.

[31] DA, 78th Session (1855), Vol. III, No. 60, p. 781, and 83rd Session (1860), Vol. I, No. 2, p. 13; DS, 80th Session (1857), Vol. III, No. 110, pp. 33–35.

Hobbled by restrictive legislation, dangerously dependent upon important but financially shaky contractors, and exposed to corruption in an era of low political morality, the prisons wallowed into debt. After the scandals of the Storms–Lockwood regime had been exposed, citizens found that the net loss to the state might run as high as $220,000. Stirred into action, the legislature prohibited the extension of credit to contractors and set up a system under which the penitentiaries were assured of a steady flow of cash from the comptroller's office upon the receipt of monthly expense estimates from prison administrators. In turn, the proceeds from penal labor were to be sent to Albany, and were expected to balance the funds disbursed from the public treasury.[32]

Citizens soon learned, however, that the goal of self-support would remain difficult to achieve. In 1855, the expenses of the penal system exceeded earnings by more than $325,000. The annual deficit was only $100,000 in 1856, but in the next two years the picture darkened appreciably. The first brought not only an adverse balance of more than $119,000 but also a national financial panic which had a severe effect upon the prison shops. At Sing Sing during the fall and winter of 1858 an average of three hundred convicts were locked in their cells without work. Despite legislation to the contrary, agents at both Auburn and Sing Sing found it necessary to extend credit to contractors. In the wake of the panic the annual deficit mounted to over $234,000. Conditions improved as the national economic outlook brightened, and by 1861 both Auburn and Sing Sing were showing small financial surpluses. The continued poor performance of the penitentiary at Dannemora, however, caused the system as a whole to show a net loss.[33]

Growing disciplinary troubles were added to the economic frus-

[32] DA, 78th Session (1855), Vol. I, No. 3, p. 5, and Vol. IV, No. 105, pp. 2–3; *Laws of the State of New-York, Passed at the Seventy-seventh Session of the Legislature . . . 1854* (Albany, 1854), pp. 542–543.

[33] DA, 82nd Session (1859), Vol. I, No. 2, p. 10, and No. 40, pp. 22, 107; DS, 84th Session (1861), Vol. I, No. 25, p. 5, and 85th Session (1862), Vol. I, No. 9, p. 7.

trations experienced by prison officials during this period. The relative mildness that had prevailed under such leaders as Mrs. Farnham, John Bigelow, and Ransom Cook was supplanted by a more stringent approach, but this did not bring about submission. Indeed, inmate behavior was clearly worsening by the end of the ante-bellum era.

Most of the penal administrators who took over after 1847 showed little or no inclination to be scrupulous in their observance of the prison act passed in that year. By and large, they honored its provisions outlawing the use of the whip, but they frequently ignored its directive to use solitary confinement on stinted rations whenever severe punishment seemed necessary. Instead, they interpreted the law to authorize any methods of correction which it did not expressly prohibit. Some convicts were, to be sure, locked up from time to time in badly ventilated and pitch-dark disciplinary cells, but many others suffered penalties which were physically afflictive.[34]

In some cases, inmates were apparently kicked, caned, or struck with fists despite all legislation to the contrary.[35] On most occasions, however, officers avoided the use of blows and resorted instead to a variety of tortures. Under the application of the pulley, one popular disciplinary device, a convict would be forced to stand with all of his weight upon one leg while his other limbs were raised by ropes.[36] Another painful punishment was "yoking," administered by placing across the shoulders of an inmate a heavy bar having staples at both ends to encircle his wrists and a larger one in the middle to fit around his neck. A variation of this treatment was described to the New York Prison Association by an

[34] See New York Prison Association, *Ninth Report* (1854), pp. 47–48; DA, 71st Session (1848), Vol. I, No. 10, p. 96; 77th Session (1854), Vol. II, No. 40, pp. 38, 118; and 78th Session (1855), Vol. IV, No. 85, pp. 242–335; DS, 84th Session (1861), Vol. I, No. 25, p. 27.

[35] DA, 73rd Session (1850), Vol. VIII, No. 198, pp. 13–21.

[36] *Ibid.*, 83rd Session (1860), Vol. I, No. 21, pp. 32, 179; Anonymous, "Torture and Homicide in an American State Prison," *Harper's Weekly*, II (Dec. 18, 1858), 808.

ex-convict who had been compelled to wear "an iron collar put around his neck with prongs about seven or eight inches in length." William Titus, a reform-minded warden and N.Y.P.A. member who managed to secure appointment at Auburn in the mid-1850's under the inspectorship of Thomas Kirkpatrick, testified that yoking made inmates complain of "soreness, headache, pains in the breast and general paralyzation," while a prison physician asserted that it could numb the arms of a victim and cause his hands to turn purple.[37] Still another ingenious punitive method was "bucking," presumably copied from military precedents. The offender who was subjected to this punishment sat with his knees drawn up against his chest and his arms fastened securely about his legs. A stick was then inserted between his knee-joints and his elbows. "Thus spitted," commented an article in *Harper's Weekly,* "the convict is helpless, and may be rolled about hither or thither, as his rulers please." [38]

By far the most common and controversial punishment in use at this time, however, was the "shower-bath," which had been introduced at Auburn in the early 1840's in an attempt to find a substitute for the lash. Louis Dwight had seen officials in Massachusetts douse inmates with water as a disciplinary method, and had recommended it to administrators at the Cayuga County prison. The latter, searching at the time for punitive techniques which would not offend humanitarian sensibilities, were willing to experiment, and in April, 1842, the punishment was given its first application in New York upon an unruly convict who was drenched with two gallons of cold well water. For a number of months after this trial, whipping was virtually abandoned at Auburn. According to the institutional physician, Joseph T. Pitney, the shower was "the most important and valuable means of enforcing prison discipline, that has ever been devised." [39] Critics of the method,

[37] Anonymous, "Torture and Homicide," p. 808; DA, 74th Session (1851), Vol. IV, No. 120, pp. 3–4; DS, 76th Session (1853), Vol. I, No. 30, p. 142.

[38] New York Prison Association, *Ninth Report* (1854), p. 165; Anonymous, "Torture and Homicide," pp. 808–809.

[39] DS, 66th Session (1843), Vol. I, No. 9, pp. 2, 72–73.

however, asserted that it was cruel, degrading, and potentially injurious.[40]

Such contrary views stemmed partly from the fact that the shower could be applied in a variety of ways, some of which were more severe than others. The typical apparatus consisted of a tank of water fixed above a booth or open stall in which a chair was placed. In a rigorous application the contents of the tank might be allowed to fall directly and with great force upon the head of a convict; otherwise, the water could be discharged through a perforated sheet of metal. If desired, ice could be added to the liquid to make it especially cold. The treatment could also be aggravated by encircling the inmate's neck with a bowllike apparatus which would catch some of the descending stream and was deliberately adjusted to drain slowly. In this way the water could be forced upward and the convict would have to strain to keep his mouth and nose above it in order to avoid drowning. The punishment could also be varied by shortening or lengthening the distance between the tank and the prisoner and by increasing or decreasing the amount of water used.[41]

Administered with moderation and care, the shower could be a mild punishment—perhaps even a refreshing one on a hot summer day. The period in which it was introduced saw the spread of a popular health fad known as the "water cure," and some exponents of showering actually believed it had a therapeutic effect upon inmates who were subjected to it.[42] There was thus no reason for

[40] *Ibid.,* 69th Session (1846), Vol. IV, No. 121, p. 5; DA, 72nd Session (1849), Vol. I, No. 243, p. 213.

[41] See especially Anonymous, "Torture and Homicide," pp. 808–809; DA, 74th Session (1851), Vol. IV, No. 120, p. 38, and 75th Session (1852), Vol. I, No. 20, pp. 136, 141. A picture of a showering apparatus used at Sing Sing between 1848 and 1875 is shown in Anonymous, "Sing Sing Prison," *Correction,* XIV (July, 1949), 6. Another device of this type, using a funnel rather than a sieve, is depicted in Fred A. Packard, *Memorandum of a Late Visit to the Auburn Penitentiary* (Auburn, 1842), p. 5.

[42] It was reported in 1853 that a Sing Sing physician had "occasionally used the same shower-bath in which the convicts are punished, as a remedial agent for disease of the head and brain, with decided benefit." (DS, 76th Session [1853], Vol. I, No. 30, p. 22.)

humanitarians to condemn the technique out of hand, especially since it offered a substitute for the whip, and some reformers did not hesitate to endorse it. Dorothea Dix, for example, was "convinced that, with due care, and under proper direction, the shower bath . . . is a very effectual means of procuring submission to proper rules and regulations." [43] Such administrators as Edmonds, Bigelow, and Mrs. Farnham had no objection to the device, and used it on a number of occasions at Sing Sing.[44]

If the shower were administered too mildly, however, its efficacy as a punishment was diminished. Realizing this, penal officials seeking a substitute for the whip after 1847 did not hesitate to aggravate the treatment by using the encircling bowl, chilling the water with ice, and drenching victims suddenly and with great force. Inmates who were showered in the 1850's described the crushing impact of outpourings which made them feel as if their necks were being broken. Some convicts were allegedly rendered deaf by the punishment, and others weakened to such an extent that they could not walk away without help after being subjected to it. One officer at Auburn admitted using four barrels of ice water upon a prisoner who was subsequently yoked for two hours before being thrown into a dungeon.[45] There was obviously great danger in applying the shower with such severity, as citizens learned in December, 1858, when an inmate named Samuel Moore died at Auburn from the effects of the device. Investigating the incident in the face of mounting public concern, the inspectors exonerated the keepers from blame and emphasized the murderousness of the offender, who had threatened to "cut the heart out" of an officer in his shop. Nevertheless, they admitted that showering was liable to misuse "even in the hands of men who will exercise the utmost prudence," and prohibited its employment in

[43] Dorothea Dix, *Remarks on Prisons and Prison Discipline in the United States* (Boston, 1845), p. 25.

[44] See DS, 68th Session (1845), Vol. I, No. 9, p. 36; DA, 69th Session (1846), Vol. IV, No. 130, pp. 105, 113–122, and 70th Session (1847), Vol. VI, No. 160, p. 5.

[45] New York Prison Association, *Tenth Report* (1855), p. 142, and *Eleventh-Twelfth Report* (1856), p. 83; DA, 75th Session (1852), Vol. I, No. 20, p. 141.

the penitentiaries of New York except "under the advice and direction of the Prison Physician." [46] At least one such official must have been willing to sanction the punishment, for in 1860 alone there were 161 showerings at Sing Sing.[47]

All the punitive ingenuity which administrators could muster, however, proved inadequate to produce the type of submission that had once prevailed in the penitentiaries of the Empire State. Except for the uprising among the female convicts at Sing Sing in May, 1843, riots and violent escape attempts had been practically unknown in New York's prisons for at least a generation. Now they became matters of common occurrence.

Why did discipline become so hard to enforce, even with the aid of torture? This question is not easy to answer, but it is clear that some of the strains in the penal system were greater than they had been in recent decades. In the first place, the penitentiaries were becoming increasingly overcrowded. When Governor Hunt reported the disheartening failure of the Dannemora ore deposits to the legislature in 1852, he was also forced to advocate sending even more convicts to the Clinton County institution because there was no room for them at the other state prisons. By the end of the decade the penitentiaries had 254 more inmates than cells. Of necessity the felons either had to share their cubicles, which made it absolutely impossible to prevent communication between them, or be put up in prison hospitals and chapels, where it was easy for them to lay plans for uprisings.[48]

Other unfavorable circumstances were also in existence. The turnover in guards and keepers was greater under the new system of inspectorships than had previously been the case, and there was more of a chance for inexperienced personnel to be placed in positions requiring seasoned judgment. Public apathy, low salaries, insecurity of tenure, and constant pressure to squeeze revenue

[46] Auburn *Weekly American*, Dec. 15, 1858 and Jan. 12, 1859; Anonymous, "Torture and Homicide," pp. 808–810.

[47] DS, 84th Session (1861), Vol. I, No. 25, p. 27.

[48] DA, 75th Session (1852), Vol. I, No. 1, pp. 12–13, and 83rd Session (1860), Vol. I, No. 21, pp. 4–5.

from an industrial system which had been hobbled by restrictive legislation sapped staff morale even when leadership was honest and competent, and the situation was much worse under administrators who, like Storms and Lockwood, tolerated drunkenness and moral laxity. The baneful effects of political pressure were especially well revealed at Auburn late in the 1850's, when the fluctuating composition of the board of inspectors kept the positions of key officials in constant jeopardy. Levi Lewis and Jacob Foshay, the agent and principal keeper respectively, quarreled bitterly and vied for the support of their superiors; discipline inevitably suffered as they worked at cross purposes and even refused to speak to one another.[49]

The convicts were not blind to what was going on around them, and it is not surprising that misbehavior in the prisons became more and more acute. Late in 1855, for example, a Sing Sing keeper who had been lured into a conversation with an inmate was set upon by a group of convicts and badly beaten before order could be restored. The next day a prisoner working in the quarries charged at some officers with a crowbar and was shot dead after a warning bullet failed to deter him. That night the felons demonstrated noisily against the administration after they had been locked in their cells. "The shaking of eight or nine hundred iron doors, and the unearthly groans of the men would be somewhat frightful," said one report in understatement, "were it not on the right side of substantial stone walls." [50]

This was not an isolated episode, for uprisings continued to occur. At Auburn, insubordination flared early in 1857 during the Lewis–Foshay controversy. When a convict in the machine shop was put in a dungeon for misbehavior, sixty of his mates armed themselves with hammers and other tools, sent a committee to negotiate with the administration, and had the satisfaction of seeing their comrade released. "This yielding by the prison officers

---

[49] See Auburn *Weekly American,* March 11 and April 15, 1857; DA, 81st Session (1858), Vol. IV, No. 143, *passim.*
[50] New York *Times,* Nov. 29, 1855.

will give the convicts new courage," predicted a newspaper correspondent, "and we may expect to hear of further trouble." [51] The soundness of this observation was shortly borne out when two attempts were made to assassinate the agent.[52]

Auburn's difficulties had scarcely died down when trouble erupted once more at Sing Sing. On a Sunday morning in May, 1857, a group of convicts broke ranks while marching to the chapel and ran from the prison yard, raising a cry of fire as they went. "Yelling wildly, and brandishing slung-shots, knives, hammers, and such other weapons as they had been able to conceal about their persons," some of the inmates tried to escape along the railroad tracks running through the institution until a group of guards managed to surround them. Ultimately the uprising was put down and the participants punished by showering. It was discovered that the riot had been concocted by ringleaders who had feigned sickness in order to get together in the prison hospital.[53]

Sing Sing was the scene of more violence early in 1858 when a column of inmates filing into the penitentiary from the saw shop received orders to halt while another group of convicts entered the prison. Suddenly a felon named Jack Haggerty sprang from the ranks, waving a knife and shouting, "Now boys, liberty or death!" Four inmates promptly followed him in a mad dash for the frozen Hudson. Two were mortally wounded by the firing of the guards, and another was clubbed with a gun-butt. Haggerty himself emerged unscathed, but none of the men got away.[54] In 1859, the wave of uprisings continued with a disturbance at the Auburn hame shop. The convicts resisted their superiors and threatened

[51] *Ibid.*, Jan. 20, 1857, citing Rochester *Advertiser*. See also Auburn *Weekly American,* Jan. 14, Jan. 28, and Feb. 18, 1857; DS, 80th Session (1857), Vol. II, No. 49, pp. 2–3.

[52] New York *Times*, March 9, 1857; Auburn *Weekly American*, March 11, 1857.

[53] New York *Times*, May 12, 1857; Auburn *Weekly American*, May 20, 1857, citing New York *Herald*.

[54] New York *Times*, Feb. 22, 1858; Auburn *Weekly American,* March 3, 1858.

their lives until the agent drew a revolver and fired among the mutineers. When it was over, two inmates lay dead.[55] Nor did Dannemora escape the growing list of outbreaks. At midnight on July 11, 1861, a keeper supervising operations in the prison rolling mill was murdered by a convict who hit him over the head with a bar of iron. Seven inmates got away, and another officer would have been killed but for the intervention of a loyal prisoner.[56]

In short, the penal system of New York was clearly in trouble as the ante-bellum period came to an end. A pattern of financial troubles, violent outbreaks, and other difficulties revealed a malaise similar to the one that had stricken the state prisons after the War of 1812. An era had ended, and few people if any held the once prevalent belief in the superiority of the Empire State's correctional methods. Indeed, in 1859 the board of inspectors registered a unanimous preference for the Pennsylvania system.[57] Three years later, Governor Morgan confessed publicly that the disciplinary and financial practices in evidence in the prisons of New York were "very faulty." [58] The heyday of the Auburn system was far behind, and the example of Newgate confronted administrators who struggled to keep an old and outmoded order from collapsing altogether.

[55] See accounts in Plattsburgh *Republican,* March 26 and April 9, 1859, taken in part from Albany *Knickerbocker.*
[56] Plattsburgh *Republican,* July 13, 1861.
[57] DS, 82nd Session (1859), Vol. I, No. 40, pp. 15–16.
[58] DA, 85th Session (1862), Vol. I, No. 2, pp. 15–16.

# Chapter XII

# Change and Continuity

AS far as the average adult convict was concerned, the pioneering period of prison reform in New York came to an end in the winter of 1847–1848. Despite important developments which took place after this in the treatment of special groups of inmates—first offenders, the criminally insane, short-term misdemeanants, and the like—the life of most prisoners remained essentially the same for more than half a century. Although defects were painfully apparent in almost every phase of penitentiary operations, the Auburn system somehow survived. In 1910, a penologist named Orlando F. Lewis visited the Cayuga County institution and marveled at the persistence of old methods and the continued use of penal facilities which had not changed since the days of Elam Lynds. By this time the lockstep and the striped uniform had been abolished—the former in 1900 and the latter in 1904—but the silent system still prevailed. It was a gloomy and disheartening situation.[1]

One should not conclude, however, that the spark of creativity and change was absent from penal affairs in New York after 1848. Despite the dismissal of such leaders as Eliza Farnham and John Bigelow, influential citizens continued to hold advanced correctional ideas and to wrestle with their implications. Although

[1] Orlando F. Lewis, *The Development of American Prisons and Prison Customs, 1776–1845* (n.p., 1922), p. 88.

administrators conducted what amounted to a mere holding operation at the state prisons, considerable progress was made during
the 1850's in the treatment of minor offenders in the county penitentiaries of Albany and Rochester under the direction of Amos
Pilsbury and Zebulon R. Brockway.[2] Offenders who were criminally insane benefited from the construction of an asylum in 1858
at which they could receive therapy instead of punishment.[3] The
humanitarianism so evident in the preceding decade, though weakened, did not pass away. When such leaders as Theodore Dwight,
John D. Wolfe, Gaylord Hubbell, and Enoch Cobb Wines came on
the scene to fight for better penal conditions in New York during
and after the Civil War, they found a situation that had been at
least partially prepared for their efforts, and drew heavily upon the
idealism that had flourished in the 1840's.[4]

One idea that found continued support among some reformers
after 1848 was the conviction that crime did not stem simply from
willful depravity. Abraham Beale, an active member of the New
York Prison Association, manifested this belief in 1856 when he
argued that convicts should be regarded as "diseased patients"
who needed care administered by "moral physicians."[5] John
Stanton Gould, another N.Y.P.A. member who did noteworthy
research on the statistical incidence of crime, was not prepared to
believe that the felon was merely a victim of disease. Nevertheless,
he did criticize pharisaical attitudes toward the offender and condemn the tendency of many citizens to tolerate such crime-
breeding evils as poverty, inadequate schools, grog shops, and
brothels. It was within the power of the people, he believed, to
eradicate many of the causes of crime through legislation.[6] A
similar outlook was displayed by Amory D. Mayo, a Unitarian

[2] See especially Zebulon R. Brockway, *Fifty Years of Prison Service* (New
York, 1912), pp. 43–67.
[3] The early years of this institution will be described later in this chapter.
[4] The activities of these and other reformers are described in Blake Mc-
Kelvey, *American Prisons* (Chicago, 1936), pp. 48–68.
[5] New York Prison Association, *Eleventh-Twelfth Report* (1856), p. 65.
[6] *Ibid., Tenth Report* (1855), pp. 113–118.

minister in Albany who held that proper penal policy should include prevention as well as cure.[7]

It is not surprising that such views persisted in the reports of the New York Prison Association or in the writings of an occasional liberal clergyman. However, there were indications that a certain amount of environmentalism was penetrating the thinking of those who had previously resisted its influence. During the 1840's, for example, the *Northern Christian Advocate,* official organ of the Genesee Conference of the Methodist Church, had uncompromisingly insisted upon the individual accountability of the offender, fought against phrenology, and ridiculed the "morbid, puling sentimentalism that would undermine with tears, and blow away with sighs, the whole fabric of the moral universe." In 1852, it was still advocating penal discipline which would be "humiliating and severe," though not cruel.[8]

By this time, however, contributors to the *Advocate* were sounding a new note. Admitting that the "higher circles" of society knew "little of the stern temptations which beset the lower walks of life," they began to discern an interconnectedness between the acts of offenders and the circumstances in which such culprits frequently lived. "The criminal is, to be sure, responsible for his crime," stated one writer, "but society is, in too many cases, not guiltless. Its own unhealthy condition contributes, year by year, to increase the number of its convicts, while it swells enormously that criminal list which punishment cannot reach." Another contributor, asserting that penury could lead men to become criminals, declared that many offenders were "more sinned against than sinning."[9] The beginnings of the Social Gospel were becoming visible as such men wrestled with the conviction "that personal sin often had communal roots."[10]

[7] Amory D. Mayo, *Symbols of the Capital: or, Civilization in New York* (New York, 1859), pp. 250–253.

[8] *Northern Christian Advocate,* June 25 and Sept. 10, 1845; Feb. 25 and Aug. 12, 1846; Jan. 6, April 21, and Oct. 27, 1847; Feb. 11, 1852.

[9] *Ibid.,* April 2 and July 9, 1851. For another article showing some environmentalist influence, see the issue of May 2, 1855.

[10] See Timothy L. Smith, *Revivalism and Social Reform in Mid-Nineteenth*

New Yorkers thus heard from a variety of sources that the group had certain responsibilities toward the individual and was blameworthy if neglect of these contributed to the spread of crime. Conversely, they learned through the New York Prison Association that the responsibility of the individual to the group in which he lived might be made the key to a new and different method of dealing with offenders. In 1854, the annual report of the Association devoted a considerable amount of space to the ideas of Captain Alexander Maconochie, a British penal reformer who had instituted a system of "marks" and other incentives for good behavior in his work among transported felons in Australia. Like the efforts of Eliza Farnham and John Bigelow, Maconochie's experiments had been terminated in the 1840's, but his ideas persisted.

The Auburn system attempted to isolate an individual, and to deprive him of all meaningful contact with his fellows; Maconochie, on the other hand, sought to inculcate within the individual a sense of responsibility toward his companions and to make him realize the need for cooperation. Under the implementation of this policy the behavior of a single inmate injured or benefited the men around him. "As I would . . . never punish an individual apart from his party," Maconochie declared, "so neither would I ever reward one. No exertion, no favor, no degree of individual merit, should carry a man through without his fellows; for on the absolute community of interest among the individuals of each party, I would rely more than on anything to make the system efficient." [11] Here was a basic challenge to American ideas as exemplified in either the silent system developed in New York or the solitary method practiced in Pennsylvania; if citizens of the Empire State were unwilling to accept it, they were at least exposed to it. Eventually the ideas of Maconochie were to have a definite impact upon American penal practices.[12]

---

*Century America* (Nashville, 1959), p. 152. My belief that the Social Gospel idea is exemplified in the two articles from which I have quoted owes much to the general themes discussed in Smith's work, especially in Chapter X, "The Evangelical Origins of Social Christianity."

[11] New York Prison Association, *Ninth Report* (1854), p. 75 and *passim*.

[12] See especially McKelvey, *American Prisons*, pp. 60–61.

Maconochie's belief that prison administrators should use rewards as well as punishments was shared by a number of New Yorkers after 1848, though without immediate effect upon penal policy. In 1851 the *Northern Christian Advocate* noted approvingly that a petition was being circulated throughout the state urging the legislature to give inmates positive incentives to good behavior. The principal idea was to allow convicts "to earn sufficient by extra labor to sustain them awhile after their discharge, so that they may not be forced into the vicious or necessitous associations of their former career." [13] The legislature refused to endorse this plan, but it did attract considerable support in other quarters. The New York Prison Association took it up, and Governor Horatio Seymour gave it his endorsement in 1854, arguing that it would encourage prudence and foresight among inmates, afford financial aid to relatives, and help ex-prisoners make a successful transition to civilian life.[14] Seymour's successor, Myron H. Clark, supported the proposal in 1855 and 1856, and the prison inspectors had swung behind it by the end of the antebellum period. Governor Edwin D. Morgan added his approval in 1862.[15] Eventually the idea of permitting offenders to earn money while confined and to save or spend it under the watchful eye of correctional officials became an important part of the system followed at Elmira Reformatory under Zebulon Brockway.[16]

Another departure from the Auburn system was recommended by the prison inspectors in 1861 in the form of systematic reductions of sentence as rewards for good behavior.[17] Tennessee had

---

[13] *Northern Christian Advocate*, Dec. 17, 1851. Dorothea Dix had spoken out for a similar policy in 1845, coupling her remarks with emphatic warnings against giving inmates gratuitous funds which might weaken their self-esteem. See her *Remarks on Prisons and Prison Discipline in the United States* (Boston, 1845), pp. 12–13.

[14] New York Prison Association, *Eleventh-Twelfth Report* (1856), p. 21; DA, 77th Session (1854), Vol. I, No. 3, pp. 12–13.

[15] DA, 78th Session (1855), Vol. I, No. 3, p. 7; 79th Session (1856), Vol. I, No. 3, p. 13; and 85th Session (1862), Vol. I, No. 2, p. 17; DS, 84th Session (1861), Vol. I, No. 25, p. 8.

[16] Brockway, *Fifty Years of Prison Service*, pp. 321–323.

[17] DS, 84th Session (1861), Vol. I, No. 25, p. 8.

been following such a policy as early as 1836, and by the time of the Civil War similar programs were working well in Ohio and Michigan. The New York legislature was thus playing the role of a follower rather than a pioneer when it enacted the Empire State's first "good conduct law" in 1863, but the step was nevertheless noteworthy.[18] Even before it was taken prison officials at Sing Sing and Dannemora had begun to use the "good behavior" technique in actual practice by issuing certificates of good conduct to support inmate applications for pardon.[19]

The state board of prison inspectors took a significant look into the future in 1862 by envisioning the establishment of a "school of industry" or "home for reform" for first offenders and other young felons. At such an institution, the members urged, the primacy of rehabilitation should be acknowledged and calculated humiliation avoided. Above all, they argued, the name "state prison" should never be used with relation to the venture, so that the subjects of the experiment could escape the stigma attaching to the ordinary convict.[20] By 1869, a site had been selected at Elmira for a trial of this plan among first offenders between the ages of sixteen and thirty. Financial difficulties prevented a quick implementation of the idea, but by 1877 the physical plant was at last ready for occupancy. Under the leadership of Zebulon Brockway, one of the most significant chapters in nineteenth-century American penology was about to begin as the Elmira Reformatory became a reality.[21]

Another group of offenders, the criminally insane, did not have to wait so long for an asylum of their own. The efforts of Dorothea Dix on behalf of convicts who were mentally unbalanced did much to awaken citizens to the need for giving such felons special treat-

---

[18] McKelvey, *American Prisons*, p. 43; DS, 85th Session (1862), Vol. I, No. 9, p. 13; New York State Department of Correction, *Sing Sing Prison, Ossining, N.Y.: Its History, Purpose, Makeup and Program* (n.p., 1958), p. 18.

[19] DS, 81st Session (1858), Vol. I, No. 4, p. 146, and 84th Session (1861), Vol. I, No. 25, p. 251.

[20] *Ibid.*, 85th Session (1862), Vol. I, No. 9, p. 18.

[21] McKelvey, *American Prisons*, pp. 67–68; Brockway, *Fifty Years of Prison Service*, pp. 161 ff.

ment; influenced by her ideas, John W. Edmonds had created a separate "out-ward" for them at Sing Sing during his term as chief inspector, but the building had to be torn down when the Hudson River Railroad was given its right-of-way through the penitentiary grounds.[22] A subsequent experiment with sending insane convicts to the state asylum at Utica failed because the officers at that institution objected to mixing free citizens with felons and insisted that they could not provide adequate security for the confinement of criminals.[23] Finally, in 1857 the legislature appropriated $20,000 to build an asylum for such offenders on the prison grounds at Auburn.[24]

Although some critics objected to placing the new institution within the confines of a penitentiary, construction quickly got under way. The first superintendent, Edward Hall, was appointed late in 1858, and the first patients were received in February of the following year. Hall plainly believed that their treatment should be designed not to punish but to cure, and allowed them to take part in activities that would have mortified Elam Lynds. In addition to receiving counseling, schooling, and religious advice, the inmates could play dominoes, draughts, cards, and quoits. They were also given music therapy and permitted to putter about in a garden which was provided for them. Hall even went so far as to advocate that the state erect a gymnasium and bowling alley for their use. Once again New York was assuming the role of penological pioneer, being the first state to provide separate facilities for the criminally insane.[25]

Even within the penitentiaries themselves, no amount of adherence to the form and spirit of old methods could restore the Auburn system in all its former rigor after 1848. Whatever the

[22] Dix, *Remarks on Prisons and Prison Discipline*, pp. 14–15, 39–40; DA, 71st Session (1848), Vol. I, No. 10, p. 2.

[23] DS, 79th Session (1856), Vol. III, No. 99, p. 12.

[24] Auburn *Weekly American*, April 22, 1857.

[25] DA, 83rd Session (1860), Vol. I, No. 21, pp. 213–216; Anonymous, "Auburn Prison," *Correction*, XIV (June, 1949), 8, 10; Albert Deutsch, *The Mentally Ill in America* (New York, 1937), p. 411. McKelvey, in *American Prisons*, p. 142, is

intentions of administrators, there was enough restrictive legislation on the books to prevent a complete return to the past. Massive walls still separated the felon from humanity, but his isolation was no longer complete. The privilege of writing and receiving letters remained from the reform period of the 1840's, and at periodic intervals convicts could be visited by relatives. Prison libraries, although usually small in size and stocked with an inferior selection of books, provided another window to the world. John Luckey, who returned to Sing Sing as chaplain in 1855, was particularly active in securing reading material and circulating it among the inmates.[26] Although underpaid and hampered in their work by a lack of educational supplies, the part-time teachers provided under the penal law of 1847 gave instruction to convicts in the evenings and on Sundays.[27] Finally, in the New York Prison Association the inmate had an organization that was committed to helping him if possible and facilitating his adjustment to free society after his release. The policy of subjecting the prisoner to a living entombment had thus been to a certain extent modified.

That policy, inaugurated after the War of 1812 by such men as Elam Lynds, John Cray, Samuel Hopkins, and Gershom Powers, had not stemmed from sheer cruelty or misanthropy on the part of its originators. The founders of the Auburn system had tried to cope with basic problems involved in what a penitentiary was, and still is: an artificially created society of criminals which is not only difficult to administer effectively but also quite likely to make those who come in contact with it worse instead of better. En-

---

technically incorrect in stating that the asylum was "outside the walls" at Auburn; it was constructed within the walled addition which had been joined to the penitentiary by 1841 as a site for new workshops. The building was used for insane criminals until 1894, after which it served for a time as a women's prison.

[26] DS, 79th Session (1856), Vol. III, No. 99, pp. 335–336, and 85th Session (1862), Vol. I, No. 9, pp. 326–327, 341.

[27] On the difficulties confronting these teachers, see especially DA, 79th Session (1856), Vol. IV, No. 85, p. 127; DS, 73rd Session (1850), Vol. I, No. 16, p. 330, and 79th Session (1856), Vol. III, No. 99, p. 353; Mayo, *Symbols of the Capital*, p. 251.

deavoring to impose order upon such a society, to prevent its members from corrupting one another, and to make the system financially self-supporting, a group of skillful and uncompromising men had established a harsh but reasonably effective mode of discipline which became widely imitated throughout the United States and in a number of foreign countries. In New York itself, the experiment was supported by a climate of opinion characterized by apprehension about the future of established institutions, a widespread feeling that special efforts were needed to secure social conformity, a profound disillusionment with previous penal policies, and a lack of sympathy for deviates. The comparative economy of the new system and the possibility of gaining revenue from the labor of convicts working silently in groups appealed to citizens imbued with a belief in governmental frugality and gave the Auburn plan an important advantage over the more expensive solitary system instituted in Pennsylvania.

As social and economic conditions changed in New York, the base of popular support for the new methods contracted. The fear and repression which existed at the state prisons, and the virtually unlimited powers which were given to the officials who administered them, led to cases of serious abuse and furnished natural targets for criticism. This was particularly true at Sing Sing, where special circumstances helped to produce an unusually severe type of regime. It also became evident that the benefits of isolating convicts from one another under the Auburn system had been won at the cost of stultifying the individual inmate. As fears about the durability of the social order became less intense, citizens no longer felt the same compulsive need to endorse a method which converted men into robots. At the same time, the industrial program carried on at Auburn and Sing Sing created hostility among various groups of workingmen who felt themselves injured by prison competition. By 1840 the times were ripe for change.

And change did come. New administrators took over at the prisons and inaugurated policies based upon reformation rather than deterrence. Restrictive legislation appeared in the law books, first with regard to penal industry and later to disciplinary methods. A reform organization, the New York Prison Association, arose to give voice to the theories and suggestions of citizens interested in correctional problems. Fresh ideas, based in part upon environmentalism and phrenology, were given a trial.

There was no real consensus, however, about the direction which prison reform should now take. Rival administrators divided into moderate and radical factions and clashed bitterly on policy matters. By 1848, it was obvious that the public was not ready for a drastic change in the treatment of convicts, and management of the prisons passed into the hands of officials who, having no mandate for a new order, contented themselves with nursing the old one along. Nevertheless, the situation was different from what it had been in the heyday of Elam Lynds. Despite growing public apathy with regard to penal affairs, the draining of reform energy into other causes, and the lack of any clear vision involving a new general approach to the treatment of felons, a leaven of ideas remained from the previous decade. From time to time limited gains could be made, especially in the care of such special types of offenders as young adults and the criminally insane. There was thus a bridge between the ferment of the forties and the time when the Empire State would once more make pioneering contributions to penology under the leadership of such figures as Zebulon Brockway, Josephine Shaw Lowell, Katharine Bement Davis, and Thomas Mott Osborne. For such reformers, and for those who supported their efforts, the past was prologue.

# A Critical Essay

# on Sources

INSTEAD of attempting to list every work which I consulted in the course of studying the prisons of ante-bellum New York, I shall here describe, with some critical comment, those sources which I found most useful and significant. Readers wishing to see an extensive listing of materials pertaining to the subject with which I have dealt should consult the bibliography of the doctoral dissertation from which the present work has grown, on file at the Cornell University Library, Ithaca, New York.

## Primary Sources

The published documents of the state of New York constitute the single most important body of sources used in the preparation of this study. Among other things, they contain the yearly reports of prison inspectors, agents, keepers, chaplains, physicians, and other officers; the laws under which the prisons operated; the findings of various investigating committees; and the policy recommendations of governors and other high state officials. Up to and including the year 1830, many materials of this sort appeared in the *Journals* of the state senate and assembly (abbreviated in this study as JS and JA); in 1831, four volumes of *Legislative Documents* were issued, after which each house of the legislature began publishing its own series of *Documents*, appearing annually in series of from one to nine volumes each and abbreviated in this study as DS and DA. The *Laws of the State of New York,* published in various editions throughout this period and afterward, provide necessary details on the legal framework within which penal policy was executed.

Although manuscript materials proved to be of secondary importance for the purposes of this study, several groups of papers did yield information of value. The Philip Schuyler Collection of the New York Public Library contains important correspondence involving Schuyler, Thomas Eddy, and Caleb Lownes; other Eddy materials, including a significant letter on penal policy written to DeWitt Clinton in 1818, are to be found in the Clinton Collection of the Columbia University Library. The major source for Eddy's writings, however, is the extensive selection of documents published in Samuel L. Knapp, *The Life of Thomas Eddy* (New York, 1834), which remains a valuable book for this reason. The New-York Historical Society possesses a small group of papers written by John Stanford, the Newgate chaplain, but most of these are drafts of reports later published in government documents. There is a highly revealing collection of letters from Eliza W. Farnham to John Bigelow in the Bigelow Papers of the New York Public Library, as well as a manuscript diary kept by Bigelow which contains a number of entries pertaining to his experiences as an inspector at Sing Sing. Finally, I am grateful to Miss Gladys Tilden of San Francisco, California, for making available to me materials from her personal collection of letters and other documents pertaining to the career of Mrs. Farnham.

Newspapers of the period contain considerable information about the penitentiaries at Auburn, Sing Sing, and Dannemora. Particularly useful to me were the Albany *Daily Argus;* the Auburn *Cayuga Patriot, Cayuga Tocsin, Free Press,* and *Weekly American;* the New York *Sun, Times,* and *Tribune;* the Plattsburgh *Republican;* and the Sing Sing *Hudson River Chronicle.* Although these had to be used with care because the political affiliations of the editors frequently colored their views on events transpiring at the prisons, such journals nevertheless provided details which I could locate in no other type of source and were therefore very valuable. A religious periodical, the *Northern Christian Advocate,* also furnished considerable information and opinion about correctional affairs in the 1840's and 1850's.

Throughout the ante-bellum era, American prisons were periodically visited by Europeans on official tours of inspection for their home governments, as well as by other travelers whose interests were more casual. By far the most important work to result from such activity was the jointly written account of Gustave de Beaumont and Alexis de Tocqueville, *Du Système Pénitentiaire aux États-Unis* (Paris, 1829), subsequently edited and translated by the German American Francis Lieber (*On the Penitentiary System in the United States,* Philadelphia, 1833). Both versions are valuable, particularly because the latter also includes an introductory essay and notes by Lieber. The inspection of prisons provided the official reason for Tocqueville's famous visit to America, and served as a means of securing funds for the trip from the French government. After the two travelers arrived, the prison project assumed secondary importance to them, but their report contains a wealth of information about the Auburn and Pennsylvania systems. Supplementary notes on penal matters which they gathered but did not include in their completed work may be found in J. P. Mayer, ed., *Journey to America* (New Haven, Conn., 1960).

The accounts of many other foreign visitors were also useful in providing details and perspective on the prisons of New York. These included E. S. Abdy, *Journal of a Residence and Tour in the United States of North America* (3 vols.; London, 1835); Guillaume Blouet, *Rapport . . . sur les Pénitenciers des États-Unis* (Paris, 1837); George Combe, *Notes on the United States of North America during a Phrenological Visit in 1838–9–40* (2 vols.; Philadelphia, 1841); William Crawford, *Report . . . on the Penitentiaries of the United States* (London, 1834); Frédéric-Auguste De Metz, *Rapport sur les Pénitenciers des États-Unis* (Paris, 1837); Basil Hall, *Travels in North America, in the Years 1827 and 1828* (2 vols.; Philadelphia, 1829); Nicolaus H. Julius, *Nordamerikas sitt-liche Zustände, Nach eigenen Anschauungen in den Jahren 1834, 1835, und 1836* (2 vols.; Leipzig, 1839); Frederick Marryat, *A Diary in America, with Remarks on Its Institutions* (2 vols.; Philadelphia, 1839); Harriet Martineau, *Society in America* (2 vols.; New York, 1837); Charles A. Murray, *Travels in North America during the Years 1834, 1835, and 1836* (2 vols.; London, 1839); and Thomas Shillitoe, *Journal of the Life, Labours and Travels of Thomas Shillitoe, in the Service of the Gospel of Jesus Christ* (2 vols.; London, 1839). Several travel accounts written in the nineteenth century but edited and published in the twentieth were also helpful, including Elizabeth H. Cawley, ed., *The American Diaries of Richard Cobden* (Princeton, 1952); Una Pope-Hennessy, ed., *The Aristo-cratic Journey: Being the Outspoken Letters of Mrs. Basil Hall Written during a Fourteen Months' Sojourn in America, 1827–1828* (New York, 1931); and Franklin D. Scott, trans. and ed., *Baron Klinkowström's America, 1818–1820* (Evanston, Ill., 1952). Although some travel accounts contain a number of unwarranted first impressions, snap judgments, and inaccuracies, this type of material is of great value when used in conjunction with other sources.

Wariness is also called for in using another group of sources dealing with the prisons of this period, the published recollections of convicts who were confined in them. Here the chance for exaggeration is obvious; nevertheless, I found most of the material contained in these accounts to be consistent with information given in other, more authoritative, sources. An exceedingly useful volume on life at Newgate is the anonymous work of W. A. Coffey, *Inside Out, or An Interior View of the New-York State Prison* (New York, 1823), written by an ex-convict of considerable in-telligence. James Bryce, *Secrets of the Mount-Pleasant State Prison, Revealed and Exposed* (Albany, 1839), gives a detailed account of the sufferings of an inmate who, like many counterparts today, thought he had been unjustly incarcerated. Particularly vivid is Levi S. Burr, *A Voice from Sing Sing* (Albany, 1833), with harrowing descriptions of starving times under the administration of Robert Wiltse. Horace Lane, *Five Years in State's Prison* (New York, 1835), is valuable in giving impressions of life at Auburn and Sing Sing as seen by a convict who had served time in both institutions.

The books and pamphlets of various prison reformers, administrators, and staff officers form an important category of source materials, sometimes contentious and invariably useful. An indispensable work dealing with Newgate is Thomas Eddy's anonymous treatise *An Account of the State Prison or Penitentiary House, in the City of New-York* (New York, 1801), containing a plan of the institution and also giving a good insight into Eddy's penal philosophy. Stephen Allen, *Observations on Penitentiary Discipline, Addressed to William Roscoe* (New York, 1827), reveals clearly the severe attitude of its author, and was written to defend the rise of the Auburn system against the attacks of William Roscoe, an English reformer. Gershom Powers, *A Brief Account of the Construction, Management, & Discipline . . . of the New-York State Prison At Auburn* (Auburn, 1826), contains an abundance of material on the physical layout of the Cayuga County penitentiary and the intricacies of the system practiced there. The same author's *Letter . . . in Answer to a Letter of the Hon. Edward Livingston* (Albany, 1829) was published for consumption in Pennsylvania, where some reformers were attempting to secure the adoption of the Auburn system; in it Powers tried to refute various objections which Livingston had raised concerning the New York method. This pamphlet is also significant because it makes a strong case for John D. Cray as primarily responsible for developing the various techniques used under the Auburn system.

A number of works by prison reformers and administrators are also important in revealing the new currents that began to work in American penology during the 1840's. An admirable statement of new ideas is Dorothea Dix, *Remarks on Prisons and Prison Discipline in the United States* (Boston, 1845), written by an author whose crusade on behalf of the insane has partially obscured her very important work for better prison conditions. Samuel Gridley Howe's trenchant *An Essay on Separate and Congregate Systems of Prison Discipline* (Boston, 1846) is a minority report submitted in defense of the revolt against the leadership of the Prison Discipline Society carried on by Howe, Charles Sumner, and Horace Mann. Despite its unrestrained polemic quality it contains some telling arguments against the Auburn system.

In New York during the same period, John Worth Edmonds, *A Letter . . . to General Aaron Ward, in Regard to the Removal of Capt. Lynds* (New York, c. 1844), is indispensable with regard to the stormy struggles during Lynds's second administration at Sing Sing. Also valuable on this and succeeding episodes is John Luckey, *Life in Sing Sing State Prison, as Seen in a Twelve Years' Chaplaincy* (New York, 1860). Luckey is curiously reticent about his battles with Eliza Farnham in this work, but otherwise gives a full account of his ideas about discipline, good material on the dispute between Edmonds and Lynds, and some fascinating details on inmate escape attempts. Eliza Farnham's views on phrenology and other topics are stated in a forthright manner in her introduction and notes to Marmaduke B. Sampson, *Rationale of Crime* (New York, 1846), which also contains the drawings of inmate head-formations that were done in Luckey's office at her direction. Georgiana Bruce Kirby, *Years of Experience* (New York, 1887), written by a friend of Mrs. Farnham's who served as an assistant matron at Sing Sing, has a section on experiences at the women's prison during the 1840's. Good material on Auburn early in the same decade, written by an admirer of the Pennsylvania system but nevertheless presented with relative objectivity, is included in Fred A. Packard, *Memorandum of a Late Visit to the Auburn Penitentiary* (Philadelphia, 1842).

The reports of various benevolent and reform societies form a rich source of information on ante-bellum prisons. The improper penal conditions prevalent in the period which followed the War of 1812 stimulated the Society for the Prevention of Pauperism, a New York City organization, to make an investigation of correctional policies and publish a notable *Report on the Penitentiary System of the United States* (New York, 1822). From 1826 until its collapse in 1854, the Prison Discipline Society published in its annual *Reports* a vast amount of material on American penal practices, heavily slanted in favor of the Auburn system, but nevertheless very useful. For the years 1844 onward, the yearly *Reports* of the New York Prison Association are indispensable.

The autobiographies of prison reformers and memoirs written by those who knew them form a small but significant group of works in the period covered by this study. I have already mentioned Knapp's *Life of Thomas Eddy;* the career of another Newgate official is recounted in Charles C. Sommers, *Memoir of the Rev. John Stanford,* D.D. (New York, 1835). A revealing autobiography is Samuel Miles Hopkins' brief *Sketch of the Public and Private Life of Samuel Miles Hopkins . . . Written by Himself,* posthumously published by the Rochester Historical Society (Rochester, 1898). Although this says next to nothing about Hopkins' activities as a prison reformer, it clearly shows the rootlessness and dissatisfaction which dogged his career until the early 1820's. William Jenks, *A Memoir of the Rev. Louis Dwight* (Boston, 1856), similarly shows how ripe Dwight was for commitment to a cause at the time of his trip for the American Bible Society. Writing shortly after Dwight's death, Jenks was particularly anxious to defend him against the aspersions of such men as Howe, Sumner, and Mann. Eliza Farnham's autobiographical work, *Eliza Woodson: Or, the Early Days of One of the World's Workers* (New York, 1864), is difficult to use because it fictionalizes proper and place names, but is especially important in showing her early desire to work with outcasts and in revealing the direct influence of Elizabeth Fry. An earlier edition of this memoir, entitled *My Early Days* and published in 1859, is quite rare. The first volume of John Bigelow's *Retrospections of an Active Life* (5 vols.; New York, 1909–1913) contains reminiscences of Bigelow's days as a prison inspector at Sing Sing. Also worth mentioning with regard to another reformer of this period is Lydia Maria Child, *Isaac Hopper: A True Life* (Boston, 1853).

A number of miscellaneous tracts and articles written during the ante-bellum era supply interesting material on penal matters. James Hardie, *Description of the City of New York* (New York, 1827), contains useful information on Newgate. A curious and entertaining piece written in biblical style is *The Chronicles of Auburn,* by Ezra the Scribe (pseudonym for Rev. Silas Shepard). Published in Auburn in 1838 during the controversy surrounding Lynds's second administration there, it alleged among other things that the famous disciplinarian had actually been the father of Rachel Welch's illegitimate child in the mid-1820's. Similarly entertaining, but for different reasons, is David Meredith Reese's *Humbugs of New-York* (New York, 1838), which satirizes various reform panaceas and theories, including phrenology. I found a number of contemporary works helpful in understanding and evaluating that pseudo-science, such as Charles Caldwell, *New Views of Penitentiary Discipline* (Philadelphia, 1829); Amos Dean, *Lectures on Phrenology* (Albany, 1834); and Roswell W. Haskins, *History and Progress of Phrenology* (New York, 1839). I have already mentioned Eliza Farnham's edition of Marmaduke Sampson's *Rationale of Crime,* the most important of all in this respect. Although I did not cover the subject of juvenile delinquents and their treatment in ante-bellum New York, a book-length topic in itself, I found Bradford K. Peirce's *A Half Century with Juvenile Delinquents* (New York, 1869) helpful for purposes of contrast and comparison. Efforts on behalf of another type of offender are interestingly recounted in Caroline M. Kirkland, *The Helping Hand: Comprising an Account of* THE HOME, *for Discharged Female Convicts* (New York, 1853).

Among contemporary periodical articles, especially significant were four essays contained in the *United States Magazine and Democratic Review:* "The Clinton State Prison, Clinton County, New York," XVII (November, 1845), 345–352; "Prison Discipline," XIX (August, 1846), 219–240; "The Rationale of Crime," XX (Jan., 1847), 49–55; and "Influence of Penal Laws," XXII (March, 1848), 233–240. Also important was the article on "Prison Discipline" in the *North American Review,* XLIX (July, 1839),

1–43, and the luridly illustrated "Torture and Homicide in an American State Prison," *Harper's Weekly*, II (Dec. 18, 1858), 808–810.

Finally, the student of penal affairs in ante-bellum New York should familiarize himself for background purposes with the writings of various European prison reformers, theorists, and humanitarians. Edward D. Ingraham's translation of Cesare Beccaria's *Dei delitti e delle pene*, under the title *An Essay on Crimes and Punishments*, is readily available in a reprinted edition published by Stanford University (Stanford, Calif., 1953). William Blackstone, *Commentaries on the Laws of England* (4 vols.; Oxford, 1765–1769), is of especially great importance for the study of penal theory. Various shades of opinion on correctional matters are revealed in William Dodd, *Thoughts in Prison* (London, 1777); William Eden, *Principles of Penal Law* (2nd ed.; London, 1771); William Godwin, *An Enquiry Concerning Political Justice* (2 vols.; Dublin, 1793); and in two tracts by Jonas Hanway: *Solitude in Imprisonment* (London, 1776) and *Distributive Justice and Mercy* (London, 1781). The greatest of all English works on prison reform is John Howard, *The State of the Prisons in England and Wales* (Warrington, 1777). Jeremy Bentham's various writings on penal matters are to be found in his *Works,* ed. Sir John Bowring (London, 1838–1843).

## Secondary Sources

The backgrounds of American prison reform can be traced in a number of secondary works. A provocative book dealing with the historical development of various penalties for crime and the motives underlying their use is Hans von Hentig, *Punishment: Its Origin, Purpose and Psychology* (London, 1937), emphasizing the human desire to propitiate deities believed to be offended by the acts of felons. Among other volumes which I found especially helpful in studying the origins of punitive practices and correctional theories were Harry Elmer Barnes, *The Repression of Crime: Studies in Historical Penology* (New York, 1926); John

Lewis Gillin, *Criminology and Penology* (rev. ed.; New York, 1935); and Ray M. McConnell, *Criminal Responsibility and Social Constraint* (New York, 1912). A thought-provoking analysis emphasizing and possibly overstating the inverse correlation between sanguinary punishments and the availability of labor is given in Georg Rusche and Otto Kirchheimer, *Punishment and Social Structure* (New York, 1939). For general perspective on various correctional problems two basic works are Harry Elmer Barnes and Negley K. Teeters, *New Horizons in Criminology* (1st ed.; New York, 1943), and Frederick H. Wines, *Punishment and Reformation: A Study of the Penitentiary System* (rev. ed.; New York, 1919).

The development of pioneer correctional institutions in early modern Europe has been studied with especially valuable results by Thorsten Sellin. This is particularly true with regard to the role played by the Roman Catholic Church, as described by Sellin in three articles in the *Journal of the American Institute of Criminal Law and Criminology:* "Filippo Franci—A Precursor of Modern Penology," XVII (May, 1926), 104–112; "Dom Jean Mabillon—A Prison Reformer of the Seventeenth Century," XVII (February, 1927), 581–602; and "The House of Correction for Boys in the Hospice of Saint Michael in Rome," XX (February, 1930), 533–553. Sellin has also made a noteworthy contribution to the history of the workhouse in his *Pioneering in Penology: The Amsterdam Houses of Correction in the Sixteenth and Seventeenth Centuries* (Philadelphia, 1944). For the relation of the church to the development of modern correctional institutions the reader should also consult the first chapter of George Ives, *A History of Penal Methods* (London, 1914). On benefit of clergy, an article especially to be recommended is Arthur Lyon Cross, "The English Criminal Law and Benefit of Clergy during the Eighteenth and Early Nineteenth Centuries," *American Historical Review,* XXII (April, 1917), 544–565.

The emergence of the modern prison-reform movement in Europe has been described in a variety of secondary works. Max

Grünhut, *Penal Reform: A Comparative Study* (Oxford, 1948), is a good general synthesis. On the enlightenment tradition the reader will find much valuable material in Coleman Phillipson, *Three Criminal Law Reformers: Beccaria, Bentham, Romilly* (London, 1923); Marcello T. Maestro, *Voltaire and Beccaria as Reformers of Criminal Law* (New York, 1942); Elie Halévy, *The Growth of Philosophic Radicalism,* trans. Mary Morris (London, 1928); and Shelby McCloy, *The Humanitarian Movement in Eighteenth-Century France* (Lexington, Ky., 1957). An authoritative and exhaustive study on its subject is Leon Radzinowicz, *A History of English Criminal Law and Its Administration from 1750: The Movement for Reform, 1750–1833* (New York, 1948).

The religious impulse underlying the activities of many early prison reformers is best revealed in various studies on English humanitarianism. Especially valuable on Quaker benevolence are Auguste Jorns, *The Quakers as Pioneers in Social Work,* trans. Thomas K. Brown, Jr. (New York, 1931), and A. Ruth Fry, *John Bellers, 1654–1725: Quaker, Economist, and Social Reformer* (London, 1935). The latter work contains a number of Bellers' own writings. The attempts of Thomas Bray and his circle to ameliorate jail conditions are described in William O. B. Allen and Edmund McClure, *Two Hundred Years: The History of the Society for Promoting Christian Knowledge, 1698–1898* (London, 1898). Hepworth Dixon, *John Howard and the Prison-world of Europe* (London, 1849), although old, is still useful; a good modern biography of the greatest of all English prison reformers is Derek Howard, *John Howard* (London, 1958). The abortive efforts to establish a penitentiary system in Britain in the late eighteenth and early nineteenth centuries are described in Beatrice and Sidney Webb, *English Prisons under Local Government* (New York, 1922).

On punishments in colonial New York, an informative and entertaining essay is Elizabeth D. Lewis, "Old Prisons and Punishments," in Maud W. Goodwin *et al.,* eds., *Historic New York: Being the Second Series of the Half Moon Papers* (New York,

1899). T. Raymond Naughton, "Criminal Law in Colonial New York," *Proceedings of the New York State Historical Association*, XXXI (1933), 235–240, can also be recommended. By all odds the most scholarly and comprehensive work on the subject is Julius Goebel, Jr., and T. Raymond Naughton, *Law Enforcement in Colonial New York: A Study in Criminal Procedure* (New York, 1944), admirable in every respect. The first chapter of Philip Klein's *Prison Methods in New York State* (New York, 1920) also contains useful information on this period. The development of prison reform in the state from which New York copied its first penitentiary system is covered in detail in Harry Elmer Barnes, *The Evolution of Penology in Pennsylvania* (Indianapolis, 1927); on the Walnut Street Jail, the standard account is Negley K. Teeters, *The Cradle of the Penitentiary* (n.p., 1955). The thought and activities of Thomas Eddy are analyzed in Arthur A. Ekirch, Jr., "Thomas Eddy and the Beginnings of Prison Reform in New York," *Proceedings of the New York State Historical Association*, LXI (1943), 376–391. For added detail, see the same author's unpublished master's thesis, "Thomas Eddy: His Ideas and Interests" (Columbia University, 1938).

The standard general account of the evolution of American penitentiaries during most of the ante-bellum period is Orlando F. Lewis' pioneering study, *The Development of American Prisons and Prison Customs, 1776–1845: With Special Reference to Early Institutions in the State of New York* (n.p., 1922). Lewis was for twelve years the General Secretary of the Prison Association of New York and an important reformer in his own right. His work is still valuable as a source of factual information and penological insight. Blake McKelvey, *American Prisons: A Study in American Social History Prior to 1915* (Chicago, 1936), covers the ante-bellum era in far less detail but is nevertheless a work of sound historical scholarship. Both Lewis and McKelvey devote considerable attention to the conflict between the Auburn and Pennsylvania systems, as do Harry Elmer Barnes and Negley K. Teeters in the previously mentioned *New Horizons in Criminology*. A long-needed treatise on the institution at which the solitary system received its most significant trial has been provided only recently in Negley K. Teeters and John D. Shearer, *The Prison at Philadelphia: Cherry Hill* (New York, 1957).

Although a number of writers have dealt with developments in the various state prisons of New York during the ante-bellum period, little has been done of a comprehensive nature, especially with regard to placing such developments within the historical context of the times in which they occurred. Chapters VI, IX, X, and XII of Orlando F. Lewis, *The Development of American Prisons and Prison Customs,* constitute the best of the previously published materials dealing with this subject. Also commendable is a series of brief unsigned articles on the history of various state penal institutions which appeared in 1949 in *Correction,* official publication of the New York State Department of Correction: see Vol. XIV, No. 2 (February), pp. 3–12; No. 3 (March), pp. 2–18; No. 5 (May), pp. 5–10; No. 6 (June), pp. 3–15; No. 7 (July), pp. 3–16; and No. 8–9 (August-September), pp. 3–16. Ralph S. Herre, "A History of Auburn Prison from the Beginning to about 1867" (unpublished D.Ed. dissertation, Pennsylvania State University, 1950), is only fair at best, and contains a number of factual inaccuracies. Much of the historical material appearing in Lewis Lawes, *Twenty Thousand Years in Sing Sing* (New York, 1932) and *Life and Death in Sing Sing* (Garden City, N.Y., 1937), written by one of the most successful and articulate prison wardens of the twentieth century, is taken from the previous work of O. F. Lewis. Philip Klein's previously mentioned *Prison Methods in New York State* is a valuable work for reference purposes, but its severely topical organization is not well calculated to facilitate historical analysis and interpretation. Clifford M. Young, *Women's Prisons Past and Present and Other New York State Prison History* (Elmira, 1932) is mainly a skeletal chronology, particularly insofar as the ante-bellum period is concerned. On the labor question, some good material is contained in E. T. Hiller, "Development of the Systems of Control of Convict Labor in the United States," *Journal of Criminal Law and Criminology,* V (July, 1914), 241–269.

Several county histories published in the late nineteenth century contain material on the prisons of ante-bellum New York, but in general this type of material should be used with caution. See especially Duane H. Hurd, *History of Clinton and Franklin Counties, New York* (Philadelphia, 1880); J. Thomas Scharf, *History of Westchester County, New York* (2 vols.; Philadelphia, 1886); and Elliot Storke and James H. Smith, *History of Cayuga County, New York* (Syracuse, 1879). An interesting and well-written work of local history which contains information on the Auburn silk craze is Henry Hall, *The History of Auburn* (Auburn, 1869).

The efforts of many recent scholars have made possible a much better understanding of the historical milieu in which the Auburn system developed than would have been attainable had I been writing even a short time ago. Like all students of events in New York during this period, I have benefited greatly from Whitney Cross's seminal work, *The Burned-over District: The Social and Intellectual History of Enthusiastic Religion in Western New York, 1800–1850* (Ithaca, N.Y., 1950). Also very helpful was David M. Ellis, "The Yankee Invasion of New York, 1783–1850," *New York History*, XXXII (January, 1951), 3–17. The conservative and religious impulse for reform is analyzed extensively in a number of recent works, including John R. Bodo, *The Protestant Clergy and Public Issues, 1812–1848* (Princeton, 1954); Charles C. Cole, Jr., *The Social Ideas of the Northern Evangelists, 1826–1860* (New York, 1954); Charles I. Foster, *An Errand of Mercy: The Evangelical United Front, 1790–1837* (Chapel Hill, N.C., 1960); and Clifford S. Griffin, *Their Brothers' Keepers: Moral Stewardship in the United States, 1800–1865* (New Brunswick, 1960). On the general intellectual milieu of the Jackson era I found Marvin Meyers, *The Jacksonian Persuasion: Politics and Belief* (Stanford, 1957), and John William Ward, *Andrew Jackson: Symbol for an Age* (New York, 1955), especially stimulating. A unique insight into American attitudes toward certain types of crimes and social deviance during this period is provided in David Brion Davis, *Homicide in American Fiction, 1798–1860: A Study in Social Values* (Ithaca, N.Y., 1957).

The intellectual currents which influenced reform activities in the 1840's are particularly well illuminated in Merle Curti, *The Growth of American Thought* (3rd ed.; New York, 1951). Other helpful treatments which concentrate especially upon literature are Carl Bode, *The Anatomy of American Popular Culture, 1840–1861* (Berkeley and Los Angeles, 1959); E. Douglas Branch, *The Sentimental Years, 1836–1860* (New York, 1934); and David Brion Davis, *Homicide in American Fiction,* previously mentioned. On phrenology, see especially John D. Davies, *Phrenology, Fad and Science* (New Haven, Conn., 1955); Arthur E. Fink, *Causes of Crime: Biological Theories in the United States, 1800–1915* (Philadelphia, 1938); and Robert E. Riegel, "The Introduction of Phrenology to the United States," *American Historical Review,* XXXIX (October, 1933), 73–78. Developments in the treatment of the criminally insane are discussed in Albert Deutsch, *The Mentally Ill in America* (New York, 1937). An admirable work on the continuing significance of the religious impulse to reform in this period is Timothy L. Smith, *Revivalism and Social Reform in Mid-Nineteenth Century America* (Nashville, 1957). Modern biographies of prison reformers active in the 1840's are not plentiful, but the reader may consult Helen E. Marshall, *Dorothea Dix: Forgotten Samaritan* (Chapel Hill, N.C., 1937) and Margaret Clapp, *Forgotten First Citizen: John Bigelow* (Boston, 1947).

# Index

LaVergne, TN USA
21 March 2011
220893LV00001B/54/P

9 780801 475481